# SUMMERS OFF

## THE WORLDWIDE ADVENTURES OF A SCHOOLTEACHER

LARRY J. SHORTELL

iUniverse, Inc.
Bloomington

# SUMMERS OFF
## The Worldwide Adventures of a Schoolteacher



iUniverse books may be ordered through booksellers or by contacting:
iUniverse
1663 Liberty Drive
Bloomington, IN 47403
www.iuniverse.com
1-800-Authors (1-800-288-4677)



Cover photo and author photo by Lisa A. E. Kaplan.

Illustrations by Denis Proulx, Shangri-La Studios.

978-1-4620-0606-9 pbk
978-1-4620-0607-6 hbk
978-1-4620-0608-3 ebk

Library of Congress Control Number: 2011907145

Printed in the United States of America
iUniverse rev. date: 05/10/11

*For Pete Gangloff*

*If one advances confidently in the direction of his dreams, and endeavors to live the life which he has imagined, he will meet with a success unexpected in common hours.*
—Henry David Thoreau

*Live as if to die tomorrow. Learn as if to live forever.*
—Mahatma Gandhi

# Contents

Contents viii
List of Illustrations ix
Preface xi
Acknowledgments xiii
Introduction 1
Aruba: Boxfish & Cocaine 3
Barrow: Bonding with Bowheads 11
Conquering the Caribbean: Cargo Boats & Cornrows 27
Dive! Dive! Dive! Belly-up & Boat-less 45
Egypt: Dead or Alive 57
Fossil Hunting: Sharks, Snakes, & Gators 69
Germany: Naked in Frankfurt 81
Hawaii: Painful Pleasures 87
Iceland: Frozen Falls & Glaciers 97
Japan: Fuji with Jimmy & Friends 103
Kenya's Chiggers: No Man Left Behind 109
Land Down Under: Walkabout Koalas 121
Mermaids: By Land or by Sea 131
New Zealand: Jump & Dive 139
Octopus: Stab or Spear 151
Pete: My Inspiration 157
Qantas: Airplanes & Airports 181
Recruit: Move Out, Not Up 195
St. Martin: Holland & Honeymoon 209
Thailand: Monkeys & Male Hookers 217
United Kingdom: Bald for Britain 229
Volcanoes: The Limb-Saving Pee 241
Wall of China: Gestures & Gastronomy 251
Xcaret: Ruins & Cenotes 259
Yasawa Islands: Cannibalistic Caterpillars 267
Zip Lines: Way to Travel 277
Afterword 285
About the Author 287

# List of Illustrations


Image A. Larry and His Boxfish Buddy 3
Image B. Bowhead and Eskimos 11
Image C. Shark Dive 27
Image D. Beached Divers 45
Image E. Camel Ride 57
Image F. The Perils of Fossil Diving 69
Image G. Naked Family in a Hot Tub 81
Image H. Hawaiian Beach Massage 87
Image I. Frozen Falls Photography 97
Image J. Atop Mt. Fuji 103
Image K. Chigger Attack 109
Image L. Park Ranger Disguise 121
Image M. Mermaids? 131
Image N. Larry's Leaps 139
Image O. Octopus Attack 151
Image P. Pete and Larry 157
Image Q. Squished and Squashed 181
Image R. Good-bye, Navy 195
Image S. Three's a Crowd on a Honeymoon 209
Image T. Elephant Trek 217
Image U. Bald-Headed Larry and the Blarney Stone 229
Image V. Larry, Two Feet Shorter 241
Image W. Onion Attack at the Great Wall 251
Image X. It's Just a Suggestion, Right? 259
Image Y. The Caterpillar Boogeyman 267
Image Z. Zip Line Around the World 277

# Preface

For some people, it is relatively easy to list off a set of accomplishments, adventures, or ideas. I do recognize that there is a commonality among entries that results from a simple recognition of things that people tend to value in our society. I am not sure, however, how much of the specifics of anyone's list is actually transferable to someone else. I think that the best I can do is explain what my life's journey has taught me to date and hope that others can benefit from what I have experienced. It may be the teacher in me, but my wish is that those of you who read this book will be inspired to travel and learn things firsthand. It is, without a doubt, the best way to understand the world and our place in it. I wrote these words to remember the details of my life, and I share these stories in the hopes that others can see the possibilities that open up when one lives life by following his or her dreams, fearing the inability to follow one's passions rather than fearing death.

# Acknowledgments

Many people have helped me in life and with this book, and the words "thank you" are nowhere near adequate to express my gratitude to those who have so significantly altered my path and helped shape the person I am today. Here are the people I recognize as being instrumental in my life:

Gloria (Glo) McCauley—my mom. You have always represented the good in my life. Thanks for your bright smile and shining personality. Thanks for being my "light" when I needed it most. Thanks for making me feel that, no matter how far I go and how long I'm gone, I will always have a place to come home to.

Lisa A. E. Kaplan—my "girlfriend plus." Your dedication, support, and true love have inspired me to produce the best book I possibly could. Thank you for accepting my complexities instead of running from them. Your rational, good-hearted being has enhanced my life exponentially.

Buzz Shortell—my dad. As a police officer and then a bounty hunter, you always had stories to tell. Thanks for keeping me entertained until I got a few stories of my own.

Cindy O'Mara. Your unconditional love allowed me to trust in others and share my thoughts and dreams with someone.

Aline Johnson. You encouraged me to go to college and thus opened up the wonderful world of teaching and learning.

Herb Kronish—my thesis professor. Your inspiring words made me believe someone would want to read my words.

Tony Pratt; Glo; John Shortell, my brother; Laurey Dangona, my sister; Cindy O.; Kitty Ringland; Jam Kristienson; Peter and Rosemary Kelly; Tom Benoit; Charlie and Cindy O'Connor; Brian Coy; and Cindy and Ray Kaplan—you are the people who have either filled your basements, attics, garages, and closets with my stuff while I was off traveling (whether it was six months or seven years) or given me a place to write. With your generosity, I was able to write while listening to the dripping of a dehumidifier in a cold basement in Massachusetts, staring out the window at a mason yard from a condo in Connecticut, admiring Bromley Mountain from a Vermont chalet, smelling the continuous flatulence of an ancient dog in a home in Georgia, watching the lazy Spanish moss trees gently blow from a trailer in Florida, glancing at an empty pool from a villa in Bonaire, perched on the sand several feet from the ocean in Curacao, and lastly, from a cottage in the Berkshires with our family dog nestled at my feet.

Finally, I'd like to acknowledge all the fellow travelers I've encountered over the last twenty years, whether we spent hours sharing photos or stories, made a train or plane ride less boring by finding a common bond, or simply exchanged a glance that sent me into a fantasy of thought that somehow shaped my future. And to the travelers whom I have not yet met, may our relationship be meaningful, may we learn from each other, and may we share that everlasting bond that connects people who wander—whether lost or otherwise.

# Introduction

I grew up very poor in Connecticut, a state considered to be one of the richest in the United States. My family's limited funds did not allow us to go anywhere or see anything. In spite of this, I never managed to get too rooted in one specific spot because my family had moved seven times before I was twelve years old. By the time I was thirteen, I was never home; but with little direction and no money, I still didn't stray very far.

I graduated from high school near the bottom of my class, thus I believed that college was not a viable option for me. Instead, when I was eighteen years old, I joined the US Navy. I planned, as the advertisements promised, to see the world. I should have known those commercials were too good to be true. In reality, I spent the majority of my time as an aviation ordnanceman on flight lines in central California and northern Florida.

Four and a half years later, with very little of the world seen, I was back in Connecticut. My days and nights were filled with work. I held many jobs, usually several at once. I worked hard and saved for a future that would never again lead me back to the poverty of my youth.

A few years after my tour in the armed forces, I landed a high-paying job at Pratt & Whitney Aircraft and thought my prayers must have been answered. With this new job, I finally had the money that I thought would bring me happiness. Unfortunately, money wasn't enough; I was still not happy. It turns out that what I thought was an early mid-life crisis was merely a lack of fulfillment.

Sadly, the true meaning of the word "crisis" was about to make itself known to me. It began with a tragic accident that would change my life forever. In those pivotal moments, I lost my best friend, and I nearly died myself. This incident did, however, put me on a path that would allow me to truly begin to live.

To date, I have had thirty-five different jobs including green bean grader, tomato picker, retail salesman, stock boy, paperboy, EMT, patient-care assistant, factory worker, bouncer, waiter, bartender, ordnanceman, landscaper, dive master and instructor, billing and collection agent, interpreter at an aquarium, and early childhood teacher at a daycare. After earning bachelors and masters degrees in education, I now have a career as a special education teacher (thus, the A through Z choice in chapter titles) that fulfills me and gives me the opportunity to teach and learn.

I have taught students in other countries and in the most northern, southern, and western regions of the United States; and I am currently teaching in the northeastern United States. While each area has its unique forms of communication and culture, one thing is clear—all students want to be understood and to understand the world around them. It is my career of choice and one that has offered me countless rewards in and out of the classroom because I have been willing to use my time to learn, explore, and share.

It also gives me the ability to wander wherever my spirit takes me. I have visited over eighty countries since I began my travels in 1990. I have just completed my second around-the-world trip where I taught, took photographs, wrote, and learned about people who do things differently than I do.

# ARUBA:
## BOXFISH & COCAINE

I found myself alone in the dark, under water, on a deep dive inside of a shipwreck. A kind of hollow, extremely uncomfortable, black hole quietly engulfed me. I was cold because I was, as usual, underdressed. It was night, and the air and water were a little cooler than I had anticipated. I was in a thin Lycra dive skin that provided protection from jellyfish stings but offered no real warmth. The dive skin was the kind that makes your butt look big, even if it's not. Since mine is, I tend to wear it only at night so the fish are the only ones thinking, *Dang, that dude has a fat tail.*

I had recently earned my SCUBA diving certification but had yet to complete the specialty training necessary to dive at night, go deeper than sixty feet, or penetrate a shipwreck. In no way, shape, or form was I remotely qualified to be doing all three at the same time, yet here I was. This dive was one of my first open-water dives as a certified diver. It was also the initial dive of my first dive vacation. Actually, at twenty-five, I was on my first vacation of any sort.

What was I doing on this momentous dive? I was freaking out because I had lagged behind and lost both the dive master and the rest of the divers in my group. I had become fascinated with a strange little fish. As I discovered later, my odd little friend was a trunkfish. Its flat belly and sides, big lips, and tiny fins made him a card-carrying member of the boxfish family. It was not a fast fish by any means, and after I had spent a couple of short minutes gaining its trust, it was relatively easy to catch it for an up-close look. At the time, I did not know I wasn't supposed to touch, let alone hold, the sea life.

I was bonding with this fish and may even have been talking to it through my regulator; when I looked around, I realized that I was utterly alone with my fish! Where had everybody gone? I turned off my underwater flashlight to see if I could see the lights of my buddies, but only darkness stared back at me.

I started sweating in my dive skin. The cold steel walls of this ancient sunken ship felt like they were closing in on me. I swore that I heard the echoes of my own heart beating. I started to breathe rapidly. Could I reach the surface in time from this depth? First things first, I commanded myself to think. Somehow, I had to find my way through this metal maze before I could even consider my ascent. I glanced down at my hand and saw my new friend calmly waiting to see what would happen next, and I had to smile. Then, I slowed my breathing, let my big-lipped buddy go, and started to high-tail it out of the ship's compartment in the direction I had last seen my fellow divers heading.

I was in such a rush and kicking so hard that my heart once again began its frantic pace. I forgot about the warning to move slowly and deliberately so as not to stir up the silt sediment that notoriously coats the floors of wrecks. My forceful, rapid kicking had created an enormous cloud of debris behind me. When I slowed down, the thick cloud caught up to me and left me blinded. I realized that I could not return to the place from which I started to reorient myself. I had to calm down. I had to breathe. I had to think.

I slowed my pace, moved my fins in small strokes with bent knees, and kept as far away from the bottom as I could. I tried to catch my breath by thinking of my big-lipped, aquatic acquaintance. With my eyes bulging out of my mask, I just kept on swimming and looking for my exit. Suddenly, a white light appeared. It looked like the sort of light described by people who have had near-death experiences. Like that light, it was mesmerizing. Was this the light that was drawing me from this life to the next? Was I dying? Should I just give in or should I, as the saying goes, "let go and let God"?

In a moment, I realized that I wasn't dead or even dying, but I did see a light. It was a dive light from another diver. Then, I saw more lights, and I knew I was safe. I looked at my dive watch and was shocked to see that only a few minutes had passed. It had seemed like a lifetime to me, and I instantly realized that it could have been.

I joined the group underwater as if nothing had happened. I finally caught my breath by thinking of slow-paced, mundane things like watching curling or golf on television. I finished the dive, as one would imagine, with my head practically attached to the backside of the diver ahead of me while simultaneously trying to hold hands with the divers on either side. I never mentioned my experience to anyone when we were back on board the dive boat because I was embarrassed. This was to be the first of several dive experiences in the years to follow that taxed my comfort zone.

Before the end of this dive vacation, though, my comfort zone would again be challenged in a very different way. This time my challenge would involve some strange land creatures. It had actually all started a few days earlier during the plane ride from Florida to Aruba. On the first leg of the journey, the 747 airplane was relatively empty. It was a late-night flight, and each of the dozen or so passengers could have had about ten seats to sprawl out and sleep. Since this was my first vacation, however, sleep was not for me. I was not going to miss a thing!

Shortly into the flight, a couple, probably thinking, *This poor single guy traveling alone could use some company*, had struck up a conversation with me. Because I was traveling to an exotic, romantic destination by myself, they probably figured that I was recently divorced, going through a midlife crisis, or just plain weird. I remember thinking at the time that there was something a little different about John and Brandy. Maybe it was the excessively friendly way that John had approached me. For some reason, I suspected that they might have been swingers.

By all outward appearances though, they seemed nice enough. Brandy was about twenty-five years old and had a great body and long blonde hair that reached all the way to her rear end. She was a bit withdrawn in manner but was always smiling, no matter what John had to say. While Brandy was clearly above average in the looks department, John was merelyan average-looking guy with a rather small frame. He had dark, slicked-back hair and wore expensive-looking clothes. His personality was outgoing enough for the both of them. I would guess John to be at least ten years older than Brandy, and I was certain that he had much more life experience than those years implied.

The situation with Brandy and John got sort of creepy when we kept bumping into each other on the island, and they kept asking me to spend time with them. On one occasion, I accepted their invitation to go horseback riding on the beach. It was a beautiful moonlit night. There I was, sitting proudly on this gorgeous animal. He was a beautiful specimen with his pure white coat and flowing mane. The white sand beach of this exotic island spread out under us and reached the water's edge. In addition to my trusty steed and me, there were three lovely couples waiting excitedly for the ride to begin. As I looked around at them, it hit me like the proverbial ton of bricks. *What was I doing here?* This was the most romantic setting I had ever been in, and I was alone. Actually, I wasn't alone. Three couples surrounded me—and that was worse. Even my horse was male. It was clear that, without a gal of my own, I did not belong here!

I stuck with it and went on the ride anyway because, well, I like horseback riding, the rental had already been paid, and it would have been more embarrassing to leave at that point—or so I thought. Besides, I reasoned at the time, maybe the other couples would continue to be too into their kissing to notice my lack of a same-species partner. As it turned out, my discomfort grew throughout the ride as I watched the happy couples pet each other, and all I could do was pet my horse.

When the two-hour ride was over, we returned to the beach, and John and Brandy asked me to join them for dinner and a trip to some casinos. I was a little suspicious because I expected them to want to be alone to continue their romantic ride in private. Since that didn't appear to be on their agenda, I figured no harm would come from eating and enjoying some slots with them. I had eaten all my meals alone since my arrival on Aruba, and I thought some table talk would be nice. Besides, I had really built up quite an appetite during my last two hours as a cowboy taming a mustang. I was very busy in my make-believe world, where I imagined that I was the ranch-hand leading a ride for six city slickers on their honeymoons. I concocted this cowboy fantasy so my brain would stop busting my hindquarters for being on that joyride with all those cooing couples.

So, although I didn't feel like it, for the second time that day, I went with John and Brandy. We ate at a nice restaurant inside a five-star hotel. It was significantly better than the places I had been eating. I started with some frou-frou drink I normally would never have ordered—I was on vacation! Brandy had a glass of white wine, and John ordered a scotch. And then he ordered another, and another, and another. They ordered prime rib, and I went crazy and spared no expense by ordering fries with my sandwich.

The three of us talked about our travels, but I had nothing major to add, as this was my first real vacation trip. Brandy had been to a couple of places with her parents, and John filled the next hour recounting his pleasure and business travels. We talked about running into each other on the flight to Aruba, and after some conversation, we realized we'd eventually share the same flight on the way back to Ft. Myers, Florida. Then, Brandy and I mentioned our careers, and that sent John into a frenzied monologue about his business that lasted well past dessert.

After dinner, Brandy claimed to have a headache and went back to the room she shared with John. Although John kind of gave me a headache too, it seemed that she really just wanted to get away from him. He seemed to grow louder and more arrogant with each drink. By the time we got our coffee, I was more than sick of him too.

Throughout the course of the evening, Brandy's comments and body language contradicted the perception that she and John were a couple, although that was the general idea that John was trying to promote. In fact, she gave me the distinct impression that she had come on the trip because John had enticed her by offering to pick up the entire tab. While I was beginning to accept that I was wrong about the swinger thing, something about them still came across as odd. In retrospect, perhaps I should have paid better attention to the small warning flags.

After dessert, it was time to make a decision: I could go back to my hotel, write in my journal about the romantic gallop I had taken on the beach, and wonder what was up with John and Brandy, or I could go on to the casino with John and see some of the nightlife that this island had to offer. Up to that point in the trip, all I had done was dive, dive, dive, night and day. I didn't feel like going back to my room alone, and, although I would have loved to continue my conversation with Brandy, I didn't think that was an option. I decided, for the third time that day, to do what I thought a person should do on vacation and go for it! In this case, going for it meant that I went with John to his favorite casino. Apparently, he had become a regular at the tables and had done little else on this island paradise since he'd arrived. On the way to the casino, John said, "Hey, before we get to the casino, let's stop for a quick drink at a little bar I know. I have to pick up something there anyway." The way he said it seemed a bit odd, but at this juncture, it was more par for the course than not.

At John's stop, I found myself walking into a dirty hole-in-the-wall bar that should have had a sign on the door that read, LOCALS ONLY. TOURISTS STAY THE HELL OUT. As we entered, I could barely see any difference made by the few working overhead lights that were pitiful in their attempts to illuminate the joint. There was broken glass from mirrors, lights, and bar glasses strewn all over the floor. Some of it had been swept or, more likely, inadvertently kicked into a corner, in the vain hope that someday someone would clean it up. Ripped benches and broken chairs were scattered around, being used as footstools rather than seats. The cloud of thick cigarette smoke made my eyes burn and tear. The smoke made it more difficult to see than if it had been pitch black and certainly made it more difficult to breathe. Maybe that was a good thing because it helped partially camouflage the foul smell of sweat, old beer, and a bathroom I would never have the courage to enter.

When we went into this place, John walked over to three guys standing in the back corner near the only intact table in the joint.

They all looked like they wanted to kill him. They were rough, scraggly characters that had probably just gotten out of prison or were destined to be there shortly. While John was conversing with these men, the rest of the bar patrons had their eyes on me. *What the heck am I doing here?* I wondered. After a brief exchange, John made his way to another group of thugs, and they followed him out of the bar. I trailed along, not really thinking what I might be getting myself into. I watched as my new Florida friend and one of the thugs exchanged a couple of bags of cocaine for some money and shook hands.

After the transaction was complete, the leader of the gang came over to me and said, "*Hola*, I am Pepe. What can I do for you?"

Because I was fairly certain he wasn't trying to make friends or buy me a beer, I just smiled and said, "No coke, Pepe."

John and I continued our walk to the casino in silence; I had nothing more to say to him. My initial gut reaction had been more on target than I gave it credit for. John, at least, was significantly more than odd. I always try to make a joke when I'm uncomfortable. A therapist would say that it's a defense mechanism, but the experience at the bar was no laughing matter. Personally, I think John needed a therapist for going into a crappy bar in a foreign country and buying drugs from a complete stranger.

I was so furious that John had put me in this situation that, halfway to the casino, I decided to separate myself from him and go back to my hotel. Still fuming, I thought about how pathetic Brandy's romantic vacation was going to be with John and his cocaine-induced, shriveled-up, impotent libido. When John had asked why I was leaving, I told him I had a headache—probably caught it from his girl.

# BARROW:
## BONDING WITH BOWHEADS

I was flying to Barrow, Alaska when the aircraft unexpectedly made a hard right banking turn. I realized that the pilot of this commercial airplane had actually just turned to give us a better look at the famed Mt. McKinley. Incredibly, after the captain circled it once, he reversed direction so the passengers on the other side of the plane could also enjoy the view of this colossal mountain.

Mt. McKinley was originally named Denali, a name still used by the Alaskan natives. Apparently this 20,320-foot mountain is usually cloud covered, especially the top few thousand feet. However, on this day, there was 100 percent visibility, and we were able to admire the snowcapped summit shimmering in the sunlight. The view of the mountain was amazing, and so was the pilot's behavior. I had never seen anything like it; whenever I had flown in the past, it was always a direct route from point A to point B without even the slightest deviation in direction.

Not only was the pilot unique, but so was the aircraft. From the outside, the plane appeared to be average in every respect, but the inside had been reconstructed to carry fewer passengers and more cargo. The back half of the plane was configured to seat about sixty people, but there were fewer than that on this flight. As for the front half of the plane, the seats had simply been ripped out and the empty space used to provide room for essentials that the residents of this small, barren town desperately needed.

Small though it may be, Barrow, the northernmost town in the United States, is home to the largest native community in the Arctic. Barrow is actually 335 miles above the Arctic Circle. It is about twenty-one square miles, and the population now is about the same as it was at the time of my visit—approximately 4,500. Of this population, more than 60 percent are Inupiat (Eskimo). The word Inupiat, or Inuit, means the "original people" or "real people." I would soon discover that this translation was very fitting.

At the time I was honored to visit these wonderful people, I was living in Seward, Alaska. Seward is in the southern part of Alaska, bordering Resurrection Bay, which pours into the Bering Sea. I had been working in this little town at the elementary school as a case manager for the special-education students.

I became friends with Jam, the kindergarten teacher at the school. One day, she showed me some photos of Barrow that her friend Pat had taken. He had just landed a one-year contract as the Barrow town attorney. After admiring these pictures of the Great White North, I was ready for a road trip. Jam admitted that, although she had been living in Alaska for eighteen years, she had never ventured that far north. This was our big chance to go; however, Jam quickly informed me that it wouldn't be a road trip since there were no connecting roads that far north.

As we stepped off the plane and onto what had to be the farthest northern tarmac, we were greeted by a bitter cold that instantly bit my nose and cheeks and made my eyes water. We were underdressed even for the thirty or so steps to the miniature luggage recovery area that looked more like a grocery store checkout counter. Luckily, Jam's friend Pat was waiting for us when we arrived. This indoor baggage area was cold enough to have doubled as a meat locker—and it probably did!

Pat had black hair and a black beard that I'm guessing he grew after he arrived in this icebox of a town. He had a Northeasterner's accent and a temperament to match. This regional temperament is either construed as abrupt and cold or as quick and efficient. Either way, it was clear that Pat's natural disposition had been influenced by the months he and his wife had been living with the friendly Alaskan people. He remained, however, first and foremost a lawyer and still possessed that profession's common gift of gab. Perhaps it was the remoteness of his new home or the fact that his wife was back in the States on business, but this man could talk.

Pat explained to Jam and me the unique Inuit culture as he took us on a tour around the small town. I was fascinated by what he'd absorbed and the stories he had accumulated in just the short time he had been in this part of the state. The unofficial tour ended at his house, but the conversation continued until just past midnight.

After everyone else had turned in for the night, I looked out the window and saw small houses with antlers hanging about and polar bear skins draped over the porch railings. I desperately hoped that I would get a chance to see a live polar bear in the short time I would be here. I also saw ladders sticking out of strategically placed holes in the front lawns to give owners access to their natural freezers. Even at this late hour, the sky was bright enough for me to make out many of the details. This far above the Arctic Circle, it stays light in the summer for more than sixty days. Each day, the sun drops down close to the horizon, then begins its climb back up without ever quite disappearing from the night sky. As I peered out at this night's midnight sun, I realized I was not used to sleeping during daylight and accepted the fact that it was going to be a long night for me. Just around 2:00 a.m., I finished reading a book on Alaska bear attacks and finally closed my eyes for the night.

The next morning, before Pat went off to the office to do some lawyer stuff, he informed us that it was the time of the year when the native people hunted bowhead whales. He suggested that we listen to the scanner to hear if they had sighted one. We expectantly turned on the scanner but instantly became frustrated because we couldn't really make out what was being said. After listening intently for a few minutes, we figured out that the transmitted conversation was a mix between English and the native language. At the time, neither of us spoke Inupiaq, but I did pride myself on being a bit more than proficient with English. Those lousy scanners, however, garbled everything to the point where I could not even understand the English part! Jam and I decided that additional effort would be futile, so we took ourselves on an unguided tour of Barrow and the surrounding area.

When we came back to the house for lunch, Pat was there to tell us the news: a crew had just caught a whale. I grabbed Pat's oversized parka, which I had just taken off, and said, "Let's go!" Pat shook his head like I'd said something crazy and laughed. Apparently, the Inuit people are sensitive about letting an outsider observe their now-controversial seasonal whale kill. The thing is, I did not want to merely observe; I wanted to participate! After some cajoling, I finally convinced Pat to phone his wife and ask her opinion. If anyone would know how the local people felt, it would be her. Pat's wife had done a lot for the rights of the locals in the short time she and her husband had been in Barrow, and the local people liked her a lot. She told Pat that she thought it would probably be all right, so the three of us bundled up in a way that only those at the North Pole do, and off we went.

The shore was just in front of where Pat was staying, but the shallower water was frozen over so we still had to walk about a half a mile to reach the open waters between the Chukchi Sea and the Beaufort Sea. The air was freezing and the wind was howling. At times, it was a total whiteout, and I could not tell the difference between the sky and the ice upon which I was walking. As the ground ice hardened and the waves crashed against it, sections of the ice shelf crushed together, forming uneven platforms like the planks on an old ghost ship. It looked violent and unstable. It was unnerving to tread on this floating ground, and I do remember being very nervous about falling through the ice into the equally cold water below it. Because this ice shelf was very difficult to walk on and over, the relatively short distance took us nearly thirty minutes to conquer.

Falling through the ice was not my only fear; I also feared the polar bears. More than with any other bear, it was a possible encounter with a polar bear that haunted me. Other bears scatter when they hear humans. It seems, according to the numerous stories I had heard and read since my arrival in Alaska, that as soon as a polar bear sees or smells a person, he wants that person for dinner. It was an eerie situation for me because we were in a wide-open space, our vulnerability compounded by low visibility. Under these circumstances, I would not have seen a polar bear's white body until it was literally on top of me, and then it would be too late.

Long before we saw the open ocean, we spotted hundreds of seagulls loitering about and patiently waiting for their shot at the fresh kill. About thirty feet from the edge of the ice shelf, a long line of about twenty Eskimos was tugging a rope. The rope was looped through the ice and was part of a pulley system that they had set up. It extended from a drilled hole in the ice to the tail of an unfortunate bowhead whale.

I felt stupid just standing there, so I joined the line immediately. I wanted them to know that I was there to help and that I was not judging what they were doing. Pat soon joined in, followed shortly by Jam. Using Pat's wife's name provided an entrée that not only forestalled rejection of our participation but actually encouraged acceptance of it. It confirmed that old saying, "It's not what you know, it's who you know."

Standing shoulder to shoulder with the Eskimos pulling on that coarse rope was nothing short of amazing! I felt like I was on the Discovery Channel. The deep blue of the distant Arctic Ocean accented the blinding white snow. The multitude of seagulls circling above filled the air with their hungry cries.

A short distance away from the power and rhythm of the pulley line, I noticed an ancient folding cot that had probably seen more than one generation of whale hunts. I observed an old, gray-haired man with dark, wrinkled skin sitting upon that cot. He methodically sharpened the blades of the long knives that were about to be used by the younger men in the group. As I watched him, I imagined this elder recalling his very first whale-hunting season. In my imagination, I watched him as he spotted his first bowhead. It probably sent chills up his spine as he and his friends paddled their handmade canoes. In my reverie, he pictures his father and older brothers, with harpoons drawn, their bodies poised and pumped with adrenaline. After the kill, he recalls helping to set the sealskin buoys to prevent the whale from sinking beneath the ocean surface and becoming lost. His face gleams with pride as he remembers the boat, with the whale in tow, reaching the edge of the ice shelf. In his mind's eye, he sees his grandfather on shore sitting on the folding cot where he currently sits. I watched as he smiled and continued to sharpen his long blades in the close companionship of his memories.

The year I participated in the whale hunt was momentous, but not because of my presence. That year was the first time small engines, instead of absolute manpower, were used to bring in the whale. The engines were attached to the back of the canoe to ease the workload for the men hauling in the whale.

While the men were busy catching and bringing in their prey, the village women, bundled in their furs and mukluks, gathered in the shelter of one of several white canvas tents. In one tent, women were busy making tea and keeping the fires burning. In another, they were making some sort of bread on an enclosed fire pit. This support station was essential for the men because it took at least twenty-four hours to dissect the whale and distribute the meat. Even to an outsider, it was clear that this ritual required the combined effort of several families.

After the whale had been pulled up onto the ice shelf, two men with rifles were stationed about one hundred feet away, on either side of the kill. They stood there to protect their people from the polar bears that were lured in by the smell. A few carefully selected men cut the whale meat, blubber, and skin, while the rest of us loaded pieces onto sleds for distribution to each family within the community. Only after all of the town's people had their take and the family that had made the catch had their *captain's cut* would the polar bears be allowed to feast. Judging by the size of the entrails pile, they had quite a meal coming. As a final act of appreciation and respect, the whale's jawbones were laid along the beach among other gifts from the ocean that had been feeding this community for centuries.

After a long day—or night, who can tell in Alaska—of doing only a small part of the dissection and distribution of one of my favorite animals, we made the long, cold, walk back across the uneven ice shelf. During that slow walk back, I could feel myself just about exploding with the thoughts that I had held in the entire time. It all tumbled riotously in my head: my observations of the people's unity and mannerisms; the sounds of screeching seagulls; the sight of the bowhead's warm, red blood splashed against the frozen, white ice; and the smell.

That terrible, putrid smell was truly hideous. Nonetheless, while I was among the Inuit people, I had hidden my reaction to it as best I could. I was too embarrassed to allow anyone to know I was on the verge of vomiting for a good part of the time, especially near the end, when they poked their long cutting spears into the belly and the whale's last meal exploded out.

Later that evening, when my thoughts were put into some semblance of order, I recognized that, beyond being overwhelmed by this awesome experience, I was especially humbled, as an outsider, to have played some small role in this traditional Alaskan scene. In the end, surprisingly, there was no mourning in my heart for the whale. I love all wild animals, especially sea creatures. Dolphins and whales, in fact, are my favorites—but a slaughter wasn't what took place here. This was a part of Inuit culture, timeless and respectful. This one animal was going to be used by the entire village. Nothing went to waste. This is the way they have always done things in Barrow. There are no McDonald's restaurants here, and I hope there never will be.

Once we were back in the comfort and warmth of Pat's temporary housing, he offered to cook up some whale meat that his wife had received from the previous season's kill. By the time I was done showering the smell of this season's kill off of me, the food was done. Pat made a traditional Inupiat dish called *muk tuk* (whale skin and blubber). He threw in some whale meat and mixed veggies. All I can say is that the veggies were great! The little bit of whale blubber and skin that I was served was probably the only bit of that entire animal that was wasted. On second thought, a stray dog, a seagull, or even a polar bear from the nearby dump probably stole it.

While the week I spent in Barrow was one of my most memorable, the entire year I lived in Alaska was filled with adventures. I lived off of Bear Lake Road in a little cabin on the edge of town in Seward,

Alaska. The start of the original Iditarod Trail was about twenty feet from my dirt driveway. The cabin was made of eight-foot spruce wood logs and a green tin roof so the snow would slide right off. It consisted of a first floor and a loft that provided me with four hundred square feet of living space. I had no phone and no cooking stove, but I was armed with a microwave and instant coffee, and this was my paradise, my own secluded, little corner of the world. I could read, think, and appreciate both the smallest and largest of details.

I thoroughly enjoyed just sitting on the porch in my green wooden Adirondack chair, staring up at the Tiehacker Glacier and drinking a cup of coffee from my favorite Alaskan coffee mug. The mug was adorned with an emblem of a bear and a moose sitting in a canoe. The moose was paddling while the bear was fishing. This cup added to the pleasure of my morning ritual. I enjoyed it so much, in fact, that my morning ritual often became my evening ritual too! I would sit on that porch almost completely surrounded by evergreens and stare up at one of the glaciers formed by the Harding Ice Field. Even with my naturally hyperactive state, I could stay peacefully in that spot for hours, just reading or doing nothing at all.

When I needed some conversation, I would drive sixteen miles out of town to share a fire with Grizzly Edna and her husband, John Lennon. They lived in a small log cabin and managed the Snow River Hostel. The hostel was unique because, unlike other log cabins where the entire length of each log is visible from the outside, only the rounded cross-sectional ends of the logs were visible on the outside of this cabin. It gave the impression that the entire building was filled with logs. In reality, the hostel did have open space inside. The upstairs had bunks, and the entire downstairs was a great room filled with *National Geographic* magazines, old bear traps, other Alaskan paraphernalia, and a giant wood-burning stove.

I liked to sit by their fire, enjoying the sweet scent of John's pipe, and listening to the stories of this heartwarming couple. They had come from New Jersey to vacation here many years back, and they'd never left. They had absorbed the nature and beauty of this great country to its fullest extent, and they glowed with it as they reminisced. Grizzly Edna and John were equally happy to share the stories of the many hostel-going travelers they had befriended over the years. They had an affinity for those who sought the same wildlife adventures. I spent many hours in their company listening to them, learning from them, and simply enjoying the company of such an interesting couple. Their friendship was a godsend in the lonely wilderness and through the long, cold, dark hours of the Alaskan winter.

When I was not working, I spent a lot of time enjoying the great outdoors. Almost every cross-country skiing, snowshoeing, or hiking adventure I went on promised the tracks, droppings, or sightings of bear or moose. One day, I nearly had heart failure when two moose ran past me in the woods. The amplified sound of their thundering hooves in the forest at such close proximity was so unexpectedly loud and frightening that I was paralyzed. I felt the blood skyrocket to my brain, and I burst out in a cold sweat. In that instant, I thought it was a bear running toward me to get his lunch. Apparently, I had simply scared the moose and sent them running for cover. I scared them? I think it is safe to say that the moose and I shared a moment of complete understanding—and abject fear!

Aside from teaching in the local elementary school, I worked at the Alaska Sea Life Center that borders Resurrection Bay. The center's beginnings are tied to the actions of one reportedly drunk captain while he was an Exxon employee. My position at the Sea Life Center allowed me free passage on any of the tour boats. I took full advantage of this perk and went on seven, eight-hour trips in that year to explore the fjords of Resurrection Bay.

Each trip was breathtaking. I witnessed sea otters eating mussels off their bellies, Orca whales on the hunt breaking the surface like a submarine, dolphins spinning through the water just beneath the surface and just off the bow, sea lions barking from their rocky islands, and puffins circling their nests like bees around their hives. The most impressive sight, however, was the exploding of the glaciers, which was followed by ice chunks breaking away from the rest of the ice field. This "calving" appeared to take place in slow motion and was always followed by a boat full of *oohs* and *aahs*. The ice would splash into the sea, causing waves that dissipated a half a mile away. The ice, now a berg, would join the many other blocks that became potential resting places for sea lions.

I also witnessed the separation of ice and snow twice on land, in the form of avalanches. The first time, I had driven down some dirt road to try out my new gun, a Smith & Wesson 44-caliber pistol. I had purchased this gun to carry with me for protection from any misinformed grizzly bears I might encounter while hiking alone. When I went hiking with someone else, as long as I was the faster runner, I didn't need the gun. Anyway, I was trying out the most powerful handgun in the world, according to Dirty Harry, and I noticed that the snow, clinging to a distant mountain, had changed color. It took me a few seconds, but I quickly realized that an avalanche was sliding down from the glacier at the top of the mountain. I expected to hear a great thundering sound like in the movies, but I didn't. This avalanche, luckily for me, was too far away to hear. Even at a distance, I could tell that it was massive. The only way to distinguish the falling snow from the standing snow was a slight color difference—and of course the bushes and trees it was wiping out on the way down. The coolest part was when the snow landed in a small valley and sprayed up over the next ledge. I often wondered if it was the loud bang of my revolver that had set it off. I also wondered why I did not have my video camera.

Although very violent in nature, the avalanche caused an odd feeling of tranquility to wash over me. I had recently been on a huge glacier in central Alaska and felt the same sense of tranquility. On my way up to North Pole, the town not the geographical location, my dentist friend Kitty and I stopped at Matanuska Glacier (Mat-Su to the locals). She was visiting from Florida and wanted to experience this glacier about which we had both heard.

As we walked out on this enormous piece of ice, we agreed that it felt more like we were on a different planet than merely in a different state. It was amazing. Pure white as far as the eye could see. In the far distance, the light blue sky met and appeared to meld with the ice so that it was impossible to tell where one began and the other ended. A few low-hanging clouds blending softly with the snow topped off the view perfectly.

After walking on the glacier for a while, careful to avoid the crevasses, we had decided that it might be cool to venture inside one. When we came across a crevasse that seemed penetrable, we carefully slithered down into an area from which we were fairly certain we could get out. It was magical. We walked through tunnels that were forty to fifty feet long and almost the same height. Some of the tunnel walls were bluish-green, some baby blue, and others speckled with various shades of red, black, brown, and gold as a result of dirt trapped inside the ice.

The walls appeared to be flowing like a calm sea with a slight breeze. I could have sworn that the walls were wet, but when I removed my mitten and slid my hand along one section, I found it was unusually dry. At times, these tunnels allowed just enough room for us to pass. Above all, it was still and quiet inside. Only the slight echo of our voices interrupted the tranquility. We had no thoughts of collapsing snow and ice, only complete peace. It was, in a most simple sense, quite a humbling experience.

Shortly after exiting the crevasse, we saw seven people walking toward us. They were all roped together, spaced at equal distances. Unlike us, they wore crampons on their feet and helmets on their heads, and they carried ice axes in their hands. As they filed past, each one looked at us in utter disbelief. "Are you guys crazy? Where's your safety equipment?" the team leader screeched. "Are you kidding me?" the second man asked, shaking his head in disgust. The third and fourth members of the hiking team simply stared with their mouths open. The next two members of the group alternated with, "Where are your ropes? Why don't you have ice axes?" The last guy exclaimed, "Look, even if you don't have ropes and ice axes to help you get out of a crevasse, you should at least be tied off to stop you from falling into one to begin with. Some of these crevasses drop down far enough so that the initial slip and fall will kill you."

We were shocked by the intensity of their concern. When we found our voices, we thanked them for the unsolicited advice, and continued our stroll back home with quite a bit more trepidation than we had felt on the first part of our hike. As we retraced our path, we explored a few more ice caves and did our best to avoid any unexpected, snow-covered crevasses.

We chatted excitedly, agreeing that our trek across the glacier had been pretty adventurous. In hindsight, it was clear that our inexperience and ignorance of safety precautions made our trip far more dangerous than we had planned. When we returned to the glacier the following weekend to retake the once-in-a-lifetime photos that we had accidentally deleted from our new digital camera, the ranger advised us to be extra careful. He informed us that on the previous Sunday, the day after our first visit, a man had in fact fallen into a crevasse and died.

The second avalanche I witnessed in Alaska was during a going-away party that had been organized by my friends and colleagues from the school. Appropriately, the party was held at my home-away-from-home, the Snow River Hostel. We were all sitting out by the campfire, and the teachers were singing a going-away song they had made up about me. This was no ordinary song: my friends had captured some of my antics over the past year and used props to act out the lyrics they had written.

Once the performance was done and we had recovered from the serious bouts of laughter that both the song and the memories had evoked, we decided to take a few pictures to remember each other and commemorate the day. A few of us were directed to line up with the glacier behind us to make a good backdrop. As the photographer readied to take the picture, the camera and her jaw dropped to her waist. An avalanche off in the distance caused us to turn and witness yet another spectacular Alaskan moment. What a great send-off!

My year was done, and I was on my way back to the lower forty-eight with my buddy Brian, who had agreed to keep me company on the five-day trip. While we were driving the famous Alaska/Canada Highway, or Alcan as it is more commonly known, we stopped to look at a bear on the side of the road. While admiring the sow, I noticed a couple of two- to three-year-old cubs in my rearview mirror. The toddlers, one brown and the other black in color—although both were brown bears—were separated by several hundred feet from their much larger mom.

I reversed the hundred or so feet on this desolate road, trying my best to avoid the potholes, and turned off my car so I wouldn't scare the curious cubs. Next, I got my camera ready, and I waited. My patience paid off because, within minutes, the two little ones approached. The black one pressed his face against my window, and I was literally shaking with excitement. It wasn't my trembling hands that caused the blurriness of the photographs however; it was something much more organic than that.

With each swipe of the black cub's curious nose, a fresh coating of bear snot was applied to my window. The bear was only a quarter of an inch away, but the dirty window was closer. Because I had the camera set to auto-focus, the camera focused on the smears on the window rather than the bear that had put them there. Stored forever in film is the image the camera picked—a runny nose with one clearly distinguished booger. The photo is interesting because it clearly depicts the individual hairs on the bridge of the bear's nose as he stood up to greet me. It also shows the saliva dripping from his mouth and what I thought might have been plaque on his teeth. In reality, the best photos from that day exist only in my mind.

For one brief moment, I wanted to roll my window down a bit to better hear the bear's low growls and the frequent smacking of his lips. I wanted to feel and smell his breath upon my face, although I was quite sure, after spying what I thought was a particularly huge glop of scale or tartar, it would not have been the freshest of smells. I imagined getting the chance to gently touch his sharp claws as he slipped his huge paws through my partially opened windows. Maybe I could even get the opportunity to pet the pads on the bottoms of his feet. In spite of all this, I was certain that our gentle bonding would have lasted about three seconds before he put his arm into the car, ripped out my window, and ate my head. All things considered, I decided to leave the windows tightly rolled up.

My regret over this lost opportunity for physical contact was short-lived, however. As I glanced away from the black bear cub and toward the back of the car, I saw the brown bear cub eating my license plate! I turned the key in the ignition, and as the car started, a big puff of black smoke from the exhaust painted him one step closer to looking like his brother and startled him enough that he took off toward the tree line.

The blast of black smoke was not typical for my car. It was a holdover from a couple of hundred miles back when I had completely filled the car with oil—well not the whole car but just that hole you pour oil into. To this day, I do not remember why I did it. I never said I knew a lot about cars, but I must have known not to top off the oil the way most people do the gas tank. Anyway, I don't want to talk about it. I heard enough about it at the time from Brian. He ragged on me for the rest of the trip, and he still does today when we get together. All I can say now is what I resorted to then, "My dipstick was broken, all right?"

Anyway, the bear at my window was, like his sibling, a bit startled and confused by all the smoke. With surprising speed and grace, he went from my window to the front of my car and climbed on top of the hood. I was snapping pictures non-stop, and Brian finally figured out how to turn on his video camera. There we were with a bear on our hood while we sat nervously laughing, photographing, and taping the encounter. Every few minutes, we looked out the side windows, expecting the other cub to return, and we glanced more frequently out the rearview mirror in case he had gone to get his mom!

The weight of the bear cub dented my hood, but I didn't care because my car was a piece of crap and one more dent really did not matter. Plus, I thought, cosmetic damage was certainly a fair price for the video footage we were sure to get. When this hairy hood ornament started eating my windshield wipers, however, I reconsidered and had to pull the plug. I backed the car up enough to help the cub slide off the hood, and we drove off before the little bears decided to taste anything more valuable.

While I would surely miss the wildlife of Alaska, it was the people I would miss the most. Just about everyone I met in Alaska was a genuinely good person, even if some were a bit eccentric and others just plain weird. Everyone in the Frontier State had stories of his or her own, consisting of hair-raising bear encounters, crashes in small bush planes, avalanches, or any of a dozen other dangers that occupy this land. After my year of teaching, traveling, and making friends in this great state, I remained thrilled with my experiences and understood why residents of Alaska often refer to their home state as its own country.

# Conquering the Caribbean: Cargo Boats & Cornrows

Crammed into a tiny prop plane ready for the short forty-five minute flight from Miami to Freeport, Bahamas, I felt like a sardine. I was in panic mode because my knees were literally pressed against the wall separating the front passenger seat of the plane from the back of the co-pilot's seat. I began to sweat, and the prescription medication I was taking to calm me down started to seep out through my pores. In an effort to relax and ignore my extreme claustrophobia, I forced myself to review my plans for this trip and how they came about.

Just one short month prior to this flight, I had finished the internship that I needed to become a certified teacher. While pursuing my degree, I had worked a series of jobs, taken a full load of classes, paid for school, and supported myself. I felt as if all I did was study and work. I had already learned that life was too short, so I had made a solemn vow that I would never use the summer months to earn extra money by teaching summer school or continuing with the litany of odd jobs. I promised myself that I would make the most of my freedom by traveling around the world and making up for lost time. Even though I had been teaching for only a month before summer rolled around, I was more than ready to make good on my vow. Having spent the previous five years in college, however, my vacation fund was a bit lower than I might have liked (okay, it was more like non-existent). Good thing I had a credit card and knew how to use it.

With only a month of my new career under my belt, I was ready and eager to hit the road when the last school bell rang for the summer. All that remained was to decide where to go. Several months earlier, when I was looking through a dive magazine, I had torn out a colorful map of the Caribbean and decided that this was a place I would love to visit. Now on the verge of a new adventure, I decided that one island would not be enough. Getting a late start as a traveler, I had some making up to do. I wanted to see it all.

I picked up the phone and started calling every local travel agent to inquire about Caribbean vacations. Then, I expanded my search throughout my home state. Nothing against travel agents, but many of them seem to deal with a relatively small number of destinations. I think that they are more likely to get a call asking to book Disney World or a nice hotel in Cozumel. I came by this opinion the hard way—by having a conversation with every agent in the Northeast. The dialogue was remarkably similar from call to call and went something like this:

Travel agent (TA): "Hello, ACME Travel."

Me: "Hi, I want to go to the Caribbean."

TA: "Where in the Caribbean, Sir?"

Me: "Everywhere!"

TA: "Uh, well, okay Sir, where would you like to go *this* trip?"

Me: "Many places!"

TA: "Um, you're going to need to go ahead and pick a place."

Me: "But I want to go to a lot of places on one trip."

TA: "Sorry, we don't do that here."

Me: "No problem, can you tell me who does?"

TA: "Yeah, nobody does that."

Me: "But …"

TA: "Thanks for calling ACME Travel." *Click!*

Not willing to admit defeat, I expanded my phone calls west. *Ask and you shall receive,* I kept thinking. I continued the calls and wondered when my telephone bill would exceed the cost of the trip I was trying to book. I think I spent more time on the phone planning this trip than I did my entire, chatty, teenage life. In fact, I was so thorough in my search that there is a good chance that if you were a travel agent in America that year, you talked to me!

Then, as I was about to give up, it happened—the voice of victory. A travel agent told me that she had a friend who knew another lady whose friend's uncle's mom's son took a trip similar to the one I was trying to arrange. She gave me the number for the Windjammer Barefoot Cruises, and I booked a trip on the ship *Amazing Grace*. This was a cargo ship that went throughout the Caribbean and supplied sailboats, as well as supplying many of the smaller islands with food and products. This particular voyage would start in the Bahamas and travel all the way down to Trinidad. As a way to help offset the cost of fuel, the shipping company had cleverly converted some of the ship's space into a few rooms. The rooms were rented out to more adventurous people who did not necessarily want all the creature comforts. One of the rooms, or at least a bunk, was waiting with my name on it—that is, it would be if I could make it to Freeport without jumping out of the plane's emergency hatch!

Suddenly, the intrusive sound of the pilot's voice over the intercom brought me back to the present with a bang, reminding me once again why I hate to fly. The only things that keep me semi-sane on a flight are the drugs I take before I arrive at the airport and the cold air that blows out of the little knob next to the light above my head.

I have this little ritual that consists of opening my air vent (and my neighbor's) full blast, tilting my head back, and sucking the cold air into my lungs for the entire flight as if it were my lifeline. I have learned to ignore the flight attendants when they ask if I am all right. I do not even mind when the little kids in the seat next to me stare at the icicles that often collect at the end of my nose.

Words cannot convey the horror I felt when the disembodied words through the intercom were, "I apologize for the inconvenience, but our air conditioning seems to be malfunctioning."

To me, an example of an *inconvenience* would be if they ran out of those tiny bags of nuts, the ones where you'd need eighty-seven bags to make up one handful. Announcing that the bathroom is out of order is an inconvenience. Telling me that the flight was overbooked and now I would have to stand for the entire trip would be an inconvenience. To take away my air, however, that was clearly a catastrophe of epic proportions!

I could not believe my ears. It was like a joke—but it was not. I instantly felt the blood drain from my head. I started sweating. I considered getting up and taking the next flight. Then, my thoughts ran rampant. *Weren't the meds supposed to be taming my anxiety? Should I take more? Should I strangle the captain, or maybe the innocent flight attendants passing by? Should I hyperventilate into the bag of peanuts? There's plenty of air in there.*

Needless to say, the flight took forever. Each moment seemed like an hour. Every part of my body was sweating. My drugs, I thought, must have been placebos. I wondered if the plane had either flown directly into a headwind or was tethered to a lodestone. At that time, I still had not learned to bring a book along on a flight to keep my mind occupied, so out of desperation, I actually read the safety card in the seat pocket … about eighty-seven times!

Forty-five long minutes later, our plane finally touched down in Freeport, and the first thing I wanted to do after getting several gulps of clean, fresh air was get wet. I had plenty of time to dive before my ship left at midnight, and I had read about a company near the airport that took clients on shark dives. I had wanted to do that sort of dive since seeing it on the Discovery Channel a year earlier. I had the opportunity to do a shark dive on another trip, but both my dive buddies backed out. This time, with only myself to please, I was not going to miss out.

First things first, though. I located my luggage on the conveyor belt. The elation of seeing my belongings come out of that hole in the wall was no less than the elation of watching a baby's little, funny-shaped head crowning at its birth. Of course, the chances are much better that the baby will come out. I checked my luggage for damage much in the same way a nurse would give a baby the APGAR test. Again, a baby has a much better chance of passing.

My old Navy sea bag contained everything I would need for my two-month trip. Inside was a day pack, water bottle, book, journal, dive card and log, a couple of pens, credit card, boat ticket, dive mask, snorkel, fins, regulator, BC, and flip-flops. Unfortunately, I had worn my hiking boots on the plane, and they had become saturated with nervous sweat, which caused them to smell for the duration of my trip. I also carried seven pairs of underwear (okay, three), a couple pairs of socks, three pairs of shorts, a bathing suit, a couple of tank tops, a sweatshirt, and a pair of colorful weightlifting parachute pants left over from the 1980s. The pants were out of style, but they were very comfortable. They had been hidden in a drawer for some time because I just could not part with them. Since I would not be running into anyone I knew on this trip, I figured it would be my only chance to wear the pants without overt ridicule and ostracism. Later, I realized that wearing those oldies-but-goodies prevented me from meeting anyone new!

I grabbed my sea bag and caught the first cab I saw. I asked the driver to take me to the place where they fed the sharks. Twenty minutes later, we were at UNEXSO Underwater Explorers' Dive Shop, and I immediately signed up for the next shark dive. Unfortunately, I had about two hours to kill before the boat was scheduled to head out. I was too excited to wait, but what could I do? I spent the first hour watching the videos of previous divers who had taken this exciting plunge. With adrenaline pumping and a smile bigger than a teenager's on prom night, I had to move around or I was going to explode. I decided to walk to Port Lucaya, a little shopping village, to make my last hour go by faster.

As I strolled along the streets looking at all the little trinkets, a behemoth of a Bahamian lady started pulling at my arm. At first, I thought she was yelling at me for some unknown offense, but I soon realized that all she wanted me to do was get my hair braided. Despite the fact that I had long hair at the time, I had absolutely no intention of getting it twisted and beaded. I mean, what if I saw someone I knew? Then I remembered that I was wearing those parachute pants, and I realized that they would overshadow anything I might have done to my hair. Could I use my choice of clothing as a justification for getting cornrows in my hair? In all actuality, I think what probably convinced me was that the big woman stroked my arm as she and her friends giggled childishly. Pathetic, I know, but I was new in this game. I am sure they saw me coming from a mile away—and they would have even if I had not been wearing those pants!

After an hour of TLC from the "Bahama mamma," I walked back to the dock, styling my classic pants and my braided and beaded hair. I was just on time to catch the dive boat. As the boat headed out to the dive site, I watched the dive master, Mitch, don his Kevlar mesh dive suit. Fully dressed, he resembled the Michelin Man. I toyed with the idea of calling him the "mesh-elin man," but I realized that harassing the person who would be guiding me on a dive with hungry wild sharks was probably not a good idea.

Once we were on the open water, I started talking with a nice Californian couple that sat on the bench across from me. Actually, the lady started talking to me first. She probably sensed a bond between us because we both had the same hair. She gave me a knowing smile and asked, "First time in the Bahamas?" Her husband and I had something in common too. He had a nice camera with an underwater housing, and I wished I had one just like it.

The shark dive was almost beyond description! It was definitely more fun than any other dive I had done up to that point. At the start of the dive, Mitch had us kneel in a half circle on the sandy ocean floor. He then opened up a tube with dead, bloody fish, and in less than five minutes, it happened: more than a hundred dark shadows appeared in the distance. Fear punctured my body like so many knives as the feeding frenzy began around me ... Actually, we had great visibility and saw a dozen or so fairly cautious sharks right away. I guess I thought I was writing fiction there for a minute.

I loved being around those Caribbean reef sharks, even when there were twelve or more sharks swimming around us. They swam closer and closer, and it was not long until the first shark got brave enough to dive in for the food. It ripped a fish out of the mesh-elin man's hands and darted right over my head. Wow! What a close-up! I would experience a dozen more fly-bys before the feeding frenzy was finished. On several occasions, sharks swam past the people to my right and left, providing me with glimpses of the predators' gills. A few times, a shark that came from directly behind me scared me half to death. My favorites were the ones that came straight at me, face to face, and then pulled up at the last second. I got some great close-ups of their teeth, followed by sweet, long glimpses of their white bellies.

At one point, a shark bit down on the dive master's hand to get the bloody fish he was holding. The shark started to thrust its head back and forth, giving the dive master a good shake. Instead of pulling harder to get his hand out, Mitch shoved his hand and arm deeper into the shark's mouth until the shark released him. It was crazy; he actually choked it. The shark swam away empty handed, so to speak, with only a small punch on his nose from Mitch by which to remember the occasion.

A few minutes later, Mitch held the fish tube between his legs to free up his hands. Considering how quickly the shark had grabbed his hand, I thought that was not the safest place to store the tube. When the next shark came sniffing, Mitch grabbed it by the snout and immediately started rapidly rubbing its belly. Mitch gradually slowed the strokes, and within about a minute, the shark was in a trance-like state. I would not have believed it if I had not seen it with my own eyes. It may sound like a fish tale, but it was real. I watched in amazement as the mesh-elin man caressed this animal as if it were the family dog or cat.

Before this adventure, I thought I might be a little anxious about diving with sharks in their own environment. The reality of the experience was so much more than I could have predicted or expected. During some moments of the dive, I laughed so hard that my mask filled with water, requiring that I clear it. At other times, I yelled into my regulator because I was so excited. At one point, if I remember correctly, a tear of joy ran down my face and was trapped by the silicone skirt of my mask.

The guy from California whose camera and housing I had had my eye on said, "Hey, I got some great shots of you with the sharks. If you give my your address, I can send you the pictures."

I decided to be proactive and take it one step further to ensure I got those once-in-a-lifetime-photos. "How about you let me go with you and your wife into Port Lucaya, and I'll even pay for a double set of prints at the one-hour photo shop?" I was so happy they agreed to my proposal that I even bought them ice cream while we waited. They got their shark pictures for free, and I got the assurance that I would actually see those pictures.

This proved to be a very smart strategy for me, and I use it whenever I can. Unfortunately, I don't always have the opportunity for instant print production. I have been given countless promises of great travel pictures from individuals and have yet to receive a single photograph. Many times I've chosen to pay the person in advance just to emphasize how much the pictures mean to me. One time, I even paid for a copy of some underwater video as well as the cost of shipping it to me. Although I have yet to receive the video, it has only been eleven years, and I remain optimistic. I do not think of these people as dishonest. It must be that it is just a hassle to get a copy, put it in an envelope, find my address, and mail it. Maybe I should start carrying self-addressed, stamped envelopes! Not to beat a dead seahorse to death, but I once stuck my hand in a ledge to scare a shark out into the open so this guy could take a great action photo of *Jaws* coming toward him. I think I more than earned a copy of that one, but despite all promises, it never materialized.

After my fantastic shark dive, I hung out in Freeport and eventually made my way to the docks to catch what would be my floating home for the next month. She was beautiful. Not beautiful in the sense of a yacht, but a "huge, steel cargo barge with cranes, forklifts, and cables" kind of beautiful. The boat was being loaded with the last of the shipping containers when I arrived, and there were dozens of people in coveralls all hard at work. Actually, it was more of a laid-back-Bahamas-type of hard work, but everyone still looked very busy. I walked around the front and side of the boat timidly, observing all the activity. When I came upon the gangplank, I hesitantly walked up and entered the boat's belly. I did not feel like I belonged there, but the greeting of a kind crewmember made my anxiety shortly slip-slide away. She welcomed me, checked my ticket, and showed me to the top bunk of a tiny room several levels below deck.

As promised, we launched at midnight, and I stayed up all night long, delighting in the gentle rocking of the huge vessel. My time on board the *Amazing Grace* took on a nice, regular pattern. In the early evenings, I would hang out in the wheelhouse with the staff. The man responsible for steering the ship was Alec. He was a tall, muscular islander, always dressed in the striped shirt appropriate for a member of a ship's crew. Alec did not talk, but Julio, the first mate from Venezuela, filled the dark hours by telling endless and fascinating stories of life at sea.

After story time, I would hang over the railings at the bow of the ship like Leonardo DiCaprio in *Titanic*. I spent most evening hours somewhere on deck just enjoying the quiet of the sea. Sometimes, I would just breathe deep, exaggerated breaths of clean, salty air and allow my body to ride every wave with enthusiasm. Other times, I was so relaxed that I was barely breathing at all. Mostly, I was just so deep in thought about every aspect of life that even a tidal wave would have been hard pressed to move me from my place. It was especially easy to fall into this meditative trance on days when there was no land in sight and we were surrounded by the endless, dark blue ocean.

Unfortunately, I found it impossible to sleep in my tiny room because of the whole claustrophobia thing. Maybe I sensed that my minuscule room was actually below the waterline. Between the claustrophobia and my enriched imagination, riotous thoughts disrupted my sense of calm like a clanging gong. *What if we started taking on water and the crew had to seal the hatches? What if we sank anyway? I would be trapped at the bottom of the ocean … forever!* Oh, God! I can't breathe just thinking about it. Take a deep breath. Take another deep breath. It is clear to see why I never wanted to leave the freedom of the deck and always tried to sleep up there.

Each night on deck, I hoped the fresh, open air and the gentle rocking of the ship would put me to sleep. Unfortunately, sleep would evade me there as well, but for a host of different reasons. Subconsciously, I think I was always afraid I would wake up dead! Or worse, what if I suddenly woke to find myself floating in the Caribbean, staring at the stern of the ship as it drifted farther and farther away?

There was one occasion when I was able to fall asleep on deck; most assuredly it was due to the "little" bottles of alcohol I had consumed late that afternoon (I blame the Dutch soccer fans in St. Martin). I woke up sometime before sunrise. I don't know if it was the smell of my drunk, rancid breath or the fact that I was freezing to death as the breeze slowly but surely sucked the heat from my body. I peeled myself away from the plastic lounge chair I had been sprawled upon, stumbled downstairs, and threw up twice before I made it to my room. After drinking most of the water in the ship's holding tanks and swallowing a few aspirin, I lay down on my bunk, and for the first time, I actually fell asleep on it.

The sound sleep lasted about thirteen minutes before the captain's voice pounded over the intercom like the shock waves of a supersonic jet. I whined for a minute, but soon realized his announcement meant that we were at another island, and I needed to check it out! I got dressed, albeit a little slowly, and slithered down the gangplank to check out the beautiful tropical island.

Over the course of two weeks, we traveled through the Caribbean, restocked a couple of sailboats, and delivered supplies to over a dozen islands. Every day, I woke up and looked out at a different island waiting to be conquered, each having its own unique flavor and color. On these islands, I hiked, checked out waterfalls or whatever the local attraction was, and snorkeled or dived.

I do my best thinking in the water whether I am diving, snorkeling, floating in a pool, or just taking a shower. On this trip, the sea was my think tank. One day, as I thought about this first big trip, I realized that my next stop or port would be the last one of this voyage. Like the rest of the travelers aboard, I was scheduled to leave the *Amazing Grace* in Trinidad. Unlike them, I had not made plans to fly back to Freeport or home. There was more summer left for me, and I wanted to continue to fill it with memorable experiences.

I thought of the other island countries that I wanted to visit. I was already far south in the Caribbean. Some islands I wanted to see were very close to the places I had already visited. I prayed for a way to extend this first trip. Could I pick up another boat going between islands, possibly a fishing boat, or maybe even another cargo ship?

My prayers were answered when the first mate, Julio, asked if I would be interested in taking the return trip with them. He remembered that my occupation allowed me to take my summers off, and he said I was a good passenger. I guess that meant I never complained about anything and was never late getting back on the boat. Julio told me we would be stopping at over a dozen different islands on the return trip. He added that the cost of the return trip would be a fraction of what I had already paid to get to Trinidad because some guests that had planned to join them for the return trip to Freeport had backed out. My excitement led to another sleepless night, and my early morning arrival in Trinidad was not a sad farewell but a gleeful event. It was merely another stopover! I was now only halfway through my Caribbean adventure. I could not stop smiling.

My smile stayed with me only for a short while as I walked the overcrowded streets of Port of Spain in Trinidad. I did not see another tourist the entire time, and if they had been anywhere, they would have been in this area among all the shops. I needed no material items and just wanted to get off the dirty streets lined with homeless beggars. After several hours of walking, observing, and getting harassed to either buy things or just hand over money, I made my way back to the boat.

After that less-than-thrilling foray into town, I decided to eat lunch on the boat. When I went into the dining area, I ran into Regina. Regina was a cook on the boat, and, like many crew members, Trinidad is where she called home. She was just getting off work and going home to visit her family. We started talking, and she invited me to come to her house to meet everybody. I gave up lunch on the boat and jumped at the opportunity.

We walked to the bus station and took the ever-so-typical, death-defying ride that seems commonplace on the islands. The trip took about thirty minutes, and once we got off the bus, we still had a twenty-minute walk before we arrived at her house. Everyone was happy to see Regina. Her mother, brothers, sisters, and friends gathered around the little local store that was part of her house. I struggled with my Spanish as I had conversations with her family, neighbors, and a friend who drove up on his motorcycle.

Regina's mom had cooked some delicious-smelling food. Unfortunately, I had a self-imposed limitation. When I go to a foreign place, food is not part of the culture I am willing to experience because I have some sort of allergy that results in a fairly violent, physical reaction to foods with any kind of spice or anything related to the onion family. This is a disadvantage for me, as food brings people together and really is a big part of the traveling experience. I also realized that my aversion to sampling food might offend certain people in some cultures. In spite of this, I figured it was less of a problem than the invariable outcome of my allergy—eight or nine hours of having one end parked on their toilet while the other end was filling the nearest sink or bucket.

I made it through dinner without insulting my hosts. I had filled up on crackers, slipped most of my meal to the family *perro*, and spread the rest around my plate like kids do when they are three years old and Mom has made spinach and meatloaf. Noticing that I had not finished all my food, Regina's mom asked if I did not like it. Regina translated as I said that I was still full from lunch. Regina knew I had not eaten lunch, but she lied for me anyway.

We talked for quite a while and decided it was time to start making our way back to the boat. Before we left, I bought four packs of cookies and a bag of chips from the family store. At first, they thought I was being nice and helping their business; that was until they realized I had eaten the entire stash before I made it out of the front door. Because some neighbors had offered to drive us back to the boat, we had some extra time on our hands. Regina and her friends decided it would be fun to take that time and stop at a club. I would have chosen differently, but I was not driving and I was greatly outnumbered.

I have nothing against clubs, but they are just not for me. The wild atmosphere, the dirty dancing, and the beautiful, sexy women with the short skirts … all right, I like those parts. As for being in a crowd of people so close together, listening to deafening music, and screaming just to be heard, these are all things I try to avoid. Witnessing alcohol-induced anger and drama is just stimulation overload for me. I know I sound like a monk, but I have always been terribly uncomfortable in that sort of atmosphere. Even during my early twenties, I would choose to do just about anything, including getting a traditional Polynesian tattoo, instead of clubbing.

When we walked into the establishment, it was everything I have previously described. However, there was an additional element; I was white—I still am, in fact—and they were not. I was in a local club in Trinidad, and I did not come even remotely close to blending in with the crowd. Therefore, I did what any person in his right mind but in an uncomfortable situation might do—drink! That's right, I wanted to get out of my "right mind," so I consumed enough alcohol to lose the uncomfortable part. It worked remarkably. Within a half hour, I was dancing and singing with my new friends, or at least I was dancing and singing with somebody's friends. It didn't matter, I was happy.

After we left the club, our final stop on the way to the boat was a roadside vendor where Regina and one of her brothers could get some chicken feet to eat. As I watched them munch on the feet, I started to feel as though I had eaten some of her mom's spicy dinner. Because we had lost track of time at the club, we arrived a few minutes late to the boat. The captain was angry, and I wondered if Julio had already regretted asking me to remain on board. Regina's excuse for being tardy was that they had to keep stopping for the tourist (me) to throw up. I'm still not sure what the final straw was for my stomach—the alcohol I sloshed into it or the sight of my friends munching on those chicken feet.

The *Amazing Grace* set sail for another glorious fourteen days at sea. Regina turned my otherwise unpleasant time in Trinidad into a momentous one. She told her fellow kitchen crew about our experience, and the gang seemed to take a liking to me. Rayen, another cook on board, began a conversation with me the following morning. Although Rayen was from the Caribbean, he had never snorkeled or even spent much time in the water. He asked me if I would I take him snorkeling at the next island if he bought me some chicken feet. I agreed to take him as long as he never mentioned the feet again.

About halfway through our return trip, we hit an island that had little to offer besides snorkeling. Rayen had the afternoon off, so I introduced him to the wonderful underwater world. After he got a spare mask and snorkel from his shipmates, I took him to a nice area where the ocean waves were calmed by some rock formations and water filtered through the gaps. We donned our gear and Rayen began to warm up. I had not realized there was a warm-up period needed for snorkeling, but all right, whatever made him feel comfortable. This six-foot-tall man bent over toward the shore and stuck his masked face in the three inches of water. He looked so bizarre, almost like a dark-black ostrich. After about four or five minutes of this, he turned toward me in the waist-deep water and reluctantly dived in. He held my arm in a vise-like grip that would tighten every time I pointed out a fish to him. When we spotted a big fish, he would actually ride on my back like a kid getting a horsy ride from his dad. I would have loved to have a video of this, but at the same time, I was very glad there was nobody around to film it.

The dive was short; it lasted about as long as it took for Rayen to warm up. He had just slid off my back for the second time, and I had just coughed up the rest of the water I had swallowed upon submersion. We had paddled out to where the surge flowed back and forth from the ocean swells. It was, apparently, about seven feet of water and an excellent spot for sharks to hang out and watch as possible prey floated by. I was tickled to see a big, but docile, nurse shark. My buddy did not share the same type of enthusiasm. He splashed through the water like he was trying to attract it. When he made it to within about ten feet of shore, he pretty much walked on water the rest of the way. I believe it will be another twenty-three years before Rayen puts another snorkel in his mouth.

I had become very attached to this small crew and the few passengers aboard the *Amazing Grace*, but after a month and over 1,670 nautical miles, I finally had to say good-bye. A couple of nights prior to our farewell in Freeport, I was eating dinner by myself in the ship's dining area, and a nice older lady approached. She introduced herself as Spock and said she was from New Zealand. She was a tour guide for a group of Kiwis and was taking a little time off. She was an amazing woman with a tremendous zest for life. She had an absolutely awesome personality and was obviously very non-judgmental. She had to be to start up a conversation with someone who had long, braided hair, a month-old scraggly beard, and a few pirate earrings, and who was wearing tiger wrestling pants.

We talked for hours that night; her spirit was the type that anyone would envy. I felt very lucky to be spending time with her and could have talked until dawn. She invigorated me with energy—true, long-lasting energy that actually revived my spirit and made me want to live my life with even more vim and vigor. I wanted to be just like her. I swore she was the kind of person whose spark was so profound that it could keep her alive forever. That is why I was so very surprised and sad when I learned that, on our last night at sea, she passed away in her sleep.

As I walked down the plank of that cargo ship, silently humming *Amazing Grace*, a song the crew traditionally played over the intercom each night, I had mixed emotions. I felt happiness for the time spent with these people and all the memorable experiences of that month. However, I also felt sadness for the end of my relationship with the passengers and crew. I especially felt sorrow for the loss of Spock. Part of me wanted to snap out of it and get on with my vacation, but instead, I spent the next couple of days thinking about her and really trying to understand the significance of our meeting and how it should influence my life. One thing was clear: the crossing of our paths was a poignant reminder of the fleeting nature of life and my need to live life with passion.

# DIVE! DIVE! DIVE!
## BELLY-UP & BOAT-LESS

From about the age of twelve, I dreamed of breathing underwater. I remember my first attempt rather vividly. It was mid-July, and I was hot—a situation that, to this day, I find quite intolerable. I set off in the direction of the Forest Park pool. Forest Park was an apartment complex down the road from the projects where I lived. I spent so much time in that pool that the residents—who had legitimate pool access—thought that I, too, lived in the complex. After slipping into the seventy-eight degree water, I cupped my hands tightly around my mouth and nose and slowly submerged my face in the chlorinated pool water. All I ended up getting from this experience was a mouth full of water. Nonetheless, it was worth it because it was still fun, and I was sure that someday I would successfully accomplish my dream.

It took thirteen years from that first attempt before I met with greater success. I was living in Connecticut when I signed up for SCUBA classes. After three weeks in the classroom and practice in the pool, the entire class drove to Jamestown, Rhode Island to do our open water certification. It was summer, but the ocean water was only fifty-five degrees. To prevent debilitating hypothermia, I had to wear a full-body, six-millimeter wetsuit. To combat my natural buoyancy as well as that of the wet suit, I needed to add about thirty pounds of weight to my belt so I could sink instead of float. I had to carry my gear down a steep embankment littered with loose rocks just waiting to give way no matter how carefully I stepped. At the water's edge, I donned my hood, a device designed to protect a diver from the cold, but that also, unfortunately, cuts off circulation to the brain. I walked into the water with the five other members of my class. We put on our fins, sank to the sandy bottom, and tried to perform our underwater skills. After twenty minutes of a dive made less-than-pleasant by near-zero visibility, we all got out of the water, dried off, warmed up, and prepared to do it all again.

Part of the PADI dive certification requires demonstrating the ability to perform a series of tasks during four dives over the course of two days. So, the next day, I found myself repeating this less-than-stellar experience and sadly discovering that additional visibility could not enhance the dive since there really was nothing at all to see. Looking back on it, I am not surprised that, for many people who take their certification dives under these conditions, their first series of dives become their last.

Shortly after I earned my certification, I wondered why we went all the way to Rhode Island to dive when we had the same ocean in Connecticut. So I grabbed Christy, the guy who had encouraged me to get SCUBA certified, and we headed down to the local shore. Christy, also known as "The Greek," had been diving for about ten years and was more than happy to be my dive buddy. We suited up just as I had done a few weeks before and started walking through the surf. The three- to four-foot waves felt never-ending. They were merciless as they beat our bodies for the ten to fifteen minutes it took us to reach deeper water. Instead of the calmer, more swimmable environment we had expected to find below the surface, we found a strong surge waiting for us. Before I had moved more than ten feet, I lost the collection bag I had optimistically brought along in case I found treasure. We rode the surge for about three minutes as the current repeatedly pushed us toward shore and then violently changed its mind and ripped us back out to sea. The effect had us both on the verge of throwing up our breakfast. During that entire nauseating time, we saw three blades of sea grass and a common three-inch shell identical to the millions I had seen on the beach as I walked into this washing machine.

With a total of about five minutes bottom time, we gave each other the signal and headed back to the beach. We kicked our fins against the current and surge until we were again floating on the surface of the shallow water. As we stood up and tried to take off our fins, three-foot waves knocked us over and stole a dive fin from each of us. During the next onslaught of larger waves, I lost my mask and snorkel. Again and again, we attempted to gain our footing. Exhausted, The Greek just rode the waves in helplessly and lay where the waves chose to deposit him on the shoreline. I got up and was able to take three solid strides before being pummeled every which way by the next set of crashing waves. I ended up on my back on the shore next to The Greek. I felt lifeless. We lay there, too tired to be embarrassed. As I gained some energy, I started trying to roll over. Unfortunately, my exit from the tumultuous ocean had been more taxing than I realized. Hampered by the weight of my SCUBA tank, I had just enough energy to start the roll—but not enough to complete it. So there I lay, on my back, much like a turtle flipped on its shell, a fine companion for my friend, who looked more and more like a stranded pilot whale. I no longer wondered why we had to go to Rhode Island to get certified. I wished I had just asked.

Within six months of getting my dive certification, I moved to Florida, where the water was warm, the visibility was good, and I did not have to wear a wetsuit—at least not in the summer. Soon after my arrival, I discovered that having the right boat was just as important as having the right dive spot.

It was Thanksgiving eve, and I was heading out into the Gulf of Mexico on a SCUBA diving trip. The one-hour boat ride to the dive site allowed me plenty of time to mingle with the rest of the divers on this excursion. Sunset was just over an hour away, and I was reminiscing about past night dives. Some of the other divers looked a little nervous. I didn't know if it was because, for some, it was their first night dive or if it was simply the result of traveling so far from shore. We were, after all, on a small twenty-foot boat about twenty-two miles off shore. In either case, I'm certain that, whatever their source of concern, it was compounded by that special eeriness that accompanies every night dive. I suspect that for some, if not all, it was a combination of both.

When we arrived at the site, I felt great anticipation as I suited up. I was excited about the dive simply because night dives were my personal favorite. My fascination with night dives involves more than a simple absence of light. It is the addition of an almost palpable mystery that raises the intensity of the experience beyond imagination. Then there is the myriad of eyes. By following the flashlight's narrow beam of light and observing even the tiniest of reefs or rocks, I could see hundreds of sets of eyes from all sorts of unknown creatures staring back through the dark night water.

"Dive! Dive! Dive!" shouted the young, naive captain. His words, like a clanging gong, broke my revere and served as my signal. This first dive of the trip would be a twilight dive. It would allow us a chance to acclimate to our unfamiliar environment. As usual, just like a kid, I rushed to be the first one into the water. My dive buddy, Jeff, the owner of the dive shop where I worked, dived in just after me.

The shockingly cold water trickled down the backs of our wetsuits as we floated for a minute trying to regain the air that had been stolen from our lungs. The time spent floating on the surface, waiting for the water that seeped between our skin and our wetsuits to warm up, was spent in vain. The cool, windy, evening air blew on our wet heads and chilled us even more. As soon as the other members of our group entered the water, we dropped toward the bottom, some sixty feet below. As we descended, the water temperature kept dropping until it was a bone-chilling sixty-five degrees.

We added a bit of air to our buoyancy compensator devices (BCD) just before we hit bottom and began our horizontal exploration of the ocean floor. We started off strong, trying to warm ourselves by kicking harder than normal. We did not stick around to watch the other divers sink to the bottom, although I did peek back to see their lights searching in all directions. This typical night dive scene reminds me of a science fiction movie and is one of the highlights of a night dive.

I usually go very slowly during a night dive because I want to closely observe the small nocturnal specimens. With natural navigation being more difficult at night, one tends to cover less ground on these dives, and I personally advocate for this because, during a couple of night dives in the past, I have been in situations that I would not care to repeat. On two separate occasions, I had to surface much sooner than I had expected. In both instances, my dive buddies had gone through air more quickly than they had anticipated because of the extra anxiety associated with a night dive. We surfaced farther from the boat than we'd planned. If we had moved more slowly and covered less ground, the air might have lasted a bit longer and, upon surfacing, our view of the boat would have been more than speck of light on the dark horizon. Although I had more than enough air, we had no choice but to stick together and swim on the surface, battling the current that is usually less prevalent on the bottom. Our dive gear, neutrally buoyant underwater, became a lodestone as we dragged it on a surface swim. Additionally, it was impossible to escape the thoughts of sharks skimming the surface for food at night.

Upon surfacing from this beautiful twilight dive, we noticed the sun just spilling its last glimmering rays into the far-off waters. Although Jeff and I had been the first divers into the water, we were the last to return to the boat. Cold was the reason the five other divers gave for returning so shortly after their plunge. Jeff and I quickly joined the shivering group in a scurry to get dry and warm. The unrelenting wind of that cold November night made it impossible for even the aggressively virile among us to hide his chill.

When the sun finally set, it added to the cold. It made most of the divers choose warmth over their second dive. There were, however, three of us too stubborn to quit. With great dread, we peeled off our warm clothes and slithered back into our cold, soaked wetsuits. Like vultures to road kill, the remainder of the group snatched up our dry clothes that still bore the warmth of our body heat. This attack was quite scary, and I felt a sense of comfort when I heard the long-awaited signal, "Dive! Dive! Dive!"

The second dive was more mysterious and spooky than usual, but it had to be cut short because of the uncontrolled shivering we were all experiencing. Upon reaching the surface, I did not find the comfort that I have typically experienced. The sky was pitch-black, and the only light was on the bow of our rocking boat. The seas had picked up a bit, making it more difficult to peel off our gear, hand it to the crew, and climb back into the boat.

The dry divers were glad to see us, but probably not for the same reasons we were glad to see them. We made our way onto the deck as if returning victorious from battle, but we had no idea of the battle that lay ahead.

First, we needed to get out of our cold, tight wetsuits. This process resembles a magician attempting to get out of a straitjacket. Getting my clothes back from the scavengers, however, was easier said than done. I probably would have asked and ultimately demanded their return if the young spunky couple who had stayed aboard had snagged my clothes, but I had left them with Sarah. Sarah was a very religious, sweet mother of eight (who has since brought that number to nine). Sarah never looked up at me, and she never offered my clothes back either. I am not a passive person, but, for whatever reason, I knew it was going to be a cold, long hour back to shore.

RRRrrrrr. RRRrrr. This vaguely familiar noise was taking on a more ominous meaning. The sound was similar to fingernails scraping a chalkboard and served as a backdrop for the drama occurring on deck with the captain. It appeared that this was his first charter trip as the captain, and Jeff was relieving the ignorant man of his duties. Jeff peppered him with questions: "Where is the backup battery? How about the spark plugs?" The spineless, soon-to-be demoted crewman slithered away speechless. At first, the drama and dead engine created a sense of inconvenience, but this quickly gave way to fear. After close to an hour—which seemed like an entire night—all attempts to bring the engine back to life came to an end.

We had to contact help, but whom? The captain claimed that Sea Tow, the equivalent to an aquatic tow truck, would charge at least $800 for coming all the way out there. He said that the owner would be livid over this cost, but he might be equally displeased with traveling twenty-two miles out to sea to pick up his newly appointed captain's first tour.

"Tough crap, just get on the radio and get us out of here!" I screamed. "We don't care how mad your boss is going to be." I felt bad for being so harsh, but I am sure the rest of the crew was glad I spoke up. My slight sympathy for the unpopular sailor would soon change.

The radio was dead. The entire crew was silent. Some of them were angry, some were deep in thought, and all of them were worried. For the first few minutes, ideas were flung about at random. Someone suggested setting off flares. This was a good thought, but the time of day, coupled with the distance to shore, probably meant that there were no other boats around to see a distress signal. Because of the many miles between our boat and shore, nobody on shore would see a flare either. Plus, a thick fog had been creeping up on us and made the flares ultimately useless. A pretentious young lady named Candy suggested paddling back to shore. We chose to be nice and not respond at all. Subsequent ideas were few and far between. The group seemed to be accepting the option of a long, cold float. We chose to float instead of anchor because the tide was coming in. Although it would have taken forever and a day to reach shore, at least we were heading in the right direction.

The soon-to-be-unemployed captain slouched on his previous throne. Jeff, Candy, and a burly man named Bill fought to get the warmest seat in the house—which was under the bow. As I left them there, nestled among the life jackets, I passed the now-quiet couple sitting on a cold, hard bench on the starboard side of the boat. Assessing my choices, I decided to perch next to the frozen mom who had not moved or said a word, except to God, throughout the whole event. This was not even close to a prime seat, and while I could have tried to join the small orgy on the bow, I felt an obligation to comfort this thin, prolific, mother of eight. Maybe she would at least give me my underwear back so I could wear it as a hat!

Time crept slowly by, making hours seem like days. At this point, we were all much colder, and most of us were visibly shivering. I was the only one still wet, but I also had the most body fat so it kind of evened out. "We're going to die out here," was the only voice I had heard from the starboard side. The young husband quickly suppressed his wife's cry of fear. I heard the captain mumbling to himself shortly after, probably something about a career change. It appeared as if the three selfish swabbies up front thought this night might be their last. It also appeared by the way they were "exchanging body heat" that one last sexual pleasure would be their chosen way to go.

Sarah stayed very quiet and dignified. Her only words to me over the course of several hours were of her regret to come on a dive trip without her husband. "This is my first dive without my Charles. Why didn't I cancel when he did? Now I will never see him again. We are going to die. We are going to die here tonight!" I had assumed with all the praying that Sarah had been doing that she was doing all right, but I was wrong. I spent the next few hours convincing her that I was not going to die tonight and neither was she. We talked of her children, and I asked lots of questions. I am sure she was aware of my good intentions, but I think we were both getting mentally drained.

Over time, my wet suit stopped keeping me warm and started acting like a refrigerator. I experienced uncontrollable, massive shivering as my body attempted to generate some heat of its own. Exhaustion was becoming a big factor. The fog engulfing us was as thick as the proverbial pea soup, and a prevailing feeling of uselessness was hovering over us all. Having no ability to influence my destiny was very discouraging, but I did comprehend that fate was beyond my control. Teeth chattering and stifled cries were the last sounds I remember. After what seemed like several days of freezing and icy silence, a dull light appeared on the horizon and simultaneously, the sound of a muffled boat engine. Some of us cheered, and others celebrated by thanking the Lord. Was this an angel? No, it was just the owner of the boat, but he was heaven-sent.

The hero supplied us with blankets. Much to our collective dismay, however, he attempted to fix the boat while we continued to wait. He installed a new battery under seven sets of resentful eyes, but it was to no avail. The engine would not start. The journey back by tow was a cold, long, slow trip, but our spirits were renewed. Though my body ached with fatigue, I enjoyed the sunrise as if I were in paradise. We reached our destination at 8:30 a.m. I felt like a steak being taken out of a freezer. My numb legs felt like clubs, and I nearly fell as I stepped onto dry land.

We all said good-bye, and Sarah gave sincere thanks. I was happy to have assisted someone who had a lot more kids and a lot less body fat than I. I cannot help but think I was warmer and stronger just by sitting next to this wonderful child of God. This event would be one of many instances in which my own faith would be challenged. Those sixteen hours had been the longest test I had ever taken, but I had passed! In my travels and adventures, I have learned to look at the bright side of almost any situation.

Although getting stranded out in the Gulf for all those hours was extremely unpleasant, I was grateful that at least there was a boat to stay afloat. During another trip, I traveled to Belize to do some diving. When I arrived at the quaint little guesthouse just off the beach in Placencia, I simply wanted to chill, and chill I did. I am usually good at chilling for about fifteen to twenty minutes before I need to plan the next event, but this was a tropical paradise. I sat in the hammock on the porch gazing at the ocean. Two days had gone by when I realized I had not done a thing except get hammock sores. I gave myself a mental shake and made what felt like a major decision. Tomorrow, I promised myself, I would walk down the boardwalk and sign up for a dive.

Even though I did not want to leave the porch the next day either, I had made a plan and decided to stick with it. By the time I got to the dive shack, however, both boats had already left. With no other option, I signed up for the following day. The young Belizean asked if I wanted to dive on the famous Blue Hole, a more aggressive dive, or just take the smaller boat and do a couple of shallow dives. "It doesn't matter to me, wherever there is more room," I responded. I could not believe my own ears. It was so unlike me not to select the coolest, most exciting choice. Maybe it was the hammock. Maybe I was still recovering from the hellish bus ride that had gotten me to Belize. Maybe it was the laid-back charm of this little town. More than likely, it was the fact that departure time for the popular Blue Hole dive was more than an hour earlier than the shallow dive option. And in my newly laid-back mode, if something meant getting up earlier, it didn't seem so appealing. Regardless of the reason, I would soon be grateful for the decision that young man made to book me on the smaller boat.

The next day, I found myself on a tiny strip of an island. I had just completed my first dive, and we pulled up to have lunch. I was dive buddies with a twelve-year-old boy and his uncle. On the way to the first dive site, the younger of my dive buddies told me all about this island.

After we ate, the boy and his uncle gathered up their food scraps and told me to take mine and follow them to the water's edge. I grabbed my scraps, and we waded knee-deep into the water. We started throwing the fish and chicken parts, the remnants of our lunch, into the water in front of us. Within a minute, I spotted shark fins coming toward us. The boy was smiling as if this was what he had expected. I glanced at the uncle to ensure that he, too, had expected this attack. He was also smiling with anticipation as the sharks neared. Within minutes, there were a dozen sharks coming from all different directions, sucking up the treats we had laid before them. As I watched the fins slice slowly and methodically through the water, heading in my direction, I was honestly scared. I could not get the theme from *Jaws* out of my head. As the sharks got close, they dashed for the food and stirred up the water inches from my feet. At times, I felt the sandpaper-like skin of the nurse sharks brush up against my legs as they swam in frenzied patterns to get their portions. The excitement ended when the food was gone. I wished I had eaten less and scrapped more.

I quickly exhausted my supply of scraps to feed the aquatic vultures and began to steal bits of food from the next hungry boatload of divers. Much to my disappointment, I was pulled away from the ever-hungry sharks by my dive boat's captain. Everyone was happy to see me onboard. My dive party was relieved because they were anxious to begin the next dive and the remaining divers were just happy that we left before I used all their food to fill the bellies of the sharks.

We completed our second dive and began our five-mile trip back to shore. Not long into our return trip, the boat's engine coughed a few times and then shut down completely. Some passengers were bummed out by the unexpected delay and started to complain. Apparently, they had something pressing to do. I was on a dive boat off shore from a beautiful country, it was daylight, and I was not cold. *Who has it better than us?* I thought. Within forty-five minutes, another boat passed by and took everyone but the captain, who stayed on board to try to fix the boat, back to shore.

The next day, we all heard the news that the dive operation's big boat, the one carrying divers to the Blue Hole, had hit a reef and sunk. The divers and crew had been floating all day and were not rescued until 3:00 that morning. A fishing boat had finally found them and brought them all safely back to shore. Under those circumstances, I imagine those divers would not have been grumbling or complaining about a boat cast adrift. They probably would have been happy to have any boat—even one with a broken engine—just as I had … twice!

# EGYPT:
## DEAD OR ALIVE

Sitting in a city bus in Cairo, I was steaming from both the Egyptian heat and utter frustration. The driver had parked the bus outside the terminal doors, and before I could even make contact with the seat, he had exited to go talk to his friend. After about fifteen solid minutes of watching them shoot the breeze, I started thinking what this scene would be like if we were in the United States. I imagined that within three minutes, some passengers would have been on their cell phones to the bus company demanding that this man be fired. Within eight minutes, at least one impatient person would be laying on the bus horn. At fifteen minutes, someone would have blown a gasket.

I did not have a cell phone, and I thought that blasting the horn—if it even worked on this dilapidated excuse for a bus—might be the start of an event that would eventually land me in an Egyptian prison. Now, I'm happy to say that I am largely unaware of the conditions in Egyptian prisons, and, while blessed with an abundance of curiosity, I was not too excited to learn. I was, however, getting exponentially more impatient every second we waited for the bus driver to return to his post. Therefore, I made my way through the maze of passengers and hopped off the bus. After all, neither I nor the famous Sphinx and Pyramids were getting any younger.

The bus driver was still in animated conversation with his friend as I strode past and probably did not hear what I said about him and the camel he rode in on. Instead of my originally planned bus ride, I found myself walking away from the airport through the security gates into a world vastly different from that of the driver and bus. There were multitudes of taxis in all different shapes and sizes lined up in rows, awaiting the arrival of desperate travelers. If I didn't know better, which at the time I did not, I would say these were just privately owned cars. As random as the scene before me initially appeared to be, upon closer inspection, it was clear that there was an order and a code. First and foremost, people looking for taxis had to choose the first car in a strategically organized line of cars. When I walked to the third taxi from the front, for example, I inadvertently started a battle that made Custer's Last Stand look like a parent-teacher conference.

Apparently, drivers who do not follow the rule are reported to the taxi gods of Cairo. I was blissfully unaware of this code when I chose the third driver from the front because he possessed the two physical characteristics I thought most important in a driver: older and heavier than I. I figured that older drivers probably had more experience than young guys and, if I was lucky, perhaps some good advice. Having a driver heavier than me was important because if he tried to get back to the car and take off with my backpack, I thought I could outrun him. Finding such a perfectly matched driver awaiting me in line, I confidently walked over to him and said with a smile, "To the pyramids, sir, and step on it."

He graciously assisted me and my backpack into his wreck of a car. He did a twelve-point-turn, whacking the bumpers of cars in front and in back of us on ten of the twelve points, and we were off! As we drove through the city, I instantly regretted the *step on it* part. Similar to everywhere else I've ever been where the safety standards are slightly less enforced than in my home country, the cabbies and bus drivers drove like psychotics. My driver, who claimed to have six children of his own, seemed to be actively trying to pick off individuals on the busy streets that were perpetually filled with a chaotic maze of people. People were walking, riding bikes, or driving cars, and they all appeared to share a single purpose: to cut in front of the cab in which I was riding.

We were on a major boulevard lined with shops, restaurants, and traffic lights when I looked to my left and saw what I had come all the way to Egypt to see. There, right before my eyes, loomed the Great Pyramids. I thought we would have been driving in the desert for hours before we came upon them. Who would have thought, after looking at all those *National Geographic* photos of Egypt, that a big, modern, thriving city was built right next to this wonder of the ancient world?

I guess that the photographers must have taken their photos from the street side facing the vast desert. So I took out my camera, lined up facing the desert, and took my shot (well, if it was good enough for *National Geographic* …). Then, I walked through the tiny little desert town where the cabby had conveniently stopped. I would like to say that I walked into a shop as a man in charge of his own destiny, but it would be more accurate, I think, to say that thirteen Egyptian salesmen carried me.

My first impression as I was pulled through door was of beaded curtains that covered the entrance to a back room filled with Egyptian papyrus paper prints. The whole scene was straight out of a classic 1940s movie. The owners began to show me how the papyrus was made. Even though I never shop, within minutes, I had bought a print of the gorgeous Cleopatra surrounded by a bunch of unidentified Egyptian hieroglyphics. A friend of mine who regretted not buying one on his last trip to Egypt had asked me to pick up a print if I had the chance. While my recently purchased masterpiece was being prepared, the shop owner arranged for me to take a camel ride around the pyramids. At the time, I did not fully understand what "prepared" meant or why the process would take so long. I later learned that it meant that the salesmen were going to replace the real print I had purchased with a fake one similar to those I could have bought from a street vendor for a dollar. In the end, I did manage to get a free sunset camel ride around the pyramids, and to me that was well worth it!

My driver, Akbar, had dropped me at a nice little hotel that his *cousin* owned. Oh the naïveté of it all! I spent part of the night and some of the next morning peeling off what felt like an infinite number of rug salesmen who insisted that I drink tea with them. They were somehow convinced that I not only needed a rug but that each one of theirs was better than the ones being sold by the eight other salesmen next to them.

After breakfast, I managed to fly through the lobby and elude the rug salesmen. I completed my escape because Akbar was waiting for me. We had arranged this meeting the previous night since I thought he was honest—probably—and he certainly needed the money. After all, as he now claimed, he had seven kids to feed. I felt good about employing him for another day.

Anyway, this time we went back down the major boulevard and drove up to the Sphinx. I first saw the paws, and then the entire body of a lion. Eventually, the head of the pharaoh with its crumbled, half-missing nose came into view. The Sphinx was a lot smaller than I had imagined. I got out of the car and lay on the ground, once again trying to reproduce the shots I had seen in the documentary that led me here.

During my explorations on site, a young Egyptian in his early twenties, who swore he did not want a thing from me, escorted me on foot to some secret tombs about a hundred yards from the Sphinx. At this point, I was so sick of being harassed and misled that I was ready to hire an Egyptian guard to keep the hounds away. For once, I was so impressed with the hidden tombs, the information he provided, and the gift of a jade scarab he said was for luck, that I gladly paid him a couple US dollars. Think he expected it?

Next, I asked my driver to take me to the most distant of the pyramids. We drove down a dirt road, and I got out to take some awesome shots of the main pyramids from far enough away to get three of those huge structures in one frame. As my foot hit the ground, more robed men approached, trying to sell me some product or service. I patiently walked away and moved to another good vantage point for my photograph, but they persisted, following me everywhere I went. I started losing my patience at this point and gruffly demanded that they leave me alone and let me take my pictures. As they stepped back, one rather innocent-looking man offered me a free camel ride; he said that I should come see him before I left the pyramids.

Finally, I had some peace. I took my photos, admired the structural mystery of these various-sized, pyramid-shaped tombs for a good long time, and then thought about how I had not quite gotten my camel fill. After all, how often can one ride a camel in its natural environment? I moseyed—yes, I actually moseyed—over to the gentleman with my tail between my legs. I asked him if he was sure that he did not want any money for this ride, and he assured me that he did not.

I said a prayer and mounted the strange desert creature. As the camel lumbered onto its worn-out knees, his actions filled the back of my hair with the ever-present sand that swirled around us. Then, it pushed up on its back legs, forcing me to kiss the sand on the ground in front of me. Finally, the camel straightened its front legs, creating a whiplash effect that was mercifully over within a few short seconds. You would definitely need an insurance policy just to get on one of these things in the United States.

I rode around the desert in true Egyptian style, admiring the view. The camel owner even offered to take my photo on the animal with the pyramids in the background. It turned out to be a real framer! Yes, indeed, I was a happy camper, trotting through the desert on my very own camel. Even after the ride was over, the nice little man with the turban clarified that while he didn't need any money, the camel charged four US dollars for the ride! I grinned, paid the camel, electing not to give it a tip, walked to my hired car, and demanded that the cab driver get me out of there.

The next morning, I met my cabby outside the hotel at the scheduled time. Yes, I used the same man three days in a row. As he reminded me, he did have eight kids to clothe! He drove me to the Egyptian Museum, where I spent almost the entire day. This was an amazing collection. The problem was getting into the joint. I stood in this long, unassembled line for … forever! I didn't know why I was waiting. The attendants were inside the booth, but nobody was selling tickets. Although it was first thing in the morning, it was already hot and the smells permeating the air were absolutely gross. People were crowded together with no semblance of organization, and there was absolutely no concept of personal space. In fact, people were not only shoulder-to-shoulder but using the backs of those in front of them as chin rests! Once tickets went on sale, certain men would push their way up front as others yelled in complaint. The attendants in the booth would sell to these pushy men first because they claimed to be representing small groups. Others simply said that they were cab drivers and the transaction was complete. It was like the floor of the US Stock Exchange. So where was my cabbie now?

When I finally managed to worm my out-of-place, little white keister to the front of the line, I was more than happy to pay the ten-dollar admission fee. Squeezing my way back through the line to get to the entrance of the museum was just as complicated as the ticket purchase feat and took almost as much time. As I gave the man at the entrance my ticket, he saw my camera, smiled, and asked me to leave it with him. Apparently it was another ten dollars to take pictures, and the line to purchase a camera ticket was just as long. I was not about to come all this way and not have photos of this museum's rare antiquities, so into the camera line I went.

The museum was amazing. I was awestruck as soon as I walked into the first exhibit. I started clicking and learned early on that I was not allowed to use my flash. I wasn't quite sure how to disable the flash of my automatic camera, so *no flash please* became such a persistent chant that, to this day, I hear it in my head every time my flash goes off.

I saw amazing sculptures, tomb equipment, furniture, jewelry, and ceramics from the eighteenth and nineteenth Egyptian dynasties. I loved the statues of the Royal Scribe, Nefertiti, the double statue of Nimaasted, Anubis, and the Ibis. The exhibits that impressed me most, however, were the relics from King Tut. Among my favorites were his gold coffin, throne, and the colossal statue of Tutankhamun. This was one of the most impressive collections I have ever seen.

After my day at the museum, it was time to get out of Cairo, and start diving. My destination, Dahab, was a seven-hour drive through the Sinai Desert. From there, I could submerge in the much-sought-after waters of the Red Sea. I hired a car and driver for the long, dusty journey across the desert. It was one of the biggest expenses of my around-the-world trip, but it was well worth it. The first part of the drive was oppressively hot, and after dark it became uncomfortably cold. My discomfort was, once again, exacerbated by my lack of appropriate clothing.

I hired a man who claimed to have ten kids, two more than the final number Akbar claimed. This new driver brought along a friend who had to out-do him by two, bringing his number of progeny to twelve. I did not understand why my driver brought a friend, but I suspected that the father of a dozen kids had simply planned to get in on the dough my supposedly rich butt was shelling out for this trip. I did know, however, that I did not like a strange man sitting behind me in the back seat of this car. I kept picturing him slitting my throat, taking my money, and buying himself his own car.

The three of us left the loud, crowded streets of Cairo. The road turned from paved to dirt, and eventually, all forms of life disappeared. The first discernable object I saw was a dead camel. I stared at this dark mound, that was a stark contrast to the white sand that extended as far as the eye could see. I wondered if I would meet the same destiny at the hands of the man in the backseat. I saw several other dead camels during the hours driving through this desert of flat land with nothing but endless sand on either side. From time to time, in the distance, I saw a lone soul dressed in a black robe, either standing or walking. I could not believe it. No water, no shade. Where on earth were they coming from or going to? And why black?

The never-ending, arid drive made me very irritable and restless. I started to see mirages myself. Is that possible from a car? There I was, swimming in an oasis, a palm tree above me and an umbrella in my iced tea. My mind was playing tricks on me because the scenery just wouldn't change. My hallucinations were a savior, something to free me from the monotony and take me temporarily away from a place where even a camel can't survive!

Halfway through our blistering road trip, the cab driver snapped me out of my daze as he banged his hand on the dash and demanded, "I think you pay me fifty dollars more." Although this was substantially more than we had agreed upon at the outset, we were already too far along to turn back. Besides, he claimed it was for his friend, and his friend was still sitting directly behind me. I was afraid that, if I didn't agree, the man behind me might bonk me on the head before they not only took the fare, but also took all of my money and abandoned me along the side of the road. If that happened, I did not think I had much of a chance of surviving; after all, I was not wearing black and the only shade available along the side of the road was the belly of a dead camel.

The night brought on a chill and the vast landscape gave way to welcoming mountains. We had finally reached the outskirts of Dahab, and even though I asked the driver for an inexpensive place to stay, he brought me to an amazing five-star hotel that stuck out from its surroundings like a red dress at a funeral. I believe it was the only hotel of any distinction in this otherwise dusty little town. I would find out the next morning that it really was a true oasis in the desert.

Although I had previously agreed to pay the extra fifty dollars that the cab driver demanded, I had no intention of actually doing it. I walked into the hotel and was greeted by the desk clerk. When he told me the daily rate, I thanked him and turned to walk away since the cost was exorbitant for both this area and my budget. Because of the late hour and his willingness to compromise, he agreed to cut the rate of the hotel room in half.

I proceeded to check in and ignored the driver as if I were not going to pay. Both the driver and his friend got very excited and began to yell, "You pay me now, you pay me now!"

I responded calmly, "No, thank you, I won't be paying you anything because you broke our deal." Being in a nice hotel, I figured I had the upper hand, as no one would want a disturbance. I was right about the disturbance part because the three of us were brought into a room by the hotel clerk to try to work things out.

The man at the desk suggested, "Listen. Negotiate with these men. They have driven you a long way and need to be paid." I was getting irritated because I felt like the sides had been drawn and it was three of them against one of me. I puffed up my chest and confidently got up to go check into my room, leaving them empty-handed. They must have realized that I was not budging and would rather fight my way out than be victim to their scam.

"Okay, okay, sir. You pay us the agreed upon amount and we are good." I guessed that they realized that they were in serious jeopardy of making this long drive and going home empty-handed.

As I paid them their money, I said, "It was dishonest and stupid of you to try to get more money out of me than we agreed upon. I probably would have given you almost as much extra in a tip for a job well done."

Needless to say, they did not receive a cent above the originally agreed fee. As one fist closed around the cash, the other reached out to try to shake my hand saying, "Okay, okay, no harm and everything is good. We are friends, good friends."

I refused their handshake and found myself getting just as angry at their suggestion that our relationship was mended. They had tried to extort me, and I am sure I wasn't the first. They had probably gotten hundreds of dollars from previous travelers over the years, maybe even thousands. I think I gained the respect of the man at the desk, as there were no additional charges when I checked out.

The hotel was amazing. It had marble everything, a huge diamond-shaped pool that appeared to pour into the ocean, and of course, a dive shop! I signed up for the following day's dives, and it was just as I had heard. After a short jeep ride through the mountainous desert area, we unloaded our gear and walked in from shore to a deep, colorful aquarium surrounded by fish I had not seen in any other place. In between dives, we drank tea that the Egyptians would prepare on an open fire and talked with the dive masters that had come from all over the world to be part of the Red Sea experience.

From our first dive, I spent every day, all day, with this group. Because I had checked out of my five-star and into a half-star hotel in town, I was able to extended my stay an extra five days. We dived, hung out at the oasis pool, and ate and drank together. I thought long and hard about not returning at all and simply joining the life my new friends had. As great as this lifestyle was, intuition told me that if I stayed in one place, no matter how great, I would miss the other oases the world had to offer.

# FOSSIL HUNTING: SHARKS, SNAKES, & GATORS

At seventeen feet below the water's surface, I had around ten feet of visibility. I thought that was a good thing. Usually, on those shallow dives off the Gulf Coast of Florida, we were extremely lucky to have ten inches! We were near a restaurant called Sharkey's, and, appropriately enough, we were searching for sharks' teeth. The teeth in this area were some sixty-five million years old and very much fossilized. They are all that remain of those cartilaginous sharks that swam the oceans as dinosaurs walked on shore.

Due to the topography in this area off of Florida's west coast, thousands of shark teeth have been washed in by waves or currents and trapped by the small reefs. Divers have been finding fossilized shark teeth here since shortly after SCUBA was invented more than sixty years ago. People have been collecting the teeth that wash up on the beaches for even longer than that. According to the old-timers, folks used to be able to find decent-sized teeth right from the beach, but these days finding a tooth bigger than a half-inch usually requires some dive gear, good navigation skills, and a little nerve.

Living in Florida for ten years opened my eyes to the wonderful world of fossil collecting. I found all types of shark teeth, wooly mammoth and mastodon teeth, and bones and teeth from extinct horses, bison, camels, alligators, and even a giant beaver. Sometimes I would go fossil-hunting alone, other times I would go with a fellow fossil fanatic. On this particular day, I was with seven other people. A couple of us had dived off Venice Beach before, and this time we decided to try an area off a fishing pier by a legendary restaurant.

We got a bit of a late start, partly because of the number of the people in our group and partly because of the varying experience levels among us. Some other divers were coming out of the water as we were suiting up, and they offered that it was, "great visibility out there!" I was eager to get started, but it seemed to take forever for the whole gang of us to make our way to the water's edge. As I stood in waist-deep water, fighting the surge and watching some members struggle to put on their fins, I became less patient. I knew that the better the visibility, the more sharks' teeth I would find.

We had agreed to go down as a group, but after we deflated our buoyancy compensators, two of the divers realized that they had not used enough weight to either compensate for the buoyancy of their wetsuits or stay down in this shallow depth. The two divers had to surface swim back to shore and sit out this first dive. Those of us remaining underwater quickly reconfigured to form smaller buddy teams.

Before long, another diver became cold and pulled the plug, taking her husband with her. None of the remaining divers had dived in this area before, so we did a zigzag search pattern to locate the reef that trapped the fossils. After about ten minutes of searching the rippling, white-sand bottom, another duo decided they had had enough and joined the others on the beach—then there were two!

My buddy, Tag, was as determined as I was to find this little rock formation that we were positive held tons of dental treasures. If we were not sure before the dive, we definitely were more convinced now, having discovered that this was a hard-to-find secret spot. We assumed (and hoped) that most novice hunters, like the rest of our team, gave up before they reached the reef.

We had been in the water for over half an hour and had spent twenty minutes of that time actively searching. In the past at this shallow depth, slowly rummaging through the sand picking up teeth, we had been able to stay under for over an hour. On this dive, however, our air was draining much more quickly because we had spent so much time propelling ourselves through the dense water trying to locate the reef. I started to believe that either we would not find the reef or that, when we did, we wouldn't have enough remaining air to collect any teeth. I had an image of us spotting the reef, thousands of beautiful fossils sparkling up at us, as we both simultaneously sucked our last breath—we'd look at each other in a fossilized stranglehold: forced to choose, teeth or air!

Every so often, we poked our heads up above the surface just to make sure we were still in Florida! I started to feel a little dizzy from the monotonous scenery. Glancing at my compass every twenty or so kicks to alter direction was my only relief. It was also the only thing that kept us from going in circles. The constant surge against my body and visual distortion caused by ripples in the ocean floor did not help matters. The sandy white bottom resembled the desert, and just when I thought I couldn't search any longer, we came across a mirage!

Luckily, this was not a mirage—it was the ocean barrier we were looking for, our dental hunting ground. In truth, this area did resemble more of an oasis than area reefs I had scrounged around in the past. Instead of a long rocky wall running parallel to the shore, it was like a little underwater island. The area was about thirty feet wide and forty feet long, and it was inhabited by many types of plants and small fish. The first thing I saw as we dropped down to hover about six inches over the grassy area was a seahorse. It was my first, and I was elated! I didn't even know that seahorses lived in this area, and even if I had, I would not have expected to see one because of the usual murky water. It was the strangest little creature. I had never seen anything like it. I gently peeled the tiny seahorse from the stem it was attached to and watched as it wrapped its tail around my pinky. I stared at the little stallion for several minutes before Tag became impatient. He tapped me on the shoulder, snapping me out of my reverie, and reminded me of what we had been really searching for.

I reluctantly said good-bye to the little stud, stroked it one more time, and replaced my pinky with a solid blade of sea grass. I nodded to my impatient buddy, and we began our hunt. The teeth were, as usual, abundant. On ordinary days, because of generally poor visibility, divers never see these treasures spread before them. Even with my head practically scraping against the ocean floor, I can rarely see more than one at a time. The day's excellent visibility, however, gave me the chance to see several at a time in all directions. Since it was difficult to find, this spot was also less picked over by other divers and it was easier to find quality teeth. It was a free-for-all, and the clear water was truly a blessing, or so I thought.

We had only been collecting for a few minutes when I got the distinct feeling that we were not alone. I looked to my dive buddy,

Tag. He had been keeping close, and was now looking over at me. He signaled that he too had the same eerie feeling. It turned out that we were right about being watched. We looked around and saw a shark circling us. As we kept our eyes on the shark, we noticed a second and then a third. We looked at each other, drew our dive knives, and pressed our backs up against one another. Now, I had seen sharks before and usually was happy to spot them, but these bad boys with their barrel-shaped bodies and blunt snouts just looked like they were up to no good.

We waited for what seemed like eternity in this defensive posture as they continued to circle us. Maybe sharks had done this in the past, on other dives here, but because of the poor water conditions, we had never seen them. Damn the good visibility! My feelings of fear were compounded by frustration when I realized that we were running out of air and had not yet collected very many teeth. These emotions quickly subsided as I continued to watch the angry (or hungry) sharks stare at us with their small, beady eyes. After watching *Jaws*, I just did not want my legs dangling in the open ocean, so we decided to avoid a surface swim back to shore. We chose to wait as long as we could. Then, cautiously, we cut through their imaginary circle. We hugged the bottom while each of us rapidly jerked our head to the right and left, sharing a constant watch of the perimeter as we kicked our way back to our safe, warm friends.

Back on shore with only a couple teeth each, Tag and I told the story of our encounter with what appeared to be bull sharks. Later research confirmed that they did, in fact, frequent those turbid waters. I am glad I did not do the research in advance because, according to the International Shark Attack Files (ISAF), at that point, the bull shark was responsible for sixty-nine unprovoked attacks on humans, seventeen resulting in fatalities.

As the years passed, Tag and I stopped telling people of our experience at Sharky's because nobody believed us anyway! Upon hearing our tale, most people just assumed we did not want to admit that our poor navigational skills led to our lack of shark-tooth bounty. At least the two of us, and the sharks, know the truth.

Although finding fossils in the oceans has its dangers, fossil hunting in rivers presents its own unique challenges. Ordinarily, when I went digging in rivers, I would stand on the shore and sift through shovels full of dirt that I had retrieved from the riverbanks or from exposed sand bars. I decided to rent a canoe and spend three days paddling down the Peace River in southwest Florida. This way, I thought I could stop periodically to dig in a variety of spots along the river. I felt that I would surely find some areas that were difficult or even impossible to get to by land. Thus, going where no man had ever gone before would increase the likelihood that I would find some really good specimens.

I convinced my friend Kevin McNally (like the map), to come along with me on this fossil hunting expedition. I decided to bring a friend because I did not know how to paddle a canoe alone—not that I do much better with a second person. I was also afraid to camp alone along the river in this area. I guess I never should have seen *Deliverance*. I specifically chose Kevin because he was greenhorn fossil hunter. I was sure he would not get more teeth than I would; after all, fossil hunting is a competitive hobby. Besides that, he had a tent, and I didn't. Plus, he had two sleeping bags, and I had none. He also had a cool machete that he had bought at an army surplus store. I thought it would come in handy if we heard banjos while camping at night. I guess one would say, then, it was pretty much just random chance that I asked him to go with me on this trip.

Anyway, we dropped off my truck at the boat launch in the town of Arcadia. We arranged a ride upriver with the canoe company that rented us our boat. We put in at Fort Meade, a place that was as far north as we could go and still paddle the boat without literally carrying it to get through the overgrown grasses. Although the Peace River is 106 miles long, only about sixty-seven miles of it is good for canoeing. Based on the distance and overall location, I predicted that we would gather tons of fossils by the time we returned to the truck three days later. I even remembered wondering how much weight the canoe would hold and how we might store the artifacts we could not tow back.

We put in at 10:00 a.m., and at 10:03 a.m. it started to rain. It was still raining twenty-four hours later when we took the canoe out of the water at our final destination. I guess a monsoon would be a more accurate description of that storm. The deluge caused the river to swell, leaving no opportunity to dig or sift through the now-flooded sand bars and riverbanks. This sped up the trip exponentially because, instead of spending any time digging, we just flew down the newly formed class II rapids.

The water rose so quickly that in no time, trees and logs were getting sucked from the riverbanks and either blocking our path or joining us on our commute. Rain gear or not, we were soaked within an hour. At times, we encountered trees that had fallen across the narrow river, blocking our path. We had to get out of the canoe, stand on the tree, chop away entangled branches with our machete, slide the vessel over the trunk, and then carefully slither back into the canoe without tipping over into the floodwaters. As I floated down the river, soaking wet from torrential rains, I wondered just how I could get any more uncomfortable; I was about to find out.

Throughout the trip, we took turns sitting in the back of the canoe. This was the preferred seat, as the guy in front usually got a face full of spider webs when we passed under clusters of low-hanging branches. At one point, I was in the front leaning back to avoid another set of branches. As I searched for the expected spiders, I spotted a big snake—right at eye level, and directly in my path. "Snake!" I shrieked. "Give me the, that, the thing!" I shouted, pointing randomly toward the back of the boat. As Kevin handed me his paddle, I shoved it back at him yelling, "No, the machete!" When I reached back to grab it, the machete came flying past me! I picked it up off the floor of the boat and started slashing at the brush above my head and screaming like the helpless child that I was. I could not wait to get past that spot, but I wasn't moving. I looked back and noticed that instead of paddling harder, Kevin had stuck the paddle deep into the muddy river bottom. "What are you doing? Get me out of here!" I bellowed.

"I'm trying to steer us away from the snake," Kevin said defensively, but I know he was delaying our progress to ensure that I had had enough time to slice up the snake before he got anywhere near it.

Although we saw no more snakes that day, I could not get rid of that creepy-crawly sensation until we pulled ashore that night to set up our tent in the rain. It turns out that our Sterno cans were not enough to boil the water needed to cook the sixteen pouches of Oodles of Noodles we had brought for all of our meals. Luck was with us, however, because we had also brought candy bars for snacks, and they would be enough to sustain us until we reached my truck the next morning. We sat in the wet tent, ate our wet candy bars, and smoked the wet cigars we had saved for the celebration of our huge cache on our final night. We took off our wet clothes, got into our wet sleeping bags, and grumbled ourselves to sleep.

The next morning, the weather was the same. We took our tent down in the rain as we both complained about not getting any sleep. We were miserable as we steered through the rapids for the short time it took us to get back to the truck. On the quiet ride home, Kevin counted a total of five half-inch sharks' teeth between us. I was sure they must had been left in the collection bag from a previous trip. To end our trip, we each took two teeth and fought over the fifth!

It is safe to say that I have had many experiences while collecting fossils over the years, some good, and some bad. Sometimes I would collect more than a hundred and fifty sharks' teeth in one day, some days none at all. Even on successful days, the fossils I collected were quite small. Then, one day in the late summer, I got the chance to search for the big ones.

For a couple of years, my fossil collecting pal Charles and I had been planning a trip to the Cooper River in South Carolina. This is where the "big stuff" is found, and now it was finally our time to cash in! We loaded up his junky Subaru hatchback that had about three hundred thousand miles on it and headed north for two weeks of fossil hunting fun.

The Cooper River is a long, winding river about seventy-five feet wide in most places. I tried not to look at the riverbank because in too many cases, I would see an alligator staring back at me. Gators on the shore meant gators in the river. When I did not see them on the banks basking in the sun, I was even more worried. These throwbacks to the past are the reason that many divers would not come here to get the big fossils. Whether we were willing to admit it or not, it may also have been the reason it took us two years to get there.

Nonetheless, I found myself on the boat discussing final plans with Charles and about to jump into the alligator-infested river. I guess that the only plans we did have were: do not leave each other's side, find big teeth, do not get eaten by gators, keep your knife out, do not stab your buddy, and again, do not leave each other's side.

We said a Hail Mary, crossed ourselves, tucked in our rabbit's feet, and jumped into the water. Of course the first thing we did was leave each other's side, but it was not on purpose. We wore twice as much weight as we normally would because we were aware of the extremely strong currents that would try to carry us down river. This extra weight still did not get me down to the bottom fast enough as I seemed to float, disoriented, in total darkness for several minutes, wondering what loomed around me.

The anticipation of connecting with solid ground at the bottom of the river did not eliminate the shock of contact. Neither did it prevent me from screaming into my regulator, much as I had screamed when I was five years old and watched *Texas Chainsaw Massacre* from the space between the seats of my parents' station wagon at the second movie of a drive-in double feature. My fins touched down, and I immediately leaned forward to lie on my belly. The current had other plans for me and pulled me backward with such force that I did a backward summersault. I took my knife, the only weapon I had against my underwater enemy, and dug it into the ground just to keep in one spot. I never did completely stop, but at least I slowed enough to gain some perspective.

The reality of being out of control in a dark environment was very stressful. As I scraped along the bottom, many horrifying thoughts entered my head, and I realized that my breathing was also out of control. I focused on taking deep, long breaths and tried only to think of the reason I was there. My knife was also supposed to be my digging tool to extract or uncover sharks' teeth. My actions, however, had disturbed the bottom sediment, causing the release of billions of particles and rendering my flashlight, tied to a lanyard and wrapped around my wrist, useless. The river floor was littered with old, dead branches and black leaves that the strong river had long ago sucked to the bottom. This made finding fossils more difficult, as they were also black. With my flashlight dragging and often getting caught on debris, I used my free hand to dig and pick up my well-deserved prizes.

With my face only a couple of inches from the bottom, I struggled to make sense of anything I found. I would blindly grab something that could have been an artifact, and put it directly on my mask to identify it (this was, of course, before age took my ability to see things within arms reach). I used a carabiner to attach a collection bag to my chest so it would not drag on the ground. I sometimes just put foreign objects in this bag for later identification, but that, too, was easier said than done.

During my dive, I constantly ran into branches or logs that had been cast into the river by floods, winds, or storms. Each time I hit a log, my heart would stop, and I would practically jump out of my wetsuit. I would pull my knife out of the sand, ready to defend myself from the alligator I was sure I had disturbed. Then I would spend the next few minutes trying to stop the somersaults, control my breathing, and determine if I had lost my bowels. It was difficult to relax when all I kept thinking about was getting bitten by an alligator, having him give me the death roll until I drowned, then tucking me neatly into a group of waterlogged trees for later consumption—after I was good and rotted.

Having endured this stress for about thirty minutes, I decided that it was time for me to come up and end the dive. Because of the situation, I had used way more air than I normally would have. Furthermore, we were supposed to limit the dive so the strong current couldn't wash us too far down river and into the ocean. According to basic dive safety, I should have surfaced after a minute of futile searching for my buddy, but Charles and I had agreed beforehand that this would probably mean aborting the dive. That was absolutely not an option. We had spent two years planning this, and we knew that the big ones were out there. It was worth being, for lack of a better term, petrified!

As I left the mucky river bottom on my way to the surface, I once again lost any sense of orientation. When I popped my head out of the water, I was glad to see that our boat had been drifting with the current too, and was not very far away from me. I do not know what was worse, bouncing off the bottom or dangling on the surface. The boat captain turned on the engine and motored toward me. I had not noticed that Charles had also popped up between the boat and me. That meant that I had to wait and drift a few minutes longer as they loaded him onboard.

Back on the boat, our adrenaline was still pumping as we laid out our bounty. We had found what we had come for: bigger shark teeth. Charles held the size record with a five incher, but I found the tooth from the oldest species. Of course, when one is talking in the millions, does it really matter?

With testosterone flying, we continued to compare the length and girth of our fossils, but we also shared our thoughts and even our fears of this experience. We agreed that this was, by far, the most stressful dive we had done, but we were glad we had accomplished it. Then, the captain came around and said it was time to suit up for our second dive! Ugh!

# GERMANY:
## NAKED IN FRANKFURT

While I was baking in a sauna in Frankfurt, a naked family walked in and joined me. I was quite surprised by their lack of attire because I was at a fairly classy hotel. I had arrived there not knowing very much about Germany or its customs, and I only had a few days to find out. I was visiting on a layover between Japan and Africa. Geographically speaking, it does not make sense to have a layover in Germany when heading to Africa from Japan, but I was caught in a case of "you can't get there from here."

I decided to make the most of my days by exploring the area. I spent the first day walking the streets and observing the churches and village homes that are unique to this country. I loved the layout of the city. The squares are lined with buildings that are a mixture of classic facades interspersed with modern storefronts. The squares are filled with people shopping, visiting, and eating at the quaint tables set out in front of the restaurants. Their manner of speech and dress fascinated me. The sounds and smells combine to paint a vivid image of what is quintessential Germany in my mind.

The second day was much the same as the first, but before I called it a night, I bought a traditional pewter beer stein. I had been admiring them in village shop windows, and I just had to have one. I am not a shopper and definitely not a souvenir kind of guy. Besides, I was on the ninth country of this particular trip and had, thus far, resisted the inclination to acquire physical reminders of the places I had visited. Now, I figured that I owed it to myself to get this beer stein. The stein I ultimately selected is made of pewter and is embossed with an image depicting a scene resembling the city square where I had spent the previous day. It captures, vividly, the essence of Germany in a way that I am unable to do with my own camera. Beyond this, the stein has a hefty weight to it. It is a manly mug, and I wanted it.

On my way back to the hotel, I thought I might order a local beer. It was probably inevitable, since I was carrying around an empty stein. I do wish I had given the waitress my pewter mug to fill because it held about a fifth as much as the glass she gave me at the quaint outside restaurant where I had stopped. I guess the word "glass" is an understatement. When the waitress brought me my beer, it was in a vessel that was, to say the least, huge! I literally could not reach the glass rim with my lips if I stayed seated on the bench. I couldn't drink that much water in one sitting, let alone beer!

About a half an hour went by, and I felt pretty pleased that I had managed to get my drink to the point were I no longer had to stand to take a swallow. My pleasure was short-lived; I realized that the German couple next to me was already on their third round in the time it had taken me to complete half of my first. In fairness, they did have size advantage over me and probably years more practice.

Now, I was starting to get a buzz and was up for a little excitement. In my wild youth, excitement may have meant a friendly little bar brawl. As I have learned from trial and error, however, it's a mistake to start a brawl with someone who can out-drink me. For old-times' sake and to illustrate my fantasy, I looked around the tables to size up possible opponents. There were only a few people present whom I thought I could drink under the table, but as any boy with a sister learns early on, you just can't hit a girl.

Then out of nowhere it came. "I'd like to order the house special, please." I could not believe my own ears. I had just ordered foreign food! I must have really been lit. Now I know that doesn't seem like much of a challenge, but I have what some might call a "sensitive" stomach. I have been hospitalized a half-dozen times for eating things like onions, garlic, and unidentified spices, so I knew the alcohol must really be kicking in when I happily ordered a smorgasbord of Germany's best.

When the food arrived, I eyed each item suspiciously. I pushed the food around my plate and occasionally took a whiff or two, but never managed to let the fork take more than four or five trips from the plate to my mouth. I hated the knockwurst, despised the bratwurst, gagged from the Wiener schnitzel, and loved the smell of the sauerkraut but could not stand the taste of it. I didn't even have the stomach to try the sauerbraten or kuchen. I took another guzzle of beer, ignored the looks from the surrounding tables, and headed back to my room, leaving about as much food on the plate as when it was served.

With a haze clouding my head and an approaching revolt in my stomach, I did what any sensible person would do under these circumstances: I went to sleep. The next day, I put on my bathing suit and headed to the top floor of the hotel to take a dip. The rooftop was quite an inspiring place. It was actually an enormous room completely encased in glass. It provided an excellent view of Frankfurt. It was quiet except for the sound of flowing water pouring into the pool. The sun beat down on me as I lounged in one of the chairs, and I felt like a cat in a sunbeam. I jumped into the cool water to wake myself up a bit, an act I would repeat periodically when the heat in that glass room got to be too much.

The lighting, of course, was great and, as any avid reader would, I seized the opportunity and opened the travel essay I was reading. I believe that books are an essential part of travel. Not only does reading fill the unavoidable waiting time with pleasure, it also allows the traveler to escape the inevitable uncomfortable periods. For some, it is romance or mystery novels that meet this need, but for me it's travel essays. Not only can I separate myself from the current situation if need be, but I can also enjoy and learn from the experiences of others. I'm entertained by their misfortunes and misadventures. I often can relate to what I am reading because of my own previous or current situations. It adds a bit of comfort knowing that others have gotten through the same situations. Most of all, I learn from travel writers. They teach me about places I plan on visiting both sooner and later. They pique my interest and teach me about people or cultures I have not experienced—yet!

After a few hours of switching between swimming and reading, I decided to try out the sauna. The experience came highly recommended by the plump lady at the front desk. She was not really clear as to why it was so great, but she certainly was enthusiastic. I'm not into heat in any form, as it drives me past irritation and into complete meltdown in no time. I definitely cannot imagine why people like to sweat on purpose. In this case, however, I said to myself, *Why not? If I can try knockwurst and bratwurst, I might as well give this a try.* I left the pool and walked down the short corridor to the bathroom area.

I strode into the bathroom and rinsed off in a shower similar to the ones found in prisons and most large US high school gyms. The bathroom was a cavernous room with four showerheads, evenly spaced, at a head-banging five feet from the floor. After my brief shower, I opened the big wooden door to the sauna, and I felt the heat singe off my eyebrows. It was the same heat you might feel if you opened the oven door to check the Thanksgiving turkey and found that the turkey was on fire! I put out my smoldering brows with the water that remained in my hair and realized that my wet body had instantly dried in the heat blast. I covered my face with my hands and buried my head in my chest while I looked for a place to sit. I chose to sit as far away from the burning coals as possible. I quickly learned that the water next to the coals was not for refreshment purposes; I am due to have my third surgery this month!

I was roasting away, admiring the fine-smelling wood panels that surrounded me in this seven-by-seven-foot sweat box. As I began to wonder if the cooking aroma was the wood or me, in walked a naked guy. In that moment, I remembered yet another reason why I had never wanted to try one of these things. Before I had the chance to decide if I was uncomfortable with the naked or the guy part of this scenario, the man's naked wife walked in with their naked teenaged son. Seeing father, mother, and son sitting a bit too close, and way too naked I might add, made the decision for me. The source of my discomfort was my typical American outlook on the public display of nudity.

The dad and I exchanged a tightened-lip kind of smile with a half-a-head nod. This international form of communication has been used for decades between males. It loosely translates into *Hi, how are you? Fine, and you? Can't complain; the kids? Doing great; how's the car running? Just great. Tell the wife hello. Will do. You do the same. See ya soon. Okay. Buh-bye.* Yes, all that is exchanged in just half a nod.

This gesture is also used when meeting complete strangers or in uncomfortable situations, and this definitely qualified. Now several thoughts raced through my head almost at once: this cannot be happening, they should have clothes on—we are in public and I can see pubic! The legal impropriety gave way to the moral part of it. This was a family, and if seeing each other naked didn't scar them—or scare them—then they should at least recognize that their open nakedness could do permanent psychological damage to me!

I wanted to leave, but somehow I had been involuntarily melded to the darn seat. My level of discomfort had grown so great that I could not even move a muscle to change positions. Plus, once I thought about it, I realized that the mom was kind of good looking. Short blonde hair combined with very sharp Germanic facial features, accompanying a surprisingly tight body for a mom of about forty. I hoped that the men did not notice me trying to get a peek. The husband would have been annoyed and the son would have wondered why I bothered—after all, it was just his mom. Anyway, as I sat there in that exceedingly hot sauna, I thought about how I was probably being stupid by judging the situation based only on the ways I was brought up. I had to accept differences such as these because I would undoubtedly encounter more of them if I was going to continue to travel.

After about fifteen minutes of sauna, discomfort, and my veiled attempts to get a better look, the family left. The father and son nodded, the mom waved good-bye, I think, but I'm not really certain because I refused to look straight at any of them. I didn't want to get caught looking at the wife—again. I waited until they were gone, and went to take another shower. I stopped in my tracks when I saw the three lined up in a row, just a few feet in front of me, showering as a family. They looked at my shorts, smiled knowingly, and said, "American, huh?"

# HAWAII:
## PAINFUL PLEASURES

It felt as if fire ants were attacking my leg as I reclined in a dentist's chair and a strange lady drilled holes in my thigh. As I sat there wearing only my underwear, part of me wanted to look, but part of me did not. One thing was certain: no part of me was about to display any sort of reaction to pain. Of course, the sweat seeping through my pores and onto this oversized chair was probably a dead giveaway.

I was used to sitting in a similar chair while someone drilled holes in my teeth. As a young boy, I was the type that wet my toothbrush and dabbed a little toothpaste in my mouth just in case my Mom checked after asking the nightly question, "Did you brush your teeth?"

I always responded with a long, drawn-out, "Yes!" whether it was true or not. As an adult who brushes often and vigorously, I still cannot keep away from the candy. Therefore, for as long as I can remember, I have always had lots of cavities. I hate everything about going to the dentist: the various smells, the piercing drilling sounds, the uncomfortable chair repelling my nervous sweat, and the pain.

My reverie was broken when the tattoo artist who looked worn and much older than her years asked, "Does it hurt?"

"No, it just feels like little bee stings," I managed to reply with a smile. Then I recalled the times I had been stung by even a single bee. I pictured myself screaming and waving my arms while running through a field like a lunatic. While my actions were not unlike those of Chris Farley's character during the bee scene in *Tommy Boy*, I like to think that any other resemblance to the character or actor stops there. As the tattoo artist continued to apply the needle to my skin, I realized that perhaps the bee sting analogy was a bit off the mark. In reality, it felt more like being stung by a bee whose stinger was the size of Chris Farley … and dipped in hot sauce.

In any event, I was careful not to expose my pain. This woman had experienced what I was going through—many times. She had tattoos on both arms beginning at her wrists and continuing as far up as the eye could see, until the ink disappeared under her shirt. She also had tattoos on her chest from her neck to as far down as I dared to look. She even had a good smattering of ink etched into her neck, which undoubtedly connected to the ones on her chest and arms. Therefore, how could I, a big, strong man, (all right, maybe just big), even break a sweat over the tattooing of this cute little petroglyph turtle the size of an actual hatchling? Talk about embarrassing!

Several months prior to this event, I was also sitting in my underwear sweating. It was, however, under very different circumstances. I had recently been informed that my teaching position was being eliminated. At first, I expected this news to be devastating. After all, I loved my job at the elementary school, and I loved living in southwest Florida. Before I shed even the first tear, though, I recalled the promises I had made to myself before arriving in Florida: to accept changes, roll with the punches, and experience all that life has to offer. During my time in college, I had refined these promises and focused on a desire to travel and teach in different schools and environments. With the loss of my current position, I decided that I had the perfect opportunity to keep my promises.

I had been told in college that, as a special education teacher, I could work anywhere I wanted. I chose to challenge that commonly held notion. I loved the water in Florida, but with highest elevation being 342 feet, that state did not allow for other activities such as climbing. Hot temperatures, sandy trails, and the constant attack of mosquitoes and *no-see-ums* also prevented me from truly enjoying any aspect of Floridian hiking trails, and I wanted it all.

I thought long and hard about what place I would consider a paradise, and the Hawaiian island of Maui was the answer. I would later find out that I was not the only one who came up with that answer. Apparently, Maui has been the number-one vacation destination in the world for many years. I did not know this when I made my choice. I did know, however, that I would never be able to afford to vacation in Hawaii—so I decided to work there!

I went online and discovered an available teaching position at a middle school in the beautiful Iao Valley. I downloaded an application, filled it out, and sent it in to the school board. Shortly thereafter, I received a phone called inquiring if I was still interested in the position.

After a few preliminary questions by a recruiter, we scheduled a phone interview with my potential principal.

Today was the day, but it was not yet time. I had just left work after a long day and was excited to be getting *the call*. I lived only a couple of minutes from my school and had given myself a good twenty minutes at home to prepare for the telephone interview. It was enough time to clear my head but not enough time to get too nervous. I had just arrived home and was in the middle of changing out of my dress clothes and into more comfortable casual clothes when the phone rang.

The simple little ring initiated a Pavlovian response of panic and confusion (plus a little salivating). My thoughts came fast and furious. *Who had the audacity to be calling me now, when I was expecting an important call in a just a few minutes? I needed time to mentally prepare. Shoot, I'm in my underwear! What if it's her, my potential principal? I'm not ready. I'm not dressed! I haven't done yoga yet. Wait, I don't do yoga. Yes, but today I was going to. Damn, the phone rang twice, is that enough? Should I have answered it on the first ring? Ouch! I stubbed my toe. Crap, I still have to pee! Stop. Breathe. Namaste. Three rings, yikes. Relax.* I sucked in a ragged breath and said, "Hello, Larry speaking." The principal's voice was as soothing as deep breathing, and I quickly calmed down.

The interview lasted almost thirty minutes, and I felt really good about it. I managed to answer all of her grueling questions in spite of my clothing situation—and my inability to use the bathroom. Thankfully, we had not set up a videoconference. I am certain that my attire, or lack thereof, would have revealed far more than either of us would have liked to see in an interview.

Now here I was, just a few short months later, willing to commit to a permanent marking on my body to represent a place that clearly was, to me, paradise. I had only been on the island for a few weeks when I experienced one of the most memorable episodes of my entire life, let alone my life on Maui. I was doing a shore dive just north of

Kaanapali in about twenty-five feet of water when I spotted a sea turtle. I instantly deflated my BCD and gently settled on the white, sandy bottom. The turtle, *honu* in the Hawaiian language, seemed unaffected by my quiet presence. I lay there on my belly and watched as it, too, settled down on the bottom for a midday snack. I saw the turtle's large, soulful eyes scan the area for both food and predators. Satisfied that the food was plentiful and predators were not, it set about the business of methodically stripping the velvety green plants off a large chunk of dead coral. Once this patch was devoured, the turtle noticed a dark green salad sandwiched between a rock and a chunk of coral just beyond its reach. The turtle's powerful beak crushed the coral, exposing a more convenient access route to the object of his desire: food. The peaceful, untroubled aura emanating from the turtle as it enjoyed life made me think about my own desire to be laid-back, unafraid, and experiencing fully all life has to offer. In the twenty minutes I lay on the ocean floor, I fought the desire to hold my breath, not wanting to exhale and risk scaring this graceful creature away with my bubbles. I noticed that my hands were folded, and I did not know if this was to ensure that they remained still or if unconsciously I was thanking God for these moments.

After this experience, I decided that an unflappable turtle was what I would tattoo on my leg as a symbol of my time in paradise. Choosing a petrogylph of a turtle was apropos for several reasons. Petroglyphs are one of the oldest forms of human expression. It is an image created by carving or digging into a rock quite similar to the way that this lady was digging into me with her needles and ink. More than anything else, though, I chose a *honu* petroglyph because it appeared honest and genuine, like the Hawaiian culture. In this culture, the sea turtle represents the navigator. It is respected for its ability to return home after roaming hundreds of miles. My tattoo would serve as a talisman to remind me of the person I wanted to be and the one I had already started to become.

In reality, if I had gotten a tattoo for every memorable experience I had in Hawaii, I would have been covered from head to toe—kind of like the lady who gave me mine. When I was not teaching, I was watching spouting whales and dolphins from a kayak or a black sand beach, diving or snorkeling in sparkling blue water abundant with incredible sea life, or hiking valleys among lush green vegetation as soft ocean breezes kept away the bugs. I climbed waterfalls, rode boogie boards through breakneck waves, explored spectacular volcanoes, and simply enjoyed life, admiring the magical sunsets.

Watching the sunset in Maui became a daily ritual. I would get out of work at 2:00 p.m., hop into my crappy little car, and drive to Makena Beach in Wailea. I would set up my chair, take out my book, and unload my cooler of Diet Coke and snacks. The snacks pretty much defeated the purpose of the "diet" part of my soft drink, but they kept me happy and balanced. I always had both my boogie board and my snorkel gear packed in the trunk of the car, but once I arrived on the sugar-sand beach, all I wanted to do was chill. From time to time, to cool off, I would take a swim, but mostly I would just sit. I became entranced with the rhythmic sounds of the waves as I read my book. More times than not, that too was a distraction, so I would put down my book and just watch.

I would stare off at the water, waves, and horizon. I could see the crater-shaped island of Molikini seven miles off in the distance. During the winter months, I would see whales here in the Alalakeiki Channel. During this time, I got even less reading done in hopes of catching a glimpse at a fin-slap, a breach (where the whale comes completely out of the water), or even a spy-hop (where the leviathan pokes its head out of the water and takes a peek). As the sunlight faded, the small jetty of rocks turned black and contrasted magnificently with the brilliant, colorful sky.

My most memorable Hawaiian sunset was not on a day when I saw wildlife in the ocean or large rhythmic waves crashing on the beach. Instead, it was the day I got my first massage. I was skinny-dipping with a stranger at a pool of water called "the aquarium." Well, she was skinny-dipping as I, with my snorkel and mask in the water, pretended to look at fish and tried hard not to get caught checking out her well-defined, red-freckled body. The natural pool we were in would refill every time a wave poured in from the neighboring ocean. With each wave, we held onto the hard lava wall and got an intense hydro massage, compliments of the surge. As my companion and I discussed the merits of this liquid massage, she compared it with a more traditional massage. After telling her that I had no frame of reference because I had never really had a massage, she recommended that I get one from a girl she knew named Meagan.

Not too long after that encounter, I had attempted, very unsuccessfully I might add, to surf. After spending the day in the sadistic sea having my body bent and twisted by the surf in ways far beyond what I had experienced even in my third grade gymnastics class, my muscles screamed for relief. The idea of a massage came back to mind, so I took the red-haired skinny-dipper's advice and called Meagan the masseuse.

Meagan told me I could get my massage anywhere I wanted to. It seems she did not have an office or even a portable massage table. Heck, I don't even think she had a home in which to set one up. I think she may have been one of the many drifters I met on Maui. Anywhere else, these people might have been construed as bums or homeless. On this island though, they were just free.

Without a doubt in my mind, I chose to have my first massage at my favorite beach. I went there after work as usual and began my ritual of relaxing and getting into my peaceful mood. As the day was ending, about an hour before sunset, the massage therapist arrived. Meagan was a young, earthy, almost sloppy woman, with *hippy* written all over her. She was perfect. We moved our things under the one large tree, just to the right of my usual spot and aligned with the jetty that

I watched each evening as it transformed from rocks to shadows. The spot was perfect.

Meagan laid me down on a blanket and positioned me so that I could comfortably watch the sunset. Her solemn voice instantly erased the bit of nervousness I had about getting a massage. And one from a female and a stranger to boot! She began to slowly and methodically rub every part of my body, including my butt. Who knew? Was this allowed? I am quite sure she did not belong to some sort of massage organization that had strict rules about this type of behavior, and for this I was glad. Even when she pulled and prodded my parts in all directions, she used a smooth, fluid motion that was relaxing. I was butter in her arms as well as her feet—which she also used to knead my sore muscles. She stood up and stroked my legs as she pulled them toward her. I snapped out of my trance long enough to regret not wearing underwear under my board shorts as I am sure she got a few flashes of my *Johnson*.

Meagan had been manipulating me for about forty-five minutes, and, as the sun began to set, she nestled up against me with her finger chimes gently ringing in one ear and her soft voice singing Hawaiian chants to me in the other. I still get goose bumps thinking about it. For that brief moment, I fell in love. Yes, with my masseuse, but also with the bright orange and red colors of the sunset, the jetty, the sounds of the sea, the lone tree, the warm breezy night air, and Hawaii. This was the day that I began to feel the spirit of Maui.

After my first year in Hawaii, my brother and my sister both announced that they were getting married in the upcoming year—not to each other, of course! In addition, my mom would be turning sixty, and there was a big surprise birthday reunion planned. Since I could not afford the time or money to fly back to the Northeast several times during the next school year, I reluctantly moved back to the mainland.

The drilling of my tattoo was pretty much the only pain I associate with this tropical paradise. Our fiftieth state's natural beauty tells only part of the story. These islands are also the home of a magnificent, unique people whose dance, music, and culture set Hawaii apart from anyplace else on earth. It was an easy lifestyle to get used to, and it was even easier to fall in love with its people. It turns out that the permanent Hawaiian icon on my leg was not really necessary; Hawaii will always be engraved in my mind and in my heart.

# ICELAND:
## FROZEN FALLS & GLACIERS

I felt trapped liked a caged animal and bored out of my mind in my condo in Connecticut. I had always found something to do in the natural wonders of Maui, the Hawaiian island where I had previously lived. Back then, if I wanted a little change, I would just fly to one of the sister islands for the weekend. Now back in New England, I was missing the beautiful adventures of the islands. It was winter, but there was no snow. Because of Martin Luther King's birthday, we had a three-day weekend coming up. I had no plans, and I needed to get away!

I had recently discovered that I had a cousin living in Iceland. Actually, I always knew I had a cousin, I just didn't know that he lived in Iceland. Anyway, I called him up and asked if he would like some company, and although he did not actually remember who I was, he told me to come on up! Obviously, people do not get too many visitors when they live in Iceland—especially in January.

I arrived in Iceland early on a Saturday morning, before the sun came up over the horizon for its brief two-hour stay. This was a good time of day and year to appreciate exactly how cold Iceland can be, especially in the center and highlands. I did not know what time it was because I refused to expose any skin, even for the briefest moment, to look at my watch. I stepped out of the Keflavik International Airport; it is about thirty miles southwest of Reykjavik, Iceland's capital, and the cold instantly took my breath away. Luckily, in the next instant, the howling fifty-miles-per-hour wind resuscitated me. The strong winds are what really add to the cold in an area like this on the Reykjanes Peninsula.

The driving wind is common here, and my cousin John was well aware of it. While leading me from the baggage area through the frosty air and into his huge four-door car, which could also have been used as a boat, he started to caution me about holding tightly to the door as I opened it. Unfortunately, because I was in such a rush to hop into the shelter of the car, his warning was a second too late. When I attempted to get in the passenger side, the wind ripped the door from my hands with such force that it hyper-extended toward the front quarter panel. It was a great start. I'm sure my cousin was very impressed and glad he accepted my self-invitation.

To break the uncomfortable moment of being with someone who was almost a complete stranger, one who had just caused his car considerable damage, John asked me a series of questions: "Why did you want to come to Iceland? Why on earth would you come in January? What made you decide to come for just a long weekend?" At that point, he explained that it was one of the coldest months, and, because of the sun's position, it was also one with the shortest amount of daylight hours. He told me that the sun would not rise until around 11:00 a.m. and then it would set just a couple of hours later. Not wanting to be let down and not yet able to get the frozen smile off my face, I told him that I really just came to see frozen waterfalls, glaciers, and Icelandic ponies.

We spent the next two and a half days exploring Iceland's frozen splendor. We did our best to drive during the dark period and be at the most spectacular sites during the daylight hours. Even after the sun had gone beyond the horizon, it lit the sky a little longer. In some ways, the scenery was like a treeless moonscape. In these moments, the only vegetation I could see was tundra grass, and the mountains and other natural features all around us were amazing.

One of the reasons I had taken this trip was to see my first glacier. Eleven percent of Iceland is covered in glaciers, so I was sure I had come to the right place. I saw Myrdalsjokull Glacier, Morsarjokull Glacier, Skaftafellsjokull Glacier, and the largest glacier in all of Europe, Vatnajokull Glacier. Most of the seven volcanoes situated under this glacier are still active. Grimsvotn, the most active of the lot, has erupted in 1996, 1998, and most recently in 2004. Even though I was there in between eruptions, it was still a blast.

Although limited, the light that was available reflected off the enormous white glaciers, making them appear brighter than they really were. I found myself underdressed for this windy winter weather, but that did not stop us from walking up as close as we could to these icy giants. Without any spikes or crampons, we were ill-prepared to scale the glaciers, but we did our best to climb up and around on them.

I love waterfalls and had seen them in several different destinations, but Iceland offered me frozen waterfalls. My cousin and I climbed alongside them and admired the patterns of ice that resembled white fingers grabbing their way outward, constantly increasing the width of the falls. We briefly visited Godafoss Falls before moving on to Gullfoss, Iceland's most popular falls. We were glad we had planned to see this two-tiered wonder during daylight. It allowed us to witness the almost ever-present rainbows. About as popular as Gullfoss is Skogafoss. This waterfall is approximately two hundred feet high and eighty feet wide. I followed a path along the Skoga River that led to many other interestingly shaped frozen waterfalls.

As we drove along Iceland's dreary roads, more than once I was blessed with the presence of mighty Icelandic ponies. After finding out that there are about fifty thousand of them on the island, I was less impressed with my luck. Legend has it that they were brought here on Viking longboats more than a thousand years ago. Their origin is undetermined: possibly Russia, northern Britain, western Norway, or Scotland. However the consensus seems to be that these ponies originated from one of the oldest horse breeds, the Celtic. Apparently, they are still used for their original purposes: work, pleasure, and food.

The cute little Icelandic ponies are so rugged and sure-footed that they are particularly well-suited for the rough terrain and fierce climate that Iceland offers. They have a stocky, compact build with a thick coat, tail, and mane. They have adapted to their environment with shorter legs, ears, head, and neck. The dominant color for these animals is chestnut, but they come in just about every horse color. Two unique features about the Icelandic pony are their fifth gait and their long lifespan.

We spotted them on open pastures or farms. Most of the farmhouses had splendid mountainous backgrounds; some were fortunate enough to have natural waterfalls flowing right behind them. The ponies were often in the foreground, digging up some forage. When these adorable creatures were close to the road, I would get out and take photos. I wanted so badly to pet their long hair and manes, but I was never able to get that close.

On the third and final day of my Nordic excursion, I had the choice of visiting the famous Iceland springs in Grindavik or going to see a hockey match. Blue Lagoon is a hot spring that is controlled by a geothermal power plant. As water passes over an underground lava flow, it is heated to very high temperatures. The temperature of the outflow water is high enough to be used to run turbines and generate electricity for the town. Besides this, the steam and hot water also pass through an exchange area, where the heat is transferred to the municipal hot water heating system. Mineral-rich water is then fed into a lagoon for medicinal and recreational purposes. Bathers enjoy this 104-degree, milky blue water while looking at fascinating views of the cliffs, cones, craters, and possibly the northern lights on a clear winter night. Although the springs are a hot spot for anyone visiting the area, I chose to go to the hockey game and spend some more time with my cousin.

We had enjoyed a very adventurous sixty hours, and then it was time for me to fly back to the States and thaw out. I thanked my cousin for his hospitality. He had allowed me to stay on-base in his home. His wife and daughter were back in the States—something about frostbite I'm sure—but his two sons were around, and he took time away from them to entertain me. John had taken at least one day off from work, and I really appreciated that; even more, I appreciated our meals of customary American food as opposed to, say, pony.

My cousin thanked me, too, for forcing him to go to all these renowned places in his own backyard. He admitted to me that many of the places we had gone were on his to-do list, but he had not done them yet. I was glad to have been of service.

The service was his reason for being there. He was in the navy and had been stationed in Iceland for over a year. I could not help but wonder what he had done wrong to be stationed in this icebox. I disliked all of my duty stations, but I never thought of any of them as a punishment. I think I would have been done with this frigid habitat about a week after my arrival—or at least after I had had long enough to witness its sights. My cousin said he had been too caught up in the military routine to really explore and enjoy the natural beauty of this island. He also admitted that he probably never would have gotten motivated enough to see these places if I hadn't lit a fire under him.

On the way to the airport, I saw signs for the Blue Lagoon hot springs, located some thirteen kilometers away. I began to wonder if I should have gone. I try not to live with regrets, but as I learned more about this place, I wished I had experienced it. John knocked me out of my musings when he began to speak of his brother Jimmy, another cousin, who was in the air force and stationed in Japan. This, of course, got me thinking.

# JAPAN:
## FUJI WITH JIMMY & FRIENDS

I placed a phone call to Japan and spoke with another long-lost relative. The conversation started innocently enough: "Hello, Jimmy? I'm your cousin from Connecticut." I was off to a good start because, unlike other kin, at least this cousin remembered me. Well, he remembered my family. More specifically, he remembered my sister. His exact words were, "Are you the one with the really hot sister?"

This comment made my skin crawl in a way that only an older brother's can when someone refers to his younger sister in any physical manner. Since I wanted to visit Japan—I mean my cousin—I decided to let the "hot sister" thing go without comment. Before I could stop myself, I blurted out a "Yes" in response to his question and instantly heard the slight sound of some banjos playing in my head. Had I just indirectly and certainly unintentionally admitted that I thought my sister was hot?

In retrospect, I can only conclude that comments about my sister caused a significantly rougher-than-expected start to the conversation. It had to have caused a temporary short-circuit in my brain because my next comment to Jimmy was, "Ahh … anyway … I'm going to be in your neighborhood; will you be around?"

What exactly is *in the neighborhood* of Japan, when one lives in Connecticut? This was pretty much the most stupid thing a person could say when wanting to visit a place almost exactly on the other side of the globe. Luckily for me and my travel plans, Jimmy was excited about my proposed visit—even after he discovered that my sister would not be with me!

Initially, I had no specific reason for wanting to visit Japan. I didn't know a thing about the country or its culture, but I just knew I wanted to go. A quick glance through a trusty travel book changed that. I went directly to the "must see" section and immediately saw what I wanted to do. I was going to climb Mt. Fuji, and, as retribution for the sister comment, I planned on dragging my cousin with me all the way to the top.

Jimmy was in the Air Force and was stationed at a military base that had a golf course on the premises. Need I say more? All right, I will. He was married to a stunning Japanese woman, had three beautiful children, and lived on base with dozens of other people who played golf and drank beer at low military exchange prices. His neighborhood was just one big party. When my cousin was not working, he was either playing golf or having a neighborhood barbeque where he drank beer and talked about golf. Life was good for Jimmy.

While consumption of beer appeared to be a requirement for living in Jimmy's neighborhood, I am not sure if it was the result of the golf or the military life. I know that the frustration I experience while trying to play golf drives me to drink. There is not enough Ritalin in all the public schools in America to get me through eighteen holes! For most others, drinking and golf go together because it is required as part of the social aspect of the game. However, being in the military had some implicit drinking requirements as well, so I would have to say that, for Jimmy, it was probably a combination of the two.

My cousin Jimmy was around thirty years old, and in his youth he would have been described as slender. Since he'd been living on this base, Jimmy had enjoyed a more sedentary life of leisurely rounds of golf and block parties. It was safe to say that he had put on a few pounds since he had been stateside.

Because of my own experiences living on base, it came as no great surprise to me when my cousin said that, although he had been in this country for twelve years, he had not yet climbed Japan's famous Mt. Fuji. My visit was just the catalyst he needed to experience this once-in-a-lifetime achievement.

At a block party my cousin had the first night I was in Japan, I met two ladies. They were college-aged Japanese women who were friends with Jimmy's wife. Through the course of conversation, I learned that they had lived in Japan their entire lives, but they had never climbed Mt. Fuji either. Combined, these women weighed less than I did and had a total height that barely exceeded Jimmy's, but their desire to climb more than twelve thousand feet to reach the summit of Mt. Fuji was equal to mine. Therefore, two days after my arrival, our little climbing party was assembled.

Japan is the land of the rising sun, and well before the sun rose, we were on our way to the parking area at Kawaguchiko fifth station on the Yamanashi Prefecture. Since it was my vacation and I was on such a high anticipating this adventure, I volunteered to spring for the toll that we had to pay to be able to drive the Fuji Subaru Line, a small stretch of road leading to the entrance. As I started pulling out a couple of singles, the toll booth attendant said "That will be twenty-three thousand yen." Because it was close to 3:30 in the morning, I thought I was dreaming. I was clearly awake when I handed him the equivalent of twenty-three US dollars.

We drove to the Kawaguchiko lot—7556 feet above sea level—parked the minivan, and walked across the street to the supply store. My three hiking mates purchased traditional Japanese walking sticks for the ascent. The sticks were nice handcrafted pieces, each with unique patterns of knots and nodes, but when all was said and done, to me they were just sticks. They were used to record a hiker's progress up the great mountain. At each thousand-foot mark was a small shack built into the cliff, and inside the shack, there was a little wooden bench to sit on and a family awaiting the arrival of hikers. They kept a fire burning in the shack and would burn a stamp into a hiker's stick, proving he or she had reached that elevation.

My friends pressured me to buy a stick, but I told them I did not want to carry it through the rest of the countries I would be visiting that summer. Actually, I chose not to purchase this stick for several reasons. First, it was just a stick. Second, I was a traveler on a budget, and buying a stick was not in my budget. I still needed to make up for the $23 toll; how many more meals would I have to skip if I bought this stick? Third, it was just a stick!

Because we were energetic at the start of this five- to seven-hour climb, we chose a fairly straight or vertical route on the Yoshidaguchi Trail rather than the longer, less-steep path that followed more of a circumference arc. We felt our energy drain immediately and noticed the burn in our legs for the first thousand feet of the ascent, but we persevered and our bodies adjusted. We followed tradition and stopped every thousand feet to take a break, catch our breath, and take the time for Jimmy and our *tomodachi* (friends) to get their walking sticks engraved, permanently recording their trek to this specific elevation.

At our next thousand-foot mark, I realized I was already at an altitude that was two thousand feet higher than my previous experiences as a native New Englander on Mt. Washington's 6288-foot peak. Although we had been climbing for a couple hours, it would take a couple more to finally forget about the $23 I had paid for the toll. However, if I am thinking and writing about it now, I still may not be over it.

By the time we reached nine thousand feet, we were no longer able to hike directly to the next thousand-foot mark without stopping. Of our little group, I was the one who felt the strain first because I was carrying so much extra weight in comparison to the others. Unfortunately, it was impossible for me to quickly unload the excess thirty pounds because it was not in my backpack—it was on my hips, thighs, and belly!

Approaching the ten-thousand-foot mark, we walked approximately twenty to thirty feet, stopping at each switchback to catch our breath. As we ascended nearer to the top of the 12,389-foot mountain, the distance between stops grew shorter and the need for oxygen became more desperate. We were all pale yellow. Three of us had terrible headaches. Two of us (the men) could barely catch our breath. One of the ladies got a bloody nose, probably from the pressure difference.

Regardless of our condition, when we reached the summit after our seven-hour climb, we became instantly energized. We cheered, hugged, and celebrated our accomplishment. The ascent of Mt. Fuji was awe-inspiring, culminating in breathtaking views from the summit. Our climb took great willpower and stamina. We toasted the transient evidence of our youthful health, and we whooped it up as if we were the first people to ever complete this daunting trek. We were secure in the knowledge that Sir Edmund Hillary, the first conqueror of Mt. Everest, had nothing on us!

Our gloating, however, came to an abrupt halt when we spotted a small Japanese man modestly crossing the threshold of the summit we had just crossed. He appeared to be about 135 years old, and he held a walking stick in each hand. Each stick had enough engravings to prove he had reached the summit dozens of times before. He had no bloody nose, he was not out of breath, and he wasn't even yellow!

After this sobering sight, we sat at the summit of this majestic peak trying to enjoy the splendid view despite the worn-out condition of our bodies. The ladies took a little nap, and Jimmy wondered aloud if this imposing summit would be a good place for a golf course. As for my musings, I decided that this accomplishment was worth swallowing the remarks Jimmy had made about my sister, and I realized that this climb would have been a lot easier if I didn't love ice cream so much. I also wondered how many more cousins I had!

# KENYA'S CHIGGERS: NO MAN LEFT BEHIND

There I was, sprawled on the dirty, lime-green bathroom floor, violently gouging a hole in my big toe with my red Swiss Army/MacGyver knife. I was determined to dig out the chigger that was, with every passing second, burrowing its way deeper into me. My toe hurt like mad, but at that point I could not tell if it was the insect penetrating deeper into my flesh or the expanding canyon I was creating with my knife blade that caused my pain. I was sweating and breathing hard, partially from the run back from the river and partially from the nervousness about what might occur if I did not get this critter out of me. All at once, I was shocked by what I was doing to myself, repulsed by the disturbing scene I had created, and afraid of what would happen if I did not continue.

Tusker, a friend and traveling companion on this trip, was laughing as he walked into the bathroom. He heard me fly past him yelling something about laying eggs. He must have thought I had eaten some very bad or unusual food and was in dire need of a toilet. His laughing came to a sudden halt when he saw the blood covering not only my foot and hands but also spilling in bright red swirls on the bathroom floor.

The thing is, I knew not to go barefoot in Kenya. My friends knew that I knew not to go barefoot in Kenya because they had yelled at me before about it. Even though I teased them about how much they sounded like my mom, I did follow their advice by wearing my hiking boots almost all of the time.

Unfortunately, on this specific occasion, I was in too much of a rush to waste even a single moment finding, let alone sliding on, my socks and shoes. I just wanted to run outside and get a better look at the crocodiles I had seen floating down the river. It was a quick, clear line to the water's edge, and I did not really see any harm in running out barefoot. Just as I felt the moist, cool mud touching the tips of my toes … *whack!* This little worm hit me with the force of a blow dart (yes, I know from experience what it is like to get hit with a blow dart, but that's a different story).

Things would not have been so bad if I had not watched so many documentaries during the few weeks prior to my arrival in Kenya. One of the last shows I had seen had documented the plight of a female traveler whose leg had grown to the size of an elephant's and was in need of amputation. Apparently, a chigger had bored its way into her body and laid its eggs. Because her wound was untreated, the eggs hatched and … well, you get the picture. With the plight of that woman firmly etched into my brain, there was absolutely no way I was going to let this happen to me.

I had wanted to see wild African animals in their natural habitat since I was eleven years old. Those were the days when I was climbing trees, swinging from vines, and pretending I was Tarzan. It had taken me twenty-eight years to make my jungle safari come true, and it would certainly take more than a chigger to take my leg or end my long-planned adventure.

Plans for this African safari had begun one rainy April night just a couple short months before our ultimate departure. I received a call from Tusker, a friend I had met when we were both living in Florida. He was able to go on another African safari because his wife had ultimately agreed to hold down the fort with the kids at home. This would be his fourth trip to Africa and his third time to Kenya.

When Tusker recalled how fascinated I had been when he showed me photos from one of his earlier trips, he called to ask if I was still interested in an expedition to Kenya. Before he finished the question, I had said enthusiastically and without any thought at all, "Yes!" Since I was not married and did not need to coordinate with a spouse, I didn't even need to give my decision a second thought.

Because I had lost touch with Tusker for a short time while he was busy in law school, I had begun to plan a safari with another friend who shared the same passion for wildlife. This guy worked on computers all day and, in my opinion, desperately needed a safari. After explaining all this to Tusker, he agreed that we could take my friend with us. Now, we were a group of three.

My roommate at the time was a young engineer who was also desperately searching for some form of escape from his job. When he, along with my neighbors and half the town, heard me shouting with joy about my upcoming adventure, he deflated like a balloon with a slow leak. I was confused at his reaction because, as my roommate for almost a year, he had listened intently and with great enthusiasm when I reflected upon my previous experiences from far-away places. Well, confused or not, I am a guy, so I ignored his lackluster response and went into another room to continue my celebratory version of an African dance.

A couple of hours later, my roommate came down into the basement where I was already beginning to pack for my trip (yes, it was a bit premature, but I was psyched). He had been doing some financial figuring, and with the eyes of a puppy dog and a lower lip hung somewhere around his knees, he asked in a quiet but hopeful voice, "Can I go with you?"

I was a bit shocked at his self-invitation because he had not ventured far from home and an African safari was a heck of a place to start. He argued that it would make sense to start taking adventures with people who had traveled before and especially if the destination was Kenya. My roommate would have to be willing to quit his job in order to go on this trip with us. He had a great job working on military airplane engines, but he was a young, vibrant dude in a stuffy profession. He was just dying for a reason to break free, and this was it for him.

I agreed to ask Tusker if there was room for one more. I was pretty hesitant because I did not want our appointed leader to regret asking me. Tusker had not planned on taking a group, and with my roommate added to the mix, we would be a group of four. I felt a bit like I was abusing my own invite, but Tusker responded that an even number of people would be better than an odd number. When I asked him why, he told me he would explain it to me later.

This trip was going to be a little different for me because I was traveling with a group of friends rather than my customary solo travel. It is not that I necessarily prefer to go solo, it is just reality. I usually hit the road for an entire summer, and not too many people are willing, or able, to do that. On one or two occasions, I have traveled for short periods with a friend or a girlfriend, but never with three other people. How would I act? How would I know what to do?

The first thing I was told we had to do was take on nicknames. We needed African nicknames or at least names that fit our destination. For Tusker, this was a no-brainer as his nickname had been in place for years. Although *tusker* is the Swahili name for elephant, it is also the moniker for a local beer in Kenya, and my friend inherited his nickname from this less magnificent source. I chose to keep my nickname, *Jungle*. Although this is not a Swahili word, I thought it fit the occasion just fine.

The name Jungle was actually given to me while I was putting myself through college by working at a daycare. Before the daycare, I had jobs that involved laying tile floors, delivering newspapers, landscaping, stocking shelves, billing and collection, making billboards, shoveling snow, grading beans for quality control, picking tomatoes, loading bombs on jets, and building commercial airplane engines. In light of those experiences, even now, I cannot believe I was getting paid to play games with kids.

At the daycare, my initial duties consisted of running around—not at all like the adult euphemism for "doing many errands" or "cheating on one's spouse," but quite literally running around. My job description included playing tag, jumping rope, and swinging on the jungle gym. The ladies I worked with concluded that I was having more fun than the kids, and when the rug rats started using me as a jungle gym, in that moment of pure child-like joy, "Jungle Larry" was born.

Our two other traveling companions were not as fortunate with their nicknames because Tusker and I chose nicknames for them. With a little research and a Swahili dictionary, we quickly learned the words for "baboon" and "jackass" and assigned the names based on a best-fit model. *Nyani* and *Punda* accepted their names with pride because we told them they were the Swahili names for their occupations.

They became a bit suspicious about the true meaning of their nicknames only after the shouts of laughter that followed their introduction to our guide—and every other Kenyan they met during our stay. Both Tusker and I insisted on the four of us solely using our African nicknames, and although Punda had no problem calling Nyani by his, and vice versa, they both hesitated every time their own nicknames were used. By the time they figured out the true meaning of their Swahili names, the safari was over.

The nicknames added to the fun of the trip, but this safari was not, however, all fun and games. This was a dangerous country with many risks: wild animals are unpredictable, bandits roam the countryside, and there is always an undercurrent of unrest in the cities. While we were in New York's JFK Airport awaiting the first flight of our journey, we put our joking aside when Tusker, the only one among us who had experience in Kenya, turned the conversation toward the precautions we would have to take. "We'll have to watch each other's backs," he said, and it was there in that different kind of jungle that our leader came up with our trip motto: no man left behind.

It was then that I learned the reason Tusker preferred four people to three. With four, when someone went somewhere, even to the bathroom, no one was ever alone. We agreed on the motto and solemnly swore a promise to watch each other's back in a manner reminiscent of little boys in a tree house. Like those same little boys, we followed our oaths and motto to a tee … for about forty-five minutes!

As we were passing the checkpoint to get on our plane, the attendant discovered a problem with my ticket, and I was temporarily prevented from boarding. I did indeed *watch their backs* as each of my comrades walked past me down the ramp, leaving me behind. One of the guys yelled back, "I'm sure we'll see you in Nairobi!" Oh well, so much for our first test of the team motto. One down!

A couple of nights later, our motto would be put to its second test. I was waiting for Tusker to come out of the tent and walk the quarter-mile distance to the main camping lodge for dinner. I started walking toward the eating area slowly following a dik-dik. A dik-dik is a tiny deer with big ears that walks as lightly and deliberately as a kung fu master. I assumed that if Tusker was not directly behind me, he would soon catch up to the dik-dik and me. I was so captivated by the dik-dik (I really like saying dik-dik) that I reached my destination without ever connecting with my tent mate.

Realizing that Tusker was nowhere in sight, I traced my route back along the path to our tent. It was totally dark out, and I had forgotten that Tusker suffered from severe night blindness. Apparently, after the poor fellow stepped out of the tent, he zipped it up, turned around, and found me already out of sight. Two steps convinced him that he could not see enough to follow me, or the path, to the eating area. He turned back around to wait inside the tent, but could not even find the tent flap's zipper.

When I got back, I found him standing in front of the tent, waiting none too patiently. When I realized what I had done, I nearly burst into tears from laughter. He followed the sound of my chuckling all the way to the lodge. I laughed even louder as I recited the story to Punda and Nyani over dinner. They cried too. We still laugh every time we get together and reminisce about that event—well, everyone except Tusker. He never actually thought this was funny. Team motto test two—failed. Two down!

A week into the trip, we went hiking in an area that required the company of several armed guards. We picked up the first one on the roadside, and he stayed with us along a dangerous stretch of road. He carried an assault rifle and reminded me of Rambo. His camouflage pants were tucked into his soldier boots, and he wore a black tank top exposing his bulky muscles and a red bandana wrapped around his head. This guard did not tell us that he was with us because this was a dangerous stretch of road. In fact, he did not say anything. He just sat there, on alert, looking like he really wanted to shoot something or someone. I decided not to push the issue when he ignored my question as to why he was in our jeep. Normally, I would just keep asking louder and louder until the person answered. He just maintained his readiness. He did not even smirk when I told him my two friends were named baboon and jackass!

Our guide would later tell us that the stretch of road we had been on was known for bandits who liked to slaughter tourists and take their belongings. "That's nice," was all I could think to say. I guess I was glad Rambo did not talk or share with me the reason for his mission. This information would have made for quite a nerve-racking, hour-long drive.

Our next guard would take us on a hike to the top of Mt. Longonot, a 9,108-foot dormant volcano in central Kenya. We never found out if this guard and his assault rifle were for protection from poachers or the wild animals around us. Upon reflection, I'm guessing probably a combination of the two.

As we started our climb at the base of the Mt. Longonot volcano, the temperature was very hot, which made sense, as we were right on the equator. The mountain was steep, and the terrain was rough and rocky, with only a narrow path winding its way across v-shaped valleys and vast craters. Because we were visiting just after the rainy season, most of the grass was waist deep. The three-foot grasses blinded us to the potential hazards spread out upon the ground before us. This would be our biggest challenge—not the heat, not the rough landscape, but our vulnerability to snakes camouflaged among the vegetation and rocks.

The black mamba and puff adder, averaging eight feet and three feet, respectively, are two deadly serpents indigenous to Kenya. The threat of their presence would keep us on alert until we reached the top of the mountain. Both snakes were plentiful in the area. We read about these two snakes before we had started our vacation and both put a healthy dose of respect (actually fear) into our hearts. The warnings we had received from the natives since the start of our safari, as well as from the naturalist we met at the base of the mountain, made our own reading seem tame.

Each bite of the black mamba delivers ten times the amount of venom needed to kill a healthy man. It is chock-full of poisons that attack a person's heart and nervous system. A victim would have to make a quick accounting of his life because death usually takes place between thirty minutes and three hours after the bite. The only good news we read dealt with the prognosis of a black mamba bite. Apparently, mortality had improved from nearly 100 percent to *only* 75 percent.

The puff adder, the shorter of the two snakes, is often considered Africa's most dangerous snake. It produces *only* three times more venom than necessary to kill a man. A victim could expect nausea, shock, and death of tissues around the bite. Although the black mamba is the more poisonous of the two snakes, it is the puff adder that wreaks the greatest havoc on the African people. Because of its camouflage, the frequency of people unintentionally coming into contact with the snake is fairly high. Now, we were about to enter into these creatures' territory.

We did not take this lightly. A bite from either snake would have serious ramifications. We were hours away from the nearest hospital back in Nairobi. If bitten, we could be dead before we got back down from the mountain. There was no carving the letter X into a pal's snakebite and sucking the poison out—especially if he were bit in the buttocks.

Tusker and Punda were so concerned about the "Puff Daddy" and "Black Momma," as they would come to be known among our group, that they bought snake pants. Snake pants are thick jeans, like Carhartts, that have strips of plastic woven inside as to not allow the snake's venomous teeth to penetrate. I was too cheap to spend the going rate of $75 on a pair. I could not, for the life of me, figure out where else I could wear them once the hike was done. Nyani, who thought the pants were a good idea, could not find a pair to fit him. In the last few years, Nyani had put on about twenty pounds … in his neck! He had also put on thirty pounds in his belly.

No one was too surprised when he stopped half-way up the trail and said he could not make it to the top. There was a moment of uncomfortable silence and looking around at one another, each man waiting for a heroic voice to say, "I'll stay back with him." That voice never came. After twenty uncomfortable seconds, Tusker, the guard, Punda, and I turned around and continued the climb. Before we left him, however, one of us—I cannot remember who but I know it wasn't me—gave Nyani a machete that had been purchased in a roadside curio shop overlooking the Rift Valley.

Nyani was left alone for hours with a dull machete among the buffalo, zebras, leopards, baboons, and poisonous, deadly snakes. Based on my experience at the airport and Tusker's experience at the campsite, Nyani was not at all surprised when nobody offered to stay behind with him. As we walked away, I thought I heard Nyani mumbling, "No man left behind. No man left behind." Three down!

On our last night in Africa, we all stayed at a really nice resort along the coast in Mombasa. During the day, we swam in the luxurious pool, played water polo, and ate our meals at the swim-up bar. It felt good after roughing it for the last fourteen days in the hot, dusty jeep. After several hours of relaxing, though, I was ready for some SCUBA diving in the Indian Ocean.

Since Punda was not a certified diver, he stayed back to hang out at the pool and talk to some European girls. Nyani was still tired from walking half way up the volcano. Tusker chose his own entertainment—relaxing on a lounge chair, smoking a cigar, and enjoying a cold beer that he claims they named after him.

One of the ladies that Punda had been talking to at the pool invited him to go dancing that night at a local bar in town. He was ticked off when none of us wanted to go, because he knew it would blow his chances of getting to know her better. Nyani did not drink, Tusker was a family man, and the three of us thought it was a bad idea to go into town and start getting crazy. Punda, however, thought it was a great idea and, after forty-five minutes of trying to convince us we would have fun, he went on his date, alone. The fourth and final man left behind!

The African safari was by far the best trip I have ever taken. I had fulfilled the dreams of my childhood; I saw every African animal in every natural setting performing every natural act that wild animals do. We taped more than twenty-two hours of video footage and took more than five thousand pictures among us. I consider these photos as one of my most valuable possessions, and I have used them to enrich the experience of reliving this trip in my mind many times.

As it turned out, traveling with three friends was a blast. We relived our youth by acting like twelve-year-old schoolboys finally let loose on the playground after hours upon hours of difficult schoolwork. It probably seemed sad to others, the immaturity of it all, but we had the time of our lives. In the world of little boys, farting was funny again (all right, it never stopped being funny, but like most gas-related noises, it's just funnier with friends). There will always be bathroom issues when one is out on safari, and we experienced plenty of them, providing fodder for the endless and sometimes crude razzing that each of us dished out and accepted from the others.

We all got along great, we shared amazing sights and sounds (and smells), and we bonded as only really true friends can. Assuming nicknames really added to the experience, especially for Tusker and me. To this day, all of us still only refer to each other by those names. At this point, I am not sure I remember their true given names. The last thing we did as a team was adjust our motto to reflect a more accurate account of our trip. It is a motto that binds us together to this day and can truly only work among good friends who genuinely know and respect each other's strengths and weaknesses: no man left behind—unless it slightly inconveniences one of us.

It would have been difficult to understand what good friends they were as they all laughed hysterically at me while I sat on that bathroom floor, widening the hole in my toe and desperately searching for the chigger. In hindsight, I am glad I was oblivious to their insensitive behavior. By this point, I felt the burning of the chigger but was oblivious to the pain from the knife. I was determined to get this bug out of me, and that is what I did. Through the blood on my knife, I saw the skinny, black body as it wiggled impotently on the tip of the blade. I carefully wiped it off on the sink counter. I sighed a breath of relief, cleared my foot and knife of blood, and did a final check to ensure that I had not left the chigger's head or tail in my sore flesh. This was a thought that bothered me for some months after.

I guess, looking back, the chigger incident was not so bad. It did not lay eggs in me, I did not have to get my leg sawed off, I did not have to miss any of the safari, and I did not die! I guess it could have been worse. Instead of getting bitten by a chigger, I could have gotten bitten by a "Black Momma" or a "Puff Daddy"! Maybe I should have worn some "chigger pants" or maybe I just should have worn my boots like my three moms told me to.

# LAND DOWN UNDER: WALKABOUT KOALAS

As I leaned up against a eucalyptus tree, gazing into her deep brown eyes, I thought I was falling in love. I had been there, alone, with my koala friend for about twenty solid minutes. Koalas were not necessarily my favorite animals by any means, but it was the most amazing experience—petting this Australian native as if it were a house cat. The image one sees of them in magazines and on television does not do them justice and in no way conveys the qualities that caused such a very profound impact on me during that time of peaceful and quiet communion.

To get an early start that morning, I had taken the first train out of Sydney. I followed this with a short bus ride and was at Koala Park just after it opened. It was a weekday, and the park was nearly empty. I had just arrived in Australia the night before, and, while this was just the first of many things I had planned to do that day, the others items on my list faded into the recesses of my memory when I found this attraction.

I wandered around the park, visiting all of Australia's unique animals. I realized early on that the koalas were residing pretty high up in the trees, so I contented myself with visiting those critters who were hanging out closer to my level. Even though I especially enjoyed the Tasmanian devils, I spent most of my time inside the kangaroo cage. I offered them little food pellets, and they ate right out of my hands. Clearly, they were used to this practice because I no sooner got the food out when about ten kangaroos surrounded me. I was able to feed and pet them for as long as I wanted without any competition from other humans. The animals were happy to remain near me as long as I had that promise of a tasty treat.

When my kangaroo food was devoured, I went searching for Australia's famous canine, the dingo. As I was looking for this dog that the aborigines call *warrigal*, I spotted a koala, just about at eye level, wedged comfortably between two small trees. I looked around for other visitors or park employees, and, as luck would have it, found myself alone with this silent creature.

I cautiously reached out my hand to touch the soft fur of its neck. When I made contact with its fur, the koala did not miss a beat or even a slow methodical chew. It was totally calm, enjoying the sweet taste of a eucalyptus leaf. I observed every bit of the koala and discovered that it was a female. She continued to munch and relax on her rather low-level perch between the branches.

I figured that, since we were alone, or more to the point, no one else was around to hear me, I could comfortably start up a conversation with my marsupial pal. So I started quietly talking to her. I complimented her on the texture of her fur, wishing that I could actually rub my face on it as a child snuggles with a favorite stuffed animal. I told her how courageous she was in selecting a spot so close to humans. I was able to get so close to her that I felt the soft puffs of her breath on my cheek. When I found myself asking if she came to this part of the park often, it dawned on me that I had been bonding a bit too long with this animal.

At that moment, some pesky tourists happened upon the scene. I was interrupted by a high-pitched squeal coming from the female half of this young European couple. Her initial screech of excitement almost caused my personal koala to leave her abode and scurry back up toward the top of the trees. As they approached, the male half of the couple asked, "Is it possible for my wife to pet your koala?" I guess because he had asked so nicely, I simply said, "Yes."

I realized that I was acting as if she were my koala. We had, after all, bonded from all that conversation and personal contact. Before I left my post at the marsupial's perch, other tourists approached me with questions, but most just wanted to pet the furry, bearlike animal. The real reason that people asked my permission to touch her was that I was serendipitously dressed similarly to park staff members. I had on my customary hiking boots, khaki shorts, and green polo-style shirt. Not surprisingly, this was similar to the employee dress code. The green in the shirt was a bit off the mark in color, but not enough for the visitors to notice, and certainly not enough for me to stop milking the situation.

I let the tourists pet the koala while I answered their questions to the best of my ability—which was not all that great at the start. I mostly learned information from one visitor and passed it on to the next. I have observed that when people know something, they usually want others to know that they know it. For example, one question I was asked was, "I know koalas sleep eighteen to nineteen hours a day, but is that true for the babies too?"

My answer was, of course, an enthusiastic, "Why, yes, they do!" I said yes not because it was true (until then, I had no idea how long baby koalas slept), but because it seemed that "yes" is the response to all questions for which people do not have the answer.

Yes is also the answer to all questions asked in a foreign language. "How do I get to the great wall of China?" I once asked while in Beijing. "Yes" was the answer I received with a smile. I have learned the hard way not to give this default answer as my response. I was visiting a Masi Mari tribe in Kenya and was making balloon animals for the children. The tribal leader said something to me in Swahili and I nodded and said "Yes" before I had a chance to get a translation from my guide. I realized very soon afterward that I had accepted an invitation to marry his daughter. Good thing I did not have the proper dowry (one sheep and one cow), or I would, at this moment, be living in a dung hut somewhere near Lake Nakuru.

Getting back to the subject at hand, I continued to answer questions based upon the knowledge I had gained from previous guests. I allowed folks to pet "my" koala, and continued to act as if I worked at the park. Why did I do this? Well, because it was fun. I also liked speaking with my version of the Australian accent. Besides, after a few minutes of petting my koala, people usually got their fill and moved on to some other exhibit where they, no doubt, shared their knowledge of that creature with the next park employee.

Although I liked the kangaroos, it was my interaction with the koala that really got to me and made me not want to leave the park at all. I spent so long with her that my legs and back hurt from standing. In fact, I think I would still be standing there if the park had longer hours. I admired every detail of the koala experience. Somewhere in the connection, I was able to feel her serenity and be utterly still, mirroring her as she drifted off into one of her blissful naps. I stared into her brown eyes, mesmerized by their drowsiness. All I wanted to do was lie down and rest. The staff would have probably frowned upon my taking a nap with a koala, so I gave my sleepy friend one last kiss and reluctantly peeled myself away from her.

Later on, I learned that my koala's drowsiness might have been caused by the fact that she was stoned—at least, that is what an Australian hitchhiker once told me. In fact, he took great pride in telling me that all koalas are stoned all of the time. I met this hitchhiker during the summer when I was living in a small southern town in Alaska. I was on my way north to Portage Glacier to do some hiking, and I picked up this guy who had apparently drunk all the alcohol in town and was now heading north to Anchorage, a bigger town, so he would not have to face this shortfall problem again.

He was a friendly Australian and asked if I had ever been to the land down under. I started to recount my memorable time spent with the koala, and that is all it took. I never said another word; I just listened and laughed as he shared a tale about his father and the koalas in his backyard.

Apparently, his father would sit on the back porch, drink all day, and admire the eucalyptus trees with their resident koalas. His dad claimed that the eucalyptus that the koalas ate kept them permanently "high." One day, my passenger's dad had decided to lure a koala onto the porch by tempting it with alcohol. I guess he figured that they both stayed in pretty much the same state of mind, so why not have some company. It was a successful maneuver—the dad and his koala friend have been sitting on the porch getting drunk every night for two years straight.

My passenger imitated his dad telling the koala he loved him. I could not tell if he was slurring because he was drunk or he was imitating his dad being drunk—it didn't matter; it was hysterical. He said he thought that his dad might also have been getting high from eucalyptus. By the time he was done with his story, I was laughing so hard that I couldn't breathe and had nearly wet my pants. I had been so enthralled and entertained by his stories that I ended up driving him all the way to Anchorage just to hear more.

After staying a few more days in Sydney to see the opera house, the bridge, and the harbor tour, I flew to Cairns to make preparations to dive off the Great Barrier Reef, the longest reef in the world. From the airport in Cairns, I got on a bus and sat down in the seat closest to the bus driver. He immediately introduced himself and struck up a conversation with me. This was not exactly the behavior I was used to from any kind of driver I had ever met, but it was a nice change from the norm, and I liked it. The bus driver appeared to be in no great hurry, as we talked the entire trip. He seemed sincerely interested in the plans I had in his town.

I had asked the driver to drop me at a good hostel near the docks. As we drew closer to the ocean I fell in love with the area. All along the front streets were rows of restaurants and stores, each having a view of the water. The sidewalks were lined with people talking at an outside café or casually walking as if they had no particular place to go. I liked the pace of this Australian town.

The nicest bus driver I had ever met dropped me off at the Walkabout Hostel, where I was immediately greeted by the nicest hostel owner I had ever met. The hostel was full, but he guaranteed that he would find a bed for me with "no worries." He allowed me to store all my gear in an oversized closet, which gave me greater hope about his ability to find me a place. The owner went on to assure me that if no beds opened up, I could sleep on the office floor. Having settled my lodging needs, I set out to make arrangements for a dive boat that would take me even further down under.

I was to leave the next morning and catch a live-aboard dive boat where I would stay for six days. Since preparations had gone so smoothly and I still had time before I needed to check back with the Walkabout Hostel, I thought I would take a bit of a walkabout myself. I wandered the streets until I came across a local pub with a cool name—I think it had something to do with a crocodile. I am not a big drinker, but I wanted to celebrate my smooth transition from airport to hostel to boat trip. God knows, these things do not usually go that easily.

I walked into this dark, dirty bar and the self-satisfied grin immediately disappeared from my face. I was so high from my anticipation of diving one of the natural wonders of the world that the excitement spilled from my every pore. I did not look like I should be in a gloomy bar in the middle of a gorgeous day. I wanted to fit in with the other patrons, so I turned my smile upside down and scowled as if I was ticked off at the world (this was actually very hard for me to do). "Give me a Fosters," I said as I sat down on a barstool. Big mistake … huge!

As I scanned the bar, I was met by the snickering stares of a dozen men that resembled Donk in the *Crocodile Dundee* movie. The thing is, in America, because of advertising, we are led to believe that Fosters is the beer of choice by Australians. In reality, all the local Australians in Queensland drink a lager affectionately called *Fourex*. By ordering a Fosters, I was instantly and irrevocably marked as a tourist. I realized my mistake and looked around to see what everyone else was drinking. They each held a bottle with four large Xs on the label. When the bartender brought me my beer, I said in a harsh, loud voice, "This is a mistake, I ordered a Fourex." He exchanged my beer with a "no worries," and, yes, he was nice about it.

The next morning, I boarded a huge cattle boat and headed to the inside reef for a day of diving amid a throng of snorkelers. These boats are meant to fit as many people as possible and, therefore, generate the maximum amount of money per trip. Add alcohol, and the passengers think it is a party. They quickly (and conveniently) forget how crowded and uncomfortable they are. Add too much alcohol, and some passengers forget—or are unable—to go snorkeling at all.

My two dives on the inner reef were fine, but nothing to write home about. The only thing that made them special was the giant wrasse, seen on many postcards, that followed us on our dive. This fish was over three feet long with bright blue and iridescent colors. It did not seem bothered by either my curiosity or my attempts to pet it. In fact, I stayed closer to it than I did to my dive buddy for almost the entire dive.

After my second dive of the day, my live-aboard arrived to pick me up for a week of diving on the outer reefs and beyond. The snorkelers, along with a few fellow divers from the cattle boat, had to head back into shore. They all jealously waved good-bye as I departed. Many looked confused, some fell down, others threw up, and a few were already passed out.

Thankfully, and to my utter delight, drinking was not the main attraction on the live-aboard boat. It was diving. This was the experience I had heard about since I first began diving. A live-aboard had the ideal itinerary: dive! dive! dive! In between dives, we ate to regain energy just to dive some more. This was what I had signed up for, and this was exactly what I got. We dived and ate all day, and slept solidly at night. Sometimes just to mix things up, we even dived at night.

Although I love night diving, I did honestly look forward to the nights when we did not dive. Because of my inability to "just say no" to any dive opportunity, I seriously needed the break. On those special nights when there was no dive scheduled, the crew would dangle fish off the back of the boat. We all watched in amazement as a feeding frenzy of sharks would rip the fish apart and bloody the water. There were at least five sharks, with their razor sharp rows of teeth, competing for the scraps of bait. All we could see were the brief glimpses of tips, tails, and teeth breaking the water's surface. Some sharks actually breached and threw themselves at the boat's platform to gain the upper hand—or fin—in the chase for an easy dinner.

I began thinking that this was the same water we had emerged from earlier and would be jumping into again the next morning. Wouldn't the sharks be looking for us the next night and expecting a tasty treat? It was a rather unsettling train of thought, but not quite enough to prevent me from diving the following night. Looking back on it, I do not recall seeing a single shark the entire time I was underwater. They were probably just beyond my line of sight. It is just as well because I hear the sharks get pretty big over there.

I was enjoying each fun-filled day on the boat and following Australia's "no worries" policy when Jessica, a fellow diver, tried to bring me "down under." One night after dinner, as we sat on deck watching the sunset and discussing how great life can be, she felt the need to burst my bubble. As the breeze gently blew across my face and the last glimmer of light bounced joyfully off the open water, she just had to tell me about a middle-aged couple who had been diving out where our boat was currently floating. Tragically, at the end of the day, their dive crew assumed they were on board and returned to the dock without them. This was before more strict policies were put in place regarding boat operator accountability.

The couple must have floated, desperate, for hours or even a couple of days in the dark waters. After several days, their dive gear washed ashore, but the two divers' bodies were never recovered. Well that was just what I needed to hear to completely ruin both my relaxing evening and my recently discovered "no worries" philosophy. I later learned that the lost couple had actually stayed in the Walkabout Hostel where I had stayed. In fact, upon my return from the live-aboard, the owner of the hostel confirmed Jessica's story and even said that he remembered giving their personal belongings to the police. When I got back to the States, I read the same story about that unfortunate couple in a dive magazine. I was a bit unnerved because, for the first time, I realized that an unknown risk existed—being left behind.

I figured that, as a single person on this boat, there would be an even greater chance of me being left behind. For the rest of the dives on this trip, my "no worries" philosophy was replaced with a "stay glued to the dive master as if she were a gorgeous mermaid" policy.

# MERMAIDS:
## BY LAND OR BY SEA

I was diving for fossils off the west coast of Florida when I saw a great shadow drift over me as some creature temporarily blocked the sunlight from above. Just like a child who refuses to look into his closet or under his bed for fear of the boogeyman, I was scared to death and did not want to look up. I did, however, want the chance to defend myself from the unknown monster should he try to remove one of my favorite limbs. Therefore, I reluctantly tilted my head and shifted my gaze upward toward the creator of that huge shadow. Even though I was certain something would be there to meet my gaze, I was not prepared for a perfect-ten reaction on the pucker factor scale. In fact, I was so startled by what I saw that I jumped about two feet, and, believe me, that is not an easy thing to do underwater!

After a few quick calming breaths, my fear quickly turned to relief when I realized it was not the large, ravenous shark that my mind had conjured. Instead, it was an unassuming, docile manatee. Rather than fear or relief, all I felt was awe and a healthy dose of respect. I was in awe of the animal's immense size. It was a good seven- to eight-footer—and that is after taking into consideration the underwater effect on objects that makes them appear 20 percent larger. The respect clearly stemmed from the uncertainty when dealing with a wild animal in an environment in which he was at home and I was the stranger.

While looking at this gentle sea cow, though, I remembered that manatees were once mistaken for mermaids. From my current perspective, I could not fathom how. The manatee was grayish in color with a humongous, torpedo-shaped body. He looked at me with small, innocent eyes, and smiled with a face more similar to a hippopotamus than a beautiful girl. The hard, wiry whiskers framing the toothless grin reminded me how glad I was that I was not looking into the sharp, saw-like smile of Carcharodon.

After this up-close experience with a manatee, I had an even greater appreciation for the lives of the originators of mermaid tales. These men, the sailors of old, had been on ships in the middle of the ocean for long periods of time. The trials and tribulations of that life clearly took their toll. Being a Navy man myself and having spent time out at sea on an aircraft carrier with a thousand other sailors, I can not only appreciate why the tales got started but also how such an outrageous misidentification could happen.

I enjoyed the manatee's company for several minutes and then turned to make the short swim back to my dive buddy, Tony from Tampa. He had been very focused with his head in the sand, hunting for fossils. I grabbed Tony's leg in the same manner a shark would and tugged with all my might. Truthfully, I have done this to him about one hundred times in different dive locations, and it never gets old. For some reason, he never expects it, and it always scares the cow dung out of him.

This time, I got even more bang for my buck. He freaked out when I grabbed him, and before he had time to collect his scattered wits, I pointed up at the hulking form above us. When Tony saw the sea creature, he literally ran away, with arms and legs pumping as if he were on a treadmill instead of underwater. Priceless!

I had an experience with a different type of mermaid on my fifth day in Roatan, one of the bay islands off of Honduras. On our way back in from an offshore dive, our boat came to a halt about a half-mile from shore. As a treat, the captain gave willing divers the option to dive through a long tunnel that stretched in a fairly straight path to an opening about seventy-five yards from shore. Of course, I accepted this offer.

I did a back roll into the ocean, deflated my BCD, and sank to the bottom. As I waited for the five other divers who had also chosen to take this challenge, I was drawn to the tunnel entrance. It was around ten to twelve feet wide, and it seemed to be softly but insistently calling my name. It was difficult to wait for the others, and I was anxious to get started. I am usually a bit apprehensive when I go into an underwater swim-through, but this one was large and inviting. I knew that my inevitable feelings of confinement would be significantly reduced.

Within a few minutes, the last diver was ready, the dive master took the lead, and we were on our way. Although the entrance was brightly lit from above and wide enough to allow five divers to pass through shoulder-to-shoulder, within seconds of entering, the tunnel narrowed down and only allowed divers to file through two-by-two. It also became dark, and we had to use our lights. Even though I had the comfort of other divers around me, I felt more claustrophobic because their presence made the tunnel appear smaller and a lot more cluttered.

The swim-through was wild. There were so many animals and so much energetic life to see. The beautiful sea fans waved a friendly welcome, and the colors radiated when the light peeked through small openings in the cave's roof. These openings gave a sense of false hope about the ease of escape should something go wrong. While fish swam carelessly through, none of the openings were big enough to allow passage of my leg—let alone my whole body. Knowing that the surface was visible but still tantalizingly beyond reach just added to the thrill and excitement of the dive. If one of us ran out of air, had equipment failure, or just had a panic attack, he or she would have been trapped and unable to reach the surface that was glistening only feet away.

There were, thankfully, no incidents that day, and we all made it safely to the end of the tunnel, where we found both the boat and crew patiently waiting to take us, as well as our dive gear, aboard. A few divers hopped on the boat that took everyone over to another beach to have a cookout. Several of us, however, chose to don our snorkeling gear and swim above the volcanic-looking bottom that led to the rock ledge wall.

The wall terrain was like no other surface I had ever seen. It appeared dark, foreboding, and certainly lifeless. In combination, however, the rocks formed thousands of tiny, clearly delineated chambers. The edges were razor sharp and the points so fine that they were like so many needles stacked in a case. Each intricate nook or cranny had been used or remodeled by some critter. Upon closer inspection, I saw that the wall was home to thousands of sea creatures. There were puffer fish and sea anemones in residence, as well as clown fish and shrimp. An extensive bed of sea fans and sea grass also served as the perfect home for lobster and octopus.

This snorkel excursion made me think about an adage I had learned about not judging a book by its cover. Contrary to initial impressions, this harsh, foreboding wall, which many people passed by and dismissed as not worthy of a second look, was actually a mural of interesting and unique life.

Not too long ago, I also would have dismissed this area as not worth my time. I needed noise and excitement and had little patience for anything else. Developing as a diver has allowed me or, more accurately, forced me to simply shut up and listen. It has also forced me to slow down, simply because it is difficult to fight against so much water pressure and weight. Once I started slowing down and making slow, deliberate moves in the water (and on land), I was able to observe small things, skittish things, and hidden treasures. Diving became my natural Ritalin and a tool to learn what I needed to really be able to "see" all that the world has to offer.

After approximately thirty minutes of exploring, my girlfriend and her friend decided to head about a half mile down the beach to where our boat had docked. The captain and dive master were preparing lunch for us there. I wanted to stay and pretend I was Jacques Cousteau without the interruption or possible criticism of humans, so the two of them trekked down to the beach, and I stayed in my underwater world.

The peacefulness and solitude allowed my imagination to run free. As I silently hovered inches off the ocean floor and inches away from the rock wall, I pretended that I was observing dozens of creatures that were yet to be discovered. In this remote location, there were many animals that I had not seen before, so it was an easy fantasy to develop. I imagined this was how the Cousteau family felt on some of their underwater journeys.

When another thirty minutes had passed, I figured it was time to leave. I was sure I had missed lunch, but I did not want to miss the boat. While clambering out of the water, I noticed a figure walking toward me. Even though I had been underwater for several hours and was pretty waterlogged, I knew I was not hallucinating. From a tree-lined glen just beyond the beach appeared a beautiful and topless goddess. The sun glistened off her body like precious jewels. Her long hair, coupled with the snorkeling fins she carried low in her hand, reminded me of a mermaid basking in the sun.

There was not another soul in sight when this vision walked directly up to me. As she stood in front of me she asked in a soft purr, "How was the snorkeling?" All I heard was a whirring in my ears. By the sound of her accent and her comfortable naked stance, it was easy to grasp that she was not from America. Since I was the one with the red face and speaking a foreign language unique only to me (I think I said, "ish smmth toe plth" in response to her query), it was fairly clear that I was.

After I picked my tongue up from the sand and brushed it off, I translated my first attempt at conversation to "it's, like, so awesome." In looking back, I guess I must have sounded like a Valley girl, but my second effort had to have been better than the first response. While that one short sentence probably suited her needs, I somehow found a way to describe the site in so much detail that it was really no longer necessary for her to do the snorkel herself.

I may have stumbled over the opening line, but what healthy American boy wouldn't have, if this sensual mermaid appeared right in front of him? Once I got started, though, the words just flowed—or gushed, as the case might be. I think I used more adjectives in that conversation than I had in the previous twenty-five years of my life. I even made up a few, but since English was her second language, I didn't think she would know the difference.

In ordinary situations, I am usually a fast talker, but this day I talked as slowly as Forrest Gump trying to answer a word problem on nuclear physics. Yeah, I wanted plenty of time to admire her great looks. I wished I was wearing sunglasses, because she asked why I did not look her in the eyes when I talked to her. I told her that I was really shy and that was the way we conversed in America. Did I mention that she was topless?

She listened patiently, but my rambling finally started to taper off. She thanked me for my insights and then slid into the water for her own peace and quiet. If I was not so shy and had not had a girlfriend, I would have asked if she wanted me to snorkel with her. Did you know things appear 20 percent larger and closer underwater? We could have frolicked around naked, made love in the sea, built a little hut on the beach, had a few kids, and fished for a living. Did I mention that she was topless?

But my girlfriend was a short walk down the beach and probably wondering where I was. In reality, I was on a magical island with a beautiful woman whom I loved very much, and it was time to get back to her. I said good-bye to my little mermaid, headed down the beach, and never looked back … well maybe just once, really quickly!

# NEW ZEALAND:
## JUMP & DIVE

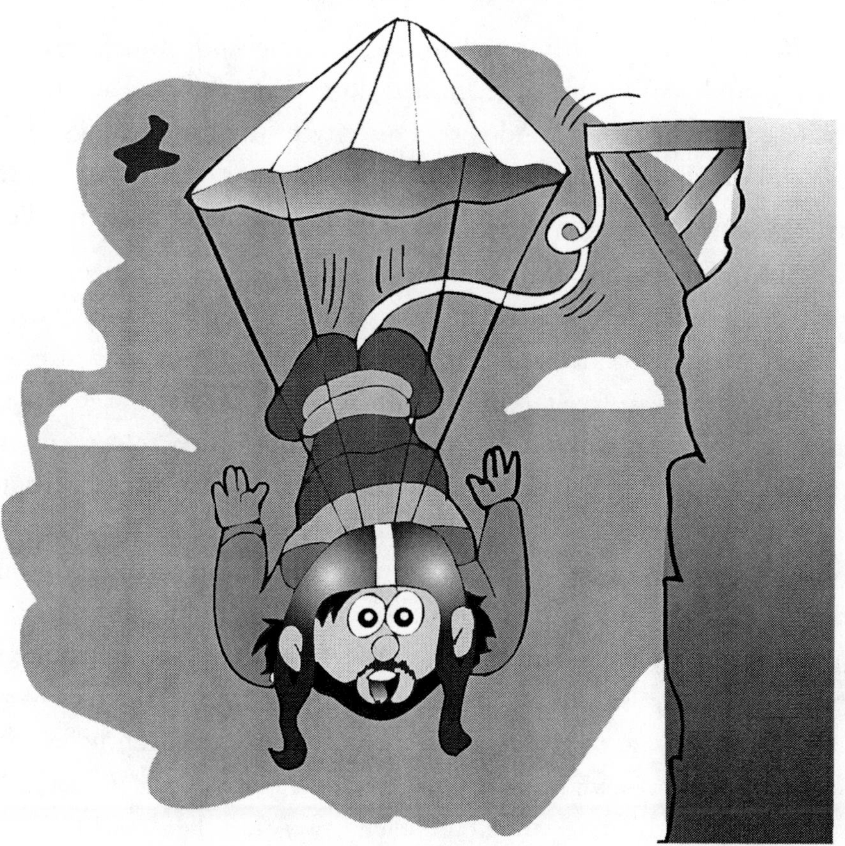

At fifteen thousand feet, I was ready to dive out of an airplane. You expected me to say a perfectly good airplane, but it was not. I was promised a big plane. In fact, that is why I chose this company to dive with instead of the many others there in Taupo, New Zealand, the self-proclaimed skydiving capital of the world. Of course, it did not hurt that it was also among the least expensive of the skydiving companies.

In hindsight, the price probably was the deciding factor and clearly not the best criterion for choosing a skydiving outfit. In my own defense, I knew that I would be on the road for two months, and my credit card did have a limit. This thrill ride, even with a low-budget group, would cost me what I usually spent during a week of traveling, but I just had to do it. I had to do it because I was deathly afraid of it.

In each of my traveling adventures, I have been fortunate to meet many people, and some of them had done crazy things. Each time I heard a thrilling story, I added that activity to my list of things to do before I die. I must admit, after looking back over that list, that a more accurate title would have been "things to do that might make me die."

Skydiving was one of those things on that list that led me to believe that the latter title might be more accurate. When I allowed myself to fully imagine participating in a skydiving jump, I developed more than just a nervous feeling in my stomach. The mental image was so disquieting that it would cause me to break out into a cold sweat. As the blood rushed to my head during the initial stage of panic, I would start to hyperventilate. Instead of helping to calm me, the excessive breathing would cause my already distressed brain to threaten to shut down and cause me to pass out. It was as if I were literally about to jump out of a plane—and this was all before I had even scheduled a jump! The only way to avoid the indignity of hitting the pavement like a dead fish was to give myself a mental shake and abruptly halt the steam train of my own imagination. I would come back down to earth, so to speak, and simply hope (and even pray) that the opportunity to skydive came later rather than sooner.

Although I believed that I would die if I skydived, I still wanted, or rather needed, to do it. I was absolutely certain that I did not want to miss out on life's adventures simply because I was scared or, in this case, terrified. I remembered never fearing a thing when I was younger.

I thought I was immortal. As age and the reality of some of life's harder lessons set in, my enthusiasm for meeting certain adventures head-on had somehow been tempered. An understanding of fear and loss had contaminated my joyful embrace of life. Without consciously deciding or marking the moment, I began to be afraid of things, such as roller coasters, that had once promised only fun. Now, I recognize that a rite of passage, understanding of mortality, is actually a clear crossroad in life. I think that too many people do not really choose a path. They are, instead, pushed and prodded in the direction that makes them fear life—or the loss of it. They stay firmly entrenched in their comfort zone, and being safe becomes the name of the game. I now believe that it is at this point that people's spirits begin to die.

One of my favorite quotes comes from Mel Gibson's portrayal of William Wallace in *Braveheart*. In the movie, he claimed, "All men die; not every man truly lives." I love that line. It means so much to me. Personally, I think that some people don't truly live; they merely exist. During the first part of my adult life, I worked, paid the bills, watched television, and periodically had the time and the money for a social event. For many people, this is enough; a regular schedule uncomplicated by change and filled with predictability. For me, that life was simply not enough. In that version of life, I had trouble determining where the "living" part was. Now, when I am fighting with the choice to do something or not, the decision will inevitably be to go for it!

After several years of avoiding the skydiving situation, as well as any conversations about skydiving, my apprehension turned to disappointment. I actually got mad at myself for letting fear rule me. When the frustration finally outweighed the fear, I decided to just make it happen. I am not oblivious to risks and hazards, but with many of the exciting things I have done, and still hope to do, I intentionally choose to focus (as I did when I was a kid) on the enjoyment as opposed to the possibility of what negative things might happen. *Fun over fear* is now my motto.

While it sounds like a perfectly good motto—short, simple, and to the point—it is sometimes hard to follow. I did not know which I was more afraid of: jumping out of the plane and taking a chance of my parachute not opening, or being crammed into a tiny plane until it was my turn to jump. I am so claustrophobic that I cannot even have my sheets tucked in on my bed. This had been my one remaining hurdle for skydiving success—to ensure that I would be jumping out of a perfectly good, big plane.

The first thing we were required to do was to watch a short video and receive a brief orientation. There were five other jumpers: one couple from Germany, another from England, and a younger, scrawny man from Switzerland. After basic instruction, we intently watched as our instructors packed our parachutes. We all donned our jumpsuits as the instructor showed us how we would be attached to them during the dive.

As I walked out onto the tarmac, still adjusting my leather helmet, I looked ahead to the plane, and my legs began to give way. It was not because I was getting close to taking the big dive. It was because the plane was the size of the first car I had ever crashed. My car had held a squashed maximum of six occupants, and now this similar-sized matchbox of a plane was about to hold twelve of us—plus a pilot!

Thinking that it was going to be like a general seating situation (first come–first served), I got into the plane first in order to secure a good seat. I wanted to sit close to the door so I could be the first one out of this tiny tin can. As I reluctantly stuck my head in, I realized that the cabin was so small that there was not even room for seats. To my personal horror, as the first person in, I had to move all the way up to the front of the plane. This meant that there would be ten bodies squashing me up against the back of the pilot's seat—five other instructors, each with his own student in tow. In my misguided attempt to avoid any extra time in tight quarters, I had landed myself in the most absolutely claustrophobic spot on the plane!

The tiny hole we entered through and would be jumping out of remained open. I assumed that was because there was not enough space to have a door that opened into the plane. Sitting there, squashed where I was, probably was a blessing in disguise since it prevented me from having the option of jumping out if I started to freak out—that and the fact that I was already clipped to my instructor and squashed between his legs.

I was nervous and my adrenaline was flowing. I needed to get out and run around, but I obviously could not. Sitting on the floor of that plane, I could barely breathe, let alone stretch a leg. It was a ride that seemed long enough to take us all the way to Easter Island, when, in fact, it took all of about fifteen minutes to steadily climb to fifteen thousand feet, where we would deplane. The other first-timers had the same kind of blank, petrified looks on their faces. I am sure each one probably wanted to say something to take his or her mind off of the impending jump, but no one could, because it was a very loud plane ride, and I had the floor the whole time.

I talk when I get nervous; it is a way to stay semi-calm and to avoid focusing on what has made me nervous. Between the prospect of jumping and the claustrophobia, I planned to spew continuously until it was time to jump. When I had totally drained the pilot by asking every possible, stupid question about skydiving and about being a pilot, I went on to get details of his family and even his pets. This man was very nice, just like everyone else I met in New Zealand. I loved talking to him because it took my mind off the crowded space I was in, and I got to listen to his delightful Kiwi accent. Actually, I was the one with the accent, right?

At first, the pilot was happy to entertain my questions, but eventually his patience wore thin, and I could not blame him. At this point, Mother Theresa would have told me to bug off. After he put his big headset on and pretended that he could not hear me anymore, I turned my attention to my instructor. Since carabiners and safety clips attached us together, he was not going anywhere. Because he did not have headphones within arm's reach, he had no convenient escape and was obligated to at least listen to my questions. Unfortunately, his patience had already worn thin before I even started with him because he had, after all, a front row view of the grilling the pilot had just endured.

I had to keep talking though, or else I would lose it. I was in a situation where my anxiety was so great I would do just about anything to get away. Under ordinary circumstances, getting away was the option I would choose, but in this case I literally could not. Ironically, when envisioning this particular situation, I had not known what I would do: panic because I did not want to stay on the plane, or freeze because I was afraid to jump.

In my worst imaginings, I saw myself clinging to the plane, crying and screaming because I was so afraid. I could picture watching everyone else jump out as I, alone, remained on board. I could see myself getting off the plane after we touched down and walking back to the hangar with the parachute between my legs. I could feel the embarrassment as the successful first-time jumpers looked away in disgust. I thought of the humiliation I would feel for the rest of my life whenever the subject of skydiving came up. Would I ever recite the story, or would I be forced to just lie and claim that I had never attempted skydiving?

In reality, when we reached our jump altitude and location, I was ready to jump. When my turn came, I scooted to the edge, looked down at an abundance of clouds through which I had a slight glimpse of land and water, and immediately started to push myself over the edge. My instructor grabbed me and pulled me back. "We must wait for the pilot's signal," he yelled as the wind whisked his voice out the door and into the clouds. He also reminded me that we needed to go on the count of three. I thought of Mel Gibson and Danny Glover in *Lethal Weapon* and wanted to ask if we count one, two, and go on three, or count one, two, three and then go. I just wanted out of that small plane, so on the count of one, I leaned forward and we dropped. So much for my fear of not being able to jump!

My stomach was in my mouth as we plummeted toward the earth, reaching break-neck speeds. It fell back into place once I reached maximum speed of 120 miles per hour. I immediately smiled and screamed joyfully. My lips flapped and my mouth dried out instantly as the rushing air flew in, blowing it up like a balloon. It was pretty uncomfortable, so just as quickly, I closed my mouth and decided to be content with smiling and laughing hysterically to myself.

I believe the free fall lasted for about forty-five seconds, although I was not looking at a watch. The dive instructor and I then spread our arms and legs like, well, skydivers. The pose was similar to someone making snow angels on his belly, except that, in this case, our arms and legs were bent. Maybe more like a monster trying to scare little kids. Anyway, after we maneuvered ourselves into this pose, the instructor pulled the ripcord.

Flap, flap, flap, *fffwwwttt*. The opening of the parachute gave a forceful jolt as it abruptly decelerated my descent. It was very reassuring though and served as a signal to let me know that I had survived the initial stage of the jump. The excitement of the uncontrollable thrill ride was over. I had tolerated the plane ride, managed to jump out, reached an incredible free-fall speed, and lived to tell about it. I was overwhelmed with adrenaline, excitement, and a bit of relief.

After the sudden opening of the parachute, a complete still accompanied us. I realized it had become soothingly silent. I had enjoyed the rush of the fall, but this was a completely different aspect of the jump, and it was, surprisingly, just as impressive. I looked around in awe, as free as I have ever felt. I realized what the literal meaning of *cloud nine* was. I wondered if my instructor had a similar feeling after his six hundred-plus dives, or if this had become just a job for him.

My instructor loosened my straps, and I quickly grabbed the ropes above as I dropped another couple of inches. It felt as though he had just cut my harness and I was about to plummet to the ground. He did this to take the pressure off my crotch and so I could use the lower straps as a seat. I was now totally relaxed and comfortable.

I removed my aviation gloves and tucked them inside my jumpsuit. I carefully pulled my camera out from a pocket and snapped a couple of pictures of the mountains and water below, and I also took a couple shots of the person who had jumped just before me. My fellow skydivers and I had made an agreement that we would each photograph the person next to us during the decent so we would all have at least one photo of ourselves during this incredible experience.

After fulfilling my end of the bargain, I put my camera away and marveled at every view I could absorb, including the incredible sight of my own colorful canopy above. I enjoyed the breathtaking scenery and absolute freedom that I had been needlessly avoiding for all these years. I was able to smile now without my lips getting ripped off and my face getting temporarily distorted, so I did. I let it all out with a huge smile that quickly turned to a *whoooo* so loud and long that I got dizzy. I was quieted only by the instructor's directions on how to land properly without ending up in a face plant. Just before touching down, I pulled the handles on each side to slow my speed, lifted my legs so they were perpendicular to my body, and began running once my feet hit the ground. I somehow nailed a perfect landing to end a perfect flight.

The skydive was over, but I was not ready to return to Kiwi Backpacker's Hostel, the place I had stayed the previous evening. I wanted to get the most out of my four-hour bus ride from Auckland, New Zealand's capitol. I was on such a high that I decided to tackle another item on my list of things to do before I die. Since Taupo was also famous for its heart-stopping bungee jumping, I decided to take a plunge. Perhaps, I reasoned, I might even get a discount for doing both on the same day!

Most of the people I had met, who had done both skydiving and bungee jumping, claimed that the jump was scarier than the dive. Since

I was already used to jumping off cliffs as a kid in Connecticut, and then later in both Hawaii and Puerto Rico, I did not think that the same would hold true for me. Besides, I seriously doubted that anything could tax my nerves like the skydiving I had just experienced.

When I told the skydiving dudes that I was interested in doing a bungee jump, they recommended a company and suggested I give them a call. A few short minutes later, a young guy arrived in a van that prominently displayed the bungee company's logo: a jumper with his eyeballs popping out of their sockets. This, surprisingly, did not intimidate me, but perhaps it should have.

It only took a few minutes to drive to the bridge where I would be taking my plunge. The river below and the majestic mountains on either side looked very familiar. I swear it had to have been the same landscape I had just observed from fifteen thousand feet above.

I stepped out of the van, and my legs still felt a little wobbly. I could not tell if I was coming down from the skydiving adrenalin rush or ramping up for the next one I was about to experience. Either way, it felt as if I had had a quadruple shot of espresso—minus the jittery part—and it felt great! I floated over to the little hut that the company used as an operations office and paid them a ridiculous amount of money to jump off their bridge and *not* hit the water with a body-splitting splat.

As I looked around the shop, I noticed that there were no other daredevils waiting to jump. For some reason, this seemed a bit unsettling. *What kind of an operation was this? Had someone died there recently? Was this place known for unexpected suicides?* Hung on the walls were photos of smiling people from all walks of life, as they were about to step off the bridge. These images helped to calm me down. It would be fine, I told myself—until I realized that there were no shots of those happy people *after* their jumps!

Not willing to think the worst for too long, I left the office and took the slow, deliberate walk across the long steel suspension bridge.

I stepped into a plastic dome where a teenage kid with acne strapped my legs to a bungee cord designed to prevent me from a landing that would mush my head as if I were high-diving onto cement. I was hoping for somebody with a little more experience. I would have preferred someone older, someone who could focus on doing the job at hand. Instead, there I was with a teenager whose main responsibility, securing me to the lifeline, was probably a distraction from the real focus of teenage life: sex! Mostly, I had wished for a person who had not been out drinking the night before and partying with his friends.

I felt justified in my reservations about this kid based upon past experience. When I had moved to Ft. Myers, Florida, it was quite the little retirement area. Over the years, however, the business owners successfully tuned the community into a spring break destination. One popular college student attraction was bungee jumping on Ft. Myers Beach. Some young entrepreneur bought himself a crane, a bungee cord, a harness, and an expensive insurance policy.

It was a big hit with both the young locals and the tourists. I never made the jump because I did not think it was worth the $80.00 to jump a short distance over the beach that I had been playing on for years. Maybe I just felt like it was more of a tourist thing, and I lived there. I would just as soon watch others fork over their cash.

Anytime I had been tempted to pay the fee and take the leap, I would look at the consistently long lines. I do not have the patience for lines, but even if I did, I just did not fit in with the crowd. The entire line seemed to consist of young, beautiful women in skimpy bikinis. My bathing suit had more material than twenty of theirs combined. Of course, I am not complaining, I'm just saying I would have felt very uncomfortable waiting in that line.

Coincidently, I never saw any of those women pay for their jumps. I had trouble believing that young college students could afford so much money for a few seconds of excitement. I also found it impossible to believe that these ladies had a place to carry a nickel, let alone eighty bucks. Based on the length and composition of the lines for his bungee, I eventually came to the conclusion that each night the owner must have partied with a lot of girls with whom he exchanged "jumping" promises—jump me tonight and I'll let you jump tomorrow.

Each morning, the bungee owner climbed up the crane, strapped himself up, and took the first dive of the day. One morning, less than a year before I was about to take my first jump, he climbed up the crane, probably still tipsy from a night of wet and wild partying, and jumped off headfirst. Sadly, he forgot an important step: strapping on the harness. While the sand on that beach was soft, it was not that soft, and the bungee owner was killed.

Anyway, this is what I thought about when the kid strapped my ankles to the bungee. The device he used looked like the leg weights that people wear to strengthen their thigh muscles. I did the best I could to ensure that he was doing everything the right way. I asked him a couple of questions about his previous night. Okay, I admit my questions were more like an interrogation. When I mentioned a breathalyzer, his patience wore out. This time I was not talking a lot because I was nervous, I really just wanted to know how much he had to drink the night before … and what time he stopped drinking … and if he had had anything to eat.

I really was not nervous about jumping. Even when the alcoholic kid connected himself by his harness to a safety line and we walked out to the platform, I was not apprehensive. I was breathing deeply to suck in all the fresh, country air. I deliberately gazed around in full circle, admiring the cliffs and mountains. I looked down at the flowing river and noticed the safety boat, which, from this height, appeared to be the size of a cookie. The youths onboard the boat were there to unhook me from the cord the after my fourth or fifth bounce.

The young kid standing next to me counted to three and then told me to jump. I slowly and calmly glanced his way, not allowing him to interrupt my bliss. Again he said, "Jump." I looked at him as if to say,

*Don't tell me what to do, punk,* but he must have missed it. He began to blurt out his expert opinion on the proper way to step off of a bridge. He explained that if I thought too much about it, I would not be able to do it. "You need to just count to three and go," he counseled. I let him know that I was not hesitant. I just wanted to savor the moment, enjoy the fear, and admire the view. He looked at me as if to say, *You're old!*

The last look I flung in his direction was enough to get him to leave me alone for a few more moments of contemplation. Then, I took a deep breath, smiled, and without hesitation leapt over the edge. I jumped off with a big, showy swan dive. Within seconds, the tingles in my stomach made my body tense up tightly. My smile immediately turned into a grimace. My brain flew through scenarios of landing with a splat and smashing my head like a watermelon as I penetrated the water. It was a slow, smooth descent and the transition between falling and bouncing was not nearly as big of a snap or jerk as I anticipated. After reaching the bottom, I started to ascend in a horizontal position. I still had not breathed. As I started to descend again, the feeling in my stomach reared its ugly head, but not in nearly so strong a way. By the time I rose from my third bounce, I intentionally spread my arms wide, took deep breaths, and enjoyed the feelings that passed over me. I tried to touch the water and admire the cliffs as I soared past them. The feelings of excitement were slowly replaced by a sense of accomplishment. I had felt as free as a bird … with its stomach in its mouth, of course.

# OCTOPUS: STAB OR SPEAR

I was being held captive by an octopus, about fifteen feet below the water's surface. We were off a near-vacant beach in Maui, five miles from the city of Lehina. The octopus was justifiably infuriated because of the spear with which I had just pierced some part of its body. I was literally face-to-dive mask with an animal whose head I could have fit in my hand but whose strong tentacles stretched to my armpits and held me underwater. Once my brain realized the potential trouble I was in, my body soon caught up and sprang into distress mode.

Just moments before, this potentially lethal weapon had simply been part of an amorphous, non-threatening blob. It reminded me of the ghost costume we used as kids for Halloween (better known as my mom's old sheet) because its head was the only thing with any true shape. I could not help thinking of all the times I had seen octopus in cartoons. I pictured this one on my television set and smiled in response to this childish image. My grin quickly disappeared as I felt the strength of this cephalopod. He was staring defiantly back at me through slanted, camouflage eyes that seemed to be saying, *Now, who has whom?*

My first mistake was thinking about this rather intelligent creature as if it were a cartoon character. My second, equally serious, error had been trying to pull the squirmy thing out of its hole using the spear. This bizarre blob appeared almost supernatural because, in its agitated state, it was changing colors right before my eyes. I was fascinated as it silently and gracefully wrapped one of its suction-cup-laden tentacles around my arm. Before I realized what it was doing, tentacle number two worked its way up to my elbow. During this process, it also wrapped two tentacles around my spear. It did manage to use three arms to brace itself in its safe haven. The remaining tentacle sort of dangled around aimlessly, as if unaware of what it was going to cling to. The octopus appeared to be looking at the situation with dozens of suction-cup eyes, but I swear that miserable sack of ink was using its last tentacle to flip me off!

I quickly realized that I was willing to give up the octopus; I wouldn't be eating it anyway. I was supposed to be capturing this octopus for my Hawaiian friend, Saito. Saito was a native of Maui and one of the first people I had met when I had moved there. He was a teacher at the school where I worked, and he was also the one that had gotten me into this predicament. One Friday, just after work, he asked if I wanted to try *taco* hunting. When I started asking questions, he said to just meet him in the morning and not worry about anything because it was just going to be "a day at the beach." I still did not know what *taco* was, but I felt pretty confident that, if it involved water, I would like it.

Around eight o'clock Saturday morning, I met him on the side of the road a few miles further north than any beach that I had previously visited. The beach was deserted and remained that way throughout the day. It was at this point that he finally explained what *taco* hunting was. "*Taco* is the Hawaiian word for octopus," he said as he pulled several spears from the trunk of the car. "These are Hawaiian slings," he proudly explained as he asked me to choose my weapon. When I ignorantly asked him why he hunted octopus, he quickly informed me that he and his mom fried up the sea creatures, shook the pieces in a plastic bag filled with coconut and sugar, and enjoyed it as a delicious snack.

Except for some childhood roadside experiments and the accidental death of a few family pets, I had never really killed anything. Because the lifespan of an octopus was very short anyway, just around a year, I thought I would give it a try. It also helped to know that Saito and his mom would be eating it; it would not go to waste. Finally, I figured that if a *taco* was going to die that day, whether by my hand or my *taco*-hunting partner's, why not mine?

As I struggled down there beneath the sea, I fervently wished I was somewhere else. I even wished that I could trade places with the owner of the spear—which, at that point, I was gladly willing to hand over to the angry octopus. In fact, it would have been my distinct pleasure to give up the spear; after all, it belonged to the man who had talked me into this potential disaster. He was the same man who had left out the details of how to retrieve the octopus, or the spear, or my arm. More important, he had omitted any reference to escaping the death grip that might be put on me. That would have taken only two, three minutes, tops, to demonstrate!

Initially, I was willing to give up the octopus. Then, I was willing to part with the spear. At no time, though, did I think I would ever be willing to give up my arm. After less than one oxygen-deprived minute of fighting with the eight-armed bandit, however, I was ready to re-negotiate on the arm thing. It is funny how a lack of air will do that to a person.

Of course, on this particular day, I had no way of cutting off one of my essential appendages. I was wearing only my board shorts, a mask, and a snorkel. I was about fifty feet from my buddy and about one hundred yards from the beach. I began to panic. I realized that I should not have been out that far, I should never have been hunting octopus, and I certainly should not have been out that far hunting octopus!

"Why me?" I said to the octopus. "Why not Saito?" I begged, "He has eaten dozens of your relatives!" *Oh my God, what was wrong with me?* I was talking to the octopus and trying to negotiate with him, and had already gotten to the "kill my friend, but spare me" plea. I was desperate. I was running out of air and struggling to free myself. I wondered what I had done to land this fate: death from an octopus on my first hunt ever. Then, I realized the answer to my own question.

On one of my first non-training dives a decade earlier, in the Dutch Antilles, I was diving with the ship's dive master, Allen. I was a neophyte and the only single diver. Allen took me under his wing, or flipper as the case may be, and showed me all the beauties of the underwater tropics. He pointed out everything and patiently wrote down the names of each of the organisms on his underwater slate.

Toward the end of the dive, we came across an octopus. It changed colors as it scurried along the rocks and wedged itself into a hole. I thought Allen put his hand into the hole to give the little fellow a pat. The octopus wrapped a couple of its tentacles around his arm. Allen then began to gently pull back his arm, as if trying to get loose from the suctioned grip. When his tug became violent, I assumed that he was in severe trouble. I quickly pulled out my shiny new, trusty dive knife and moved in with full intent to cut the octopus's limbs off and save my dive buddy. I would be a hero, an underwater hero, like Aquaman! I could have almost seen the headlines: NOVICE DIVER SAVES DIVE MASTER'S LIFE FROM TERRIFYING SEA CREATURE—RECEIVES THE "DIVER OF THE YEAR" AWARD. Maybe I would get free diving for life, I thought! At the very least, Allen would be forever indebted to me.

Well before I even nicked, let alone severed, any part of that octopus, my ungrateful buddy frantically intercepted the play. He grabbed my hand with his free hand, and gently but expediently relieved me of my knife. Even through his mask I could read his eyes. They said, *Hey rookie, what are you thinking?* I gave an embarrassed, underwater shrug and tried unsuccessfully to explain myself through my regulator. My explanation would have to wait until we both surfaced, but I was still confused as to why Allen did not want me to dissect this marauding sea baggy. How often does one actually have a real-life situation and have the right tool?

Next, Allen calmly demonstrated how to properly peel the animal's arms back, releasing the suction of the dozens of cups. With Allen's assistance, I began to relax and slip out of survival mode and back into the tranquil underwater zone that most dives provide. Back on the boat, we both laughed about the miscommunication. However, because of this incident, I'm still not allowed to carry a knife while diving.

Now I found myself in this predicament, and the shoe (tentacle) was on the other foot (arm). I was without a weapon to amputate the two slimy arms of the predator that was trying to drown me. All I had was the amount of time I could hold my breath, but I had used most of the air in my lungs reflecting on that Dutch Antilles incident. However, this reflection turned out to be time well spent. I had recalled the knowledge required to engineer my escape from this Hawaiian octopus. I knew what to do. I haphazardly peeled back its powerful arms, just as Allen had demonstrated so many dives ago—although with a lot less grace and absolutely no patience. I sprang to the top like a rocket and broke the surface like a submarine. I gulped for air and cherished the first few breaths like never before.

I left the Hawaiian sling underwater with the octopus still attached—or was it the other way around? It did not matter to me either way; that resilient fellow deserved to keep it. The Hawaiian sling was not mine, and even if it had been, it was not worth dying for. I'm sure the slippery rascal thought of it as a trophy.

I never went *taco* hunting again. In fact, that was the first and last time I did any kind of hunting. Saito and I are still friends because he went back, found his Hawaiian sling with my trophy still attached, and he and his mom enjoyed that octopus with some coconut and sugar sprinkles on top.

# PETE:
## MY INSPIRATION

I was literally freezing and doing the best I could to stay afloat in the January New England water. Chunks of ice floated by, but I could not find one big enough to grasp onto for buoyancy. It was difficult to tell—and more difficult to remember—which was colder, the water or the air. One thing was certain, the air temperature and the wind offered no relief for my wet face and soaked hair. The current was slowly carrying me downstream. I was in an area of the river that was not very populated by houses. The darkness obliterated the safety of shore. The sky was without light and the river was without noise, except for the screams of my best friend, Pete, calling out my name.

I had first met Pete at the beginning of seventh grade at the middle school in Rocky Hill, Connecticut. Students were grouped into cohorts called "packages," and both Pete and I were in package number four. Because of this assignment, we had every one of our classes together throughout the year. In less than a month, we became friends and started hanging out together, both in and out of school.

Like most kids at that age, we played sports, talked about girls, and tried to fill the countless hours in between by doing fun, exciting (or as the less adventurous say, stupid) things. Until that January evening, the things we did might have caused a few bumps and bruises, possibly even a stitch or two, but never any major damage. To us, it appeared that our antics were well worth the risk if it meant that we could avoid a situation I would later coin: teenage boredom syndrome (TBS).

Shortly after the start of seventh grade, Pete's mom was tragically killed in a horrific car accident. As a result, Pete was out of school for a long period of time and missed a good part of that school year. I did not have much contact with him during those months, and this I regret. At twelve years old, I certainly did not know what to say or how to act to help my friend feel better. This was far beyond the realm of a very immature seventh grader. In fact, it would be well into my adulthood before I became even a little better at coping with the subject of death.

When Pete did return to school, he had lost the childlike certainty that everything was going to go on forever and somehow be all right. In the years that followed, he mentioned several times that he did not feel that he was going to live a long life. He felt that his life, like his mom's, would be cut short.

We continued to spend time together, but as we grew, our hijinks became less about fun and more about challenge. Our conversations were very deep and serious. We talked about meaningful things that we probably should not have had to tap into until many years later. The events surrounding Pete's loss forced him to grow up instantly and in a way that very few of us middle school or high school students could even fathom. As a result, the bond between Pete and me strengthened and we forged a relationship that was far deeper and more private than the typical teenage friendship.

Throughout much of junior high school, we lived with the notion or philosophy that we were personally indestructible. Pete and I constantly challenged each other and pushed each other to do more. Sometimes the contests were small, like racing up a small mountain or completing a given number of push-ups. Many times, however, our teenage immortality complex required that the challenge be of a dangerous nature, like crossing a pond, in early winter, when it might—or might not—be frozen enough to support our weight.

When I was fifteen, Pete turned sixteen and got his driver's license. He had already been working as a cook for a year in anticipation of this event and managed to save enough money for a car. This car meant freedom for both of us. When he was not working, we would be driving. We could go anywhere, any time. Often, we had no destination in mind at all—we just drove.

Whether the sun was shining or the rain was falling, we had all the windows down and the moonroof open. In the winter, when it was freezing, we would crank up the heat so we could crank open the moonroof. The best times were when it snowed. We would sit at a red light and allow the snowflakes to fill the car. It was especially memorable at night, when we could look up at the blackness and see, in contrast, as each unique, fluffy white snowflake decorated the sky.

Regardless of the weather, only Bruce Springsteen was allowed to blast through the speakers in Pete's car. Pete and I would sing along with Springsteen at the top of our lungs on all our little road trips.

Early one evening, we picked up three other friends for an impromptu escapade. We each told our parents that we were staying at the others' houses for the weekend. Without a concern in the world, we left Connecticut and headed in the general direction of our nation's capital. Pete was always a very proud American and had always wanted to visit this historic area. We were aware that Washington, D.C. was south of us, but that was about it. Luckily, by simply following interstate 95 south and driving straight through, all night (except for a potty break under a bridge in the Bronx), we arrived at our destination.

It was very early in the morning when we pulled into a parking lot and tried to catch a nap until attractions started to open. We began our day by riding pedal boats in the Tidal Basin near the National Mall. Although this activity had nothing to do at all with learning about the men and women who had died for our country, it looked like the most fun. It was extremely beneficial because the laughing, splashing, and ramming of one another's boats really re-energized us after that long drive.

When our hour was over, we dried off, and grabbed some pretzels and Sunkist from a vending cart. We were thoroughly convinced that because the soda was orange, it would be an excellent substitute for orange juice. We enjoyed our breakfast while strolling among the aisles of white tombstones at Arlington Cemetery. We stopped our progress only once, briefly, at the Tomb of the Unknown Soldier.

At the time of my first visit, the Vietnam Memorial Wall had not yet been constructed. We did, however, visit monuments commemorating other wars. We each posed in a playful manner by the statues of soldiers while the others took pictures. Initially, our gang was goofing around next to the figures, but I think all of us, eventually overcome by pride, were honored to stand next to even the statue of a hero. This place must have made quite an impression because four of the five of us would later serve in the military as members of the United States Navy.

In high school, Pete and I signed up for all the same classes, just as we had done throughout junior high. However, with high school came a lot of changes. Pete met a girl and fell in love. I started hanging out with different crowds—some good, some not so good. I was now busy with a job, and Pete continued to work all the time. He missed a lot of school because of work, and even when he was there, he was rarely awake. Needless to say, he was voted the superlative "Class Sleeper." I spent a lot of time nudging him and telling him to stop snoring and clean up the drool on his desk. I should have been voted "Most Likely to Wake Up the Class Sleeper."

Pete fell asleep all the time, and not just at his desk in school. One night, shortly after dark, restlessness got the best of us, and he and I decided to go sleep at the beach. We gathered up three friends and headed to the coast. After playing a small game of football, we challenged each other to a midnight swim. I believe this trip took place in the spring, but New England's Atlantic Ocean is cold all year long. We had no towels with which to dry off or warm up, so when we finally did try to go to sleep, we were freezing. The ocean breeze was in full swing, and one third of a torn and tattered Deputy Dog blanket did not cut it. I believe that, for me, the worst part was the sandy, salty residue that encrusted my body.

Around 2:00 a.m., when it became apparent that sleep was not going to happen, we pulled the plug. The five of us–sleepy, grumpy, sandy, salty, and chilly—crawled back to Pete's car in a haze of bickering. Once in the vehicle, an exhausted silence overtook even the toughest among us, and one by one we drifted off to sleep. My friends and I awoke to the scraping sound the car made as Pete, fast asleep at the wheel, drove us along a guardrail.

He did this to me again several years later while we were driving from California to Florida in a U-Haul. I had been driving for nine hours straight when I asked him to switch with me. He had been driving for nine minutes before he fell asleep and drove off the road. Fortunately, I am a light sleeper. He was not. In both incidents, whether we were bouncing off-road or scraping along the guardrail, Pete did not wake up. Both times, just like in the classroom, I had to shake him until he regained consciousness.

Pete wanted great things out of life, and that was why he worked so much. He had talked about really making a mark in this world. I wanted the same and had many dreams of fortune and fame; I just did not know how I would go about it. Work became the focus of my efforts to ensure I would at least obtain the fortune. Fortune, at a minimum, would bring me the freedom to go and do what I wanted. With that shared logic, school became less and less of a priority (if that was possible) for Pete and me. What we were trying to do was learn the minimum we had to in order to get away from the institution with its rules and control.

With our steadfast belief that work was significantly more beneficial than school, college was not an option. With our life goals set high, however, a menial job in our hometown would not get us on to the fast track to success. For that, we needed to make a big move. So after graduation, Pete and I joined the US Navy. Now, I realize the irony of joining the Navy to escape the rules of high school, but back then, the huge step seemed like something we needed to do to get us jump-started.

Pete went to San Diego, California, and I, on the advice of my recruiter, held out for Great Lakes, Illinois. With the recruiter's support I also held out for a December 22 entry date to make sure I would be in boot camp during the holiday season and during the coldest months of the year. I am being sarcastic, of course, about both these decisions. It did not take me long to realize that my recruiter was full of it, but let's not open up that can of worms—at least not yet!

Although we were always stationed at different locations, Pete and I kept in touch the entire time we served, exchanging letters and tapes detailing the things we did and the trouble we got into. The majority of the time, trouble found us, because neither Pete nor I believed in the system or the way the system was run. We shared these thoughts and accepted that the military was not the place for us for the long haul. We agreed that we would be getting out as soon as our four-year term was done.

When Pete and I were home on leave after being away for a couple years, we decided that we had better start planning for our successful future, so we took another step toward our financial success and bought a condominium in Hartford. Even though we had not made much money, with the Navy providing us with room and board, we had been able to save a good portion of what we had earned in the previous two years. We had talked about real estate as a way to get ahead, and both of us began reading books on the subject. We thought that we would get started by investing in a condominium and renting it out until we returned from our tour in the US Navy, at which point the value would have gone up considerably.

When we got out of the service, we moved back to our home state and began the rat race. I got several jobs so that I could build a big bank account. Before I started my job as a billing and collection agent (a far cry from loading bombs onto fighter jets), I first had to spend money on nice clothes. For the previous four years, all I had worn besides T-shirts and jeans was my Navy working uniform—navy jeans. My day job was a source of decent, steady money, but I worked from nine to five, in an office, on a computer—and wished that somebody would just shoot me!

Every morning, several hours before the start of my day job and well before the chickens woke, I delivered the bulk newspapers for the *Hartford Courant*. I was not, I repeat *not*, a paperboy. I delivered to the paperboys who would in turn deliver the papers to the subscribers. I was a paper-man, but not really proud of it. Luckily, this second job was at a time that guaranteed that no friends or acquaintances would ever catch me—unless they were just returning from the bar in the wee hours of the morning.

I also worked as a bouncer on the weekends at a local establishment called The Smuggler's Inn Restaurant and Bar. Being a bouncer was more exciting than the other two jobs combined. In addition, I got free meals out of the deal, and I made a lot of friends. Of course, I learned that many of those "friends" were just people that did not want to wait in long lines to get in on those busy Friday and Saturday nights.

To continue to ensure my solid financial future, my brother and I bought an old, junky house that we planned to totally rebuild and then sell for a profit. The only time I was not already working was during daylight hours on the weekend. This was my only spare time, and reconstructing the house would, of course, have to be done during those hours. The house needed to be completely gutted, and we had a lot to do before the winter. Shortly after we began the restoration, I found myself needing to squeeze in repairs at night during the week. The to-do list at our fixer-upper was so extensive that I eventually had to quit my paper-man job and sleep at the trashed house so I could work on repairs during every spare moment.

The house, conveniently located next to where my brother was residing, was very far from the condominium in Hartford. I cannot really complain about the location of the property we fixed up. My brother was the expert on construction; I was merely the dumb workhorse that did most of the destruction. I was very appreciative that he had given me the opportunity to turn this house over and make great money. I was even more grateful when he stopped me from using a chainsaw to slice through the wall that held the live 220-volt electrical wire to the stove.

Pete had gotten a couple of jobs as well. He made billboards during the week and painted houses on the weekends. One day, he visited me at my collections job. I was typing away on my computer, staring at the screen, dressed in my miserable dress clothes. He walked in wearing jeans and a white thermal shirt with the sleeves ripped off. I was so jealous. He made fun of my pointy shoes and pulled me around my office by my tie a couple times as he tried to convince me to quit and get a job where he worked.

It sounds absurd that I would even consider this offer, but the computer, phones, nasty customers, and nice clothes were just not for me. I was working all hours on the fixer-upper house, and my commute was killing me. Because Pete and I were working so much and in strict get-ahead-mode, we never had time to hang out or even get together to update each other on the progress of our financial goals. Thus, it did not take much thought when I looked at my pros and cons list (thanks, Ben Franklin), to realize that it was time to quit my daytime, "grown-up" job.

I started working at the billboard factory with Pete, and we were both happy to have time to compare notes about our futures. I started staying at the fixer-upper full time. There was no heat except for a little kerosene space heater that I purchased and put in a bedroom. It was big enough to give some heat in the one room, but I dreaded going to the bathroom. Once winter hit, I just could not stay any longer; I feared waking up like a Popsicle, frozen to the sheets.

Pete, aware of my dilemma, asked me to move in with him and his brother. Although it was not an ideal situation, I gladly accepted because it was warm and closer to the fixer-upper than the condominium was. Since Pete's apartment boasted only two bedrooms, I had to sleep on the floor. Before long, I got bored making billboards. Luckily, in less than a year, my fixer-upper sold, and I had a good chunk of money to invest and a little bit of financial breathing room.

I started searching for a better job, and, thanks to my military service, I landed one at Pratt & Whitney Aircraft assembling commercial jet engines. I really was not overly qualified for this position since I had spent the majority of my time in the Navy building bombs, but I quickly caught on to this assembly work. Before long, I moved off of Pete's floor and back into the condominium in Hartford. It was a lot closer to my new job, and it had a bed!

Pete soon opened his own painting business, something he had wanted to do from the beginning of his painting days. He started dating Kim, a high school friend of ours. They got an apartment together, and before long he asked her to marry him. Pete had always been a family kind of guy. He was always the rock that held his family together throughout the rough times in their lives. At this point, he was ready to start a family of his own and so was Kim.

Over a year went by, and I was not seeing very much of Pete. I attended his wedding—the first one I had ever been to—but as is usually the case with weddings, there was not very much time to hang out with the groom. Pete was married now and trying to have a baby. I was happy for him but concerned for our friendship because our paths were no longer parallel. Looking back, I see that on the occasions when we did get together, it was as if nothing had changed, even when at that point, everything *had* changed. We still had the same everlasting bond, though; our connection transcended time and place.

In a fairly short amount of time, I grew unhappy with my factory job. Although the money and benefits were very good, it was menial and not at all challenging. I had a small, specific part in the construction of the engine. It was very routine and repetitious. It was also a union job, so I was only allowed to work for what felt like two out of my eight hours. While others who had adapted to this pace read the paper, smoked their cigarettes, and drank coffee, I was cringing at the boredom. I could not seem to get used to this lifestyle and was not really sure that I wanted to.

With good wages and investments, I was on track for the future that I had planned for myself. My job definitely was not stressful (or thought-provoking), so I had the time and energy to set and reach goals outside of work. In the end, all I kept doing was spending money to try to make myself happy. I bought two motorcycles: one for the street, and one for the dirt. I had even taken up SCUBA diving, a childhood dream, to try to fill the growing void in my life.

I had not seen Pete in a few months, and I needed to see my friend. Pete had new changes and challenges in his life and was content; I was not. Reminiscing about the "glory days" and planning for future ones would surely bring my spirits up and confirm that this was still the right path for me. I needed to talk with Pete almost as if he were a touchstone for me. He had been such a pivotal part of my development; the drive, the work, the future plans and dreams. In fact, he was the only real person with whom I ever talked about these things. All of my growth outside our relationship came from books and tapes rather than personal interactions. At the very least, this adventure would serve as a reminder that I was still alive.

The plan was for his wife to play cards with some mutual friends of ours while we went to have a long-overdue adventure. I picked Pete up at his apartment and watched as he kissed his bride good-bye. We went back to my condominium, and around 6:30 p.m. we headed to Chuck's, a local restaurant and hangout. Before we could map out our entire evening, we ran into my sister and her friend. We exchanged small talk with them for a while, but Pete and I wanted to focus on what we could do to make our infrequent reunion really exciting. We had a plan that could not be discussed in front of my sister—or any family or friends for that matter. As with most of our capers, it would probably be met with disapproval. Therefore, at around 7:30 p.m., we said good-bye and went next door to Friendly's Restaurant to discuss our night and get an ice cream. We joked about the fact that we were getting a frozen treat as the bank sign across the street read thirty-three degrees.

As we devoured our ice cream, Pete shared with me that he had recently bought a five-foot wooden rowboat. The vessel was old and decrepit. It appeared as if it had spent the last ten years supporting plant life as opposed to supporting fishermen or the like. He was unsure if the old boat could keep both of our 180-pound bodies afloat, but we decided it was high time to test it out. This caper was nothing out of the ordinary for us. It was part of what made us feel alive, and it was just what I had been craving.

Our most immediate impediment was that the boat was kept in the garage of our mutual friends, the same place where his wife was playing cards. So to complete our stunt, we had to smuggle the boat out of there as if we were thieves in the night, which only added to the excitement.

We left Friendly's and arrived at our friend's house just before 8:00 p.m. Pete wanted to go inside and say hi to his wife and our friends. I was anxious to get the night started but agreed to the slight deviation from the plan. We ended up playing cards and having a beer. We left a few minutes before 9:00 p.m. and drove to the next street over to figure out our next move.

Unfortunately, our escape route was not very direct. We parked down the road from their house so as not to be seen by either our friends or Pete's wife. We cut through two yards and arrived back at the house on foot. The door to the garage was locked, but because, as kids, we had spent so much time there, we knew where the key was hidden. The dining room window was literally five feet from the small garage door, and for several heart-stopping moments, we were in full view of our friends and Pete's wife. Once we gained access to the inside of the garage, we felt safe.

At that point, all we had to do was lift the old garage bay door up and lug the heavy load out. Fortunately, the main garage door faced the road and reduced our chances of being seen or caught. We put the boat on the side of the garage away from the house and quietly pulled the big door back down. We replaced the door key and snagged a six-pack of beer from the garage refrigerator. We giggled, thinking about our "grand theft beer"—and then reminded ourselves to replace the beer the next day.

We threw the boat over our heads and retraced our steps through the two backyards. The neighbors whose yards we were traipsing through would have been very confused at the sight of an upside-down boat, with six beers, four legs, and two paddles, all sticking out from beneath as it blindly staggered by their windows. When we made it back to the road, we threw the boat into the back of my Isuzu pickup truck. The boat fit in length but not in breadth. We were not concerned with it staying on during the mile or so drive to the Rocky Hill ferry launch.

Our goal was a bit incoherent; we had the boat, we had succeeded in smuggling it out, but we had no real supplies and certainly no detailed plan of action. Realizing this, we picked up a Maxwell House coffee can and gathered some sticks. We planned on using them to make a fire later in the night if we got cold. Without matches, we had to drive back to the center to bum some matches from a stranger. With the sticks, matches, can, and beer, we felt that we had all the supplies we needed.

We decided to float, and occasionally paddle, down the icy Connecticut River to the mouth of the ocean—into Long Island Sound. We had no idea how many miles it was or how long it would take, but that was our plan. The lack of detail made it feel good from the start because it instantly brought back so many youthful memories and feelings that had been overshadowed, almost to the point of oblivion, by insurance, bills, responsibilities, and, most of all, the need to get ahead.

Pete and I really connected with Bruce Springsteen's words, "You gotta stay hungry." We understood the intent of the lyrics and vowed to keep on struggling and always do more to be successful. I had already begun to notice that, for many people, the need to get ahead was often and sadly replaced with just the need to survive or settle for what they had.

As we talked and planned, it became evident that we viewed our mini-adventure, like many of our previous ones, as a way to remind ourselves that we still needed to feel life. It was also our way to reconnect with each other, the past, and, probably more importantly, the future. We reminded one another of our desire to get ahead rather than merely stay afloat, even if it meant fighting against all odds.

Neither of us had ever rowed a boat before, but that just added to the fun. We were so excited and pleased with the prospect of doing something novel that we actually chuckled as we launched. We slipped and slid down the icy ramp and fumbled with the awkward oars. A slight adjustment in our launch site, from the sloping ramp to the edge of the grass, prevented us from beginning our trip with soaked sneakers.

Once we were on the water, Pete and I each immediately cracked open a beer to begin our epic journey. All it did, however, was make our hands cold. We emptied the next two cans out into the water, urinated into them, and held them tight to keep our hands warm. Each time we had to empty our bladders—for me this was quite a bit—we would dump the contents of the can into the river and replace it with fresh, warmer urine. We did not want to drink any cold beverages, so we just let the two remaining cans roll uselessly around in the bottom of the boat.

It was very cold that winter night, so cold that the air instantly pulled the heat from our hatless heads and our gloveless hands. Within the first half-hour, we pulled out the rest of our supplies and attempted to make a fire in the coffee can. I struggled for a good ten minutes to get the fire started. The slight wind that had picked up was constantly trying to blow the small flames out. Even after it started, the fire was so small and provided so little heat that it was not worth keeping our hands out of our jacket pockets. As our portable fire proved worthless, I filled the can with water, and let it sink to the bottom of the river. While doing this, for the first time that the evening, I felt the numbing sting of the frigid water.

We began the evening underdressed, as usual, for the winter conditions. It was January 12th, a day I am not likely to forget any time soon. We were on the Connecticut River in Connecticut (yes, it flows through other states too). We wore only jeans, sneakers, T-shirts, and leather jackets. Being underdressed in these circumstances was just another challenge for us. In light of this, when I saw Pete take off his extra pair of socks, I called him a wimp for overdressing, but as I watched him put one on each hand as mittens, I was very jealous. When I apologized for teasing him, he took one off and gave it to me, so we each had some sort of hand-muff.

During the first part of our journey, we just flowed down river with the current as we alternated telling stories—each of which started with "Remember when …?" We constantly cut each other off to add to the other's version or to switch blame. We kept warm by throwing a football back and forth as we sat in that five-foot rowboat. As I think back, no matter what we did or where we were, we always had that ball.

Ice floated along the river, and, at one point we got out of the boat and pulled it onto an iceberg about the size of a big car. We passed the football back and forth to each other while trying foolishly to keep our balance. The iceberg was slippery and unsteady, but that just seemed to add to the thrill. I felt like a cross between Huckleberry Finn and Tom Sawyer.

Moving around felt good and seemed to get our blood flowing a bit, but standing on the ice with the additional exposure to the wintry night air seemed to exacerbate our decreasing body temperatures. Therefore, after about fifteen minutes, we slid the boat off the berg, and haphazardly climbed back in to continue our journey.

We soldiered on, drifting and reminiscing. When the stories tapered off, we started to sing well-memorized Bruce Springsteen songs. "Born in the USA" was always our favorite, but on that night, "The River" seemed much more fitting, so we sang that mellow song, happy with the break from the more energetic ones. We were starting to get fatigued and decided to change plans and try to land at Harbor Park in Middletown. It was only two towns away from where we had started, and was a lot easier to get to than the ocean.

Within thirty minutes of that decision, we changed our minds once more. The moon that had been providing light and some ability to get our bearings was now covered with clouds. The wind had picked up and seemed to suck the last vestiges of warmth from our bodies. We agreed that the next time we had the opportunity to pull out we would. Although we had not seen any such place, we anticipated passing a bridge or a road soon. We thought that either structure would provide a good enough place to disembark. Once we were back on land, we figured that it would be fairly easy to hitchhike back to the truck.

We decided to start rowing. It would get us to our anticipated destination much sooner and would have the added advantage of allowing us to warm up a bit. Even when it was not my turn to row, I would move around as much as possible to keep warm. After several hours of being on the river, we were not only fatigued, we were also chilled to the point of shivering. Still very far from our destination, we were becoming dangerously exhausted.

Initially, we did not care who rowed because we both enjoyed warming up, as well as resting from the awkward motion of rowing. After the first few switches, we gained confidence and the process began to seem easy. We would both stand up simultaneously and casually change seats. Not once did we think of the freezing water below us as a real danger. Even earlier, when we had bounced up and down on the iceberg, we did not foresee the dangers. As exhaustion took its toll, we were each more hesitant to begin our turn at the oars. Alternating rowers became trickier because our legs were tight and tired, and our moves were awkward and uncoordinated.

At twenty-five, however, I still felt the security and invincibility that many teenagers do about life; I was still too young to even think about it ending. Were we being cool and macho, or was it just plain stupidity? Either way, it was this mentality that led us to consciously decide not to take the life vests that had actually been stored in the boat. That decision about a seemingly small precaution drastically changed both of our futures.

I do not remember how or why the boat tipped. We were changing positions, and that is all I recall. Were we unstable due to exhaustion? Did one of us trip? No matter how many times I replay the event in my mind, I just do not recall. What remains perfectly clear, though, is the pain that shot through my veins and the memory of the ice crystals that seemed to form in my blood. The freezing water engulfed my entire body and quickly robbed all of the air from my lungs as I submerged.

Somehow, I drew my head back out of the water and swallowed a gulp trying to capture some air, as my breath was again snatched away by the shock. Because of the weight of my drenched clothes, my head was barely above water. As if programmed, I immediately began to swim for land on the west side of the river. We were dead in the middle, so shore was of equal distance to either side. Earlier in the evening, when the moonlight still shone, I noticed that the east side was devoid of civilization. Perhaps subconsciously, I had thought of the need for a possible escape route.

Pete had grabbed onto the capsized (but still floating) boat, and he yelled for me to grab onto it too. As soon as I stopped to turn around, I began to sink again. With huge effort, I pulled myself above the water once more, and I took only a couple of strokes before I reached the boat. It instantly started to go under with the weight of both of us, so I abandoned it and again headed for shore.

I quickly realized that I could not swim freestyle fashion because my heavy wet coat would not allow it. I loved my jacket. It was my first leather anything and my first article of clothing that had any value, but the weight of it was now dragging me under. Fortunately, I was never really attached to any material items, so I quickly decided to ditch it. However, one failed attempt at removing my coat was enough to prevent any additional efforts in that area. The cold water had severely diminished any strength and control that I had, and when I stopped treading water even for an instant, I sank quickly toward the bottom. I realized later that if I had dressed appropriately for winter (boots, heavy jacket, gloves), I would have been in even more danger.

When I surfaced for what was now the third time, I screamed at the pain from what felt like thousands of needles pricking my face, like they had been doing to the rest of my body. I vowed to continue the combination of sidestroke and doggy paddle that had kept me afloat thus far and not to deviate from these simple movements again.

Then, Pete's screams began to overpower my own as he yelled for help. Initially, I thought he was better off because the boat offered him some sort of floatation, and I had nothing. The wooden vessel was not that seaworthy after all, though—now it could not even hold his weight. If we had spotted our football, which had provided us countless hours of entertainment, it may have provided at least one of us adequate floatation. Pete abandoned the boat and attempted to move toward shore. I heard him call out in a panicked voice, "Talk to me, Larry." I tried to tell him to just keep on swimming in the fashion that I was, but because I was floating so low, I kept getting mouthfuls of water.

Pete was begging for help from anybody, but I knew it could not be from me. How could I support another when I could barely keep my head above water and my body from sinking to the bottom? As I continued to instinctively, almost mechanically, swim in a modified sidestroke, I heard my friend's cries for help become weaker and more desperate. I heard the exhaustion in his voice yelling, "Larry, help me!"

I was not just physically numb, but emotionally numb too. While a million thoughts went through my head over the next twenty minutes or so, I remained disturbingly calm. My arms and legs were on autopilot from the minute I touched the water. They never stopped moving and neither did my brain. Our motto to "keep on pushing" and our creed to "never say die" kept me going. I went from fear to anger to sadness and then to some indescribable state of emotion for which I have no words.

I thought about life, my life. I thought about death and its finality. I thought about my mom and what my death would do to her. I wanted to apologize for doing such a dumb thing and maybe for all the dumb things I had done in the past. I could not believe I was going to die, in that most immediate moment, and in that way. I could not conceive that I only had a few more minutes to do everything I always wanted to do. In an instant, I relinquished my teenage immortality complex. As I faced my own mortality, I started to make a deal with God but immediately stopped because I felt dishonest even making promises. I knew from past experiences in similar, but less severe, situations that I would only keep my word until shortly after I dried off. I did, however, continue to pray an honest, simple prayer as I looked up at the dark sky. I just wanted to live. I just wanted some more time.

In that moment, though, I had let go. I was emotionless and had just accepted my fate. It was fine. It was so unbelievably quiet. I was calm. I was content. I was at peace. It was over, and it was all right. Even at this lowest period of motivation when I had given in spiritually, my body had not quit. My emotions were tested when I heard, off in the distance, the last thing Pete said before his permanent silence, the words I still hear even today as I write these words, "Larry I'm gonna drown, Larry!" I really wished he had not used my name.

I did not react at that time. It did not sink in that I had lost my best friend. I did not feel a thing. All the thinking and feeling and praying was over. Now I was just moving. I visualized my pale white, even bluish hands just pushing the water and keeping my nose skimming just above the surface. I fought to move my feet, toes, and fingers. I would not stop. I saw nothing. I heard only the sound of my breathing as I forced air in and out, disregarding my body's uncontrollable shivers. I was in a zone that was probably my last phase of survival.

I awoke from this life-ending trance when something grabbed my foot. I jerked my leg up, and something touched my other leg. It was the river bottom. Touch down! I had been certain I would reach the bottom, but I thought it would be with my cold, dead body. Instead, I was near shore and in only about three feet of water. I was alive.

I made it! I could not believe it. I had no idea how much, if any, progress I had been making. Because of the river current, I thought I might be just drifting down the river and not getting any closer to the edge. I could not even see the icy bank, and yet there I was. As I felt the shore under my hands and feet, I dragged myself onto it. I collapsed from sheer exhaustion, but some force or reserve helped me to pull myself up. I looked out at the black river that had taken my friend and began to cry. Again, I immediately snapped out of anguish. I did not allow myself to feel the pain. I was not yet in the clear.

I took off my heavy leather jacket and began to crawl up a steep embankment. My wet clothes turned the cold dirt to mud, and I began to struggle even more to scale the more than one hundred-foot high, steep embankment. I lost one of my sneakers as I pulled myself up by grabbing onto small tree branches and bushes. When I reached the top, I was near the backyard of a house that, thankfully, had its porch light on. I crawled toward the house and eventually pulled myself up and began to stagger closer to my destination. Before I reached the house, a police officer came running from the side yard. This neighbor had called the police at 1:14 a.m. after hearing screams coming from the river. As the officer approached me, I realized the fight for my life was over, and I collapsed into his arms from the swelling mix of exhaustion, hypothermia, shock, and relief.

As the policeman helped me to his car, I told him that the man yelling for help was still down there, and the officer called for a search. Moments later, an ambulance came and EMTs cut off my clothes and wrapped me in blankets. They hooked me to an IV of warm saline and brought me to Middlesex Memorial Hospital, where I was treated for hypothermia.

While I was being treated, two police officers climbed down the embankment I had just scaled. They searched for any signs of Pete but found only my jacket. Two other officers checked a boat launch some forty feet south of where I came ashore. Cromwell and Portland fire departments were dispatched as well as a helicopter from Old Saybrook. At 2:11 a.m., the Cromwell fire department found Pete's capsized boat about a hundred yards south of the launch. The Middletown dive team was called to the scene at 2:45 a.m., but they never did enter the water. At 4:00 a.m., the search was called off because of a combination of the floating ice and other debris in the river, extreme dark, and no concrete last reference point. Because of the water temperature and length of time Pete had been missing, the officers determined that it was a recovery rather than a rescue mission. Based on all these factors, the search would not resume until first light.

I did not know what to feel. I realized that my best friend was dead, but I also knew that I had made it out alive. Regardless of the emotions that were flowing through me, I did not allow myself to focus on or really feel any of them. I lay there in the hospital bed, thawing out physically but remaining emotionally frozen and numb.

Some time later, the same police officer that had come to my rescue arrived at the hospital and informed me that the search had been called off until morning. My friend Birdsey came to the hospital and brought me some of his clothes to wear home. I did not know how he found out I was there; I thought he might have known someone who worked for the ambulance crew. I later remembered that we had told Pete's wife that we planned on being at his house for the evening. Apparently, the police had called him to get a statement, and he came down.

The hospital released me at 3:15 a.m., and the police took me directly to the Cromwell police department to fill out all of the required paperwork. Although I understand the need for the detailed paperwork and statements from all parties even remotely involved, I was angered by some of the loaded, accusatory questions the officer asked. I finished giving my statement at approximately 5:00 a.m. and then Birdsey drove me to the ferry to retrieve my truck. As I drove myself home, I began to realize my loss.

At around 7:00 a.m., authorities began to gather support for the recovery efforts. The same officer called me and asked me to meet him at the station. Aside from the local police and fire departments, a US Coast Guard helicopter was dispatched from Brooklyn, New York. The Connecticut State Police assembled their dive team to search the river bottom.

The officer drove me to a boat launch in Cromwell, just downriver from my exit point. It seemed to take forever for all the personnel involved in the search to get organized and begin. Eventually, the state police picked me up in their Zodiac, and we went out onto the river. I assisted divers by pointing out the approximate spot where our boat had gone down. Because it had been so dark, I really did not feel like I was much of a help in approximating where we fell in. It was 1:00 p.m. before the divers dropped into the water with their sleds, and it took just over thirty minutes for them to find what they were looking for. At 1:32 p.m., the divers pulled Pete's body out of the water. I watched from shore, motionless. At 2:10 p.m., my friend was officially pronounced dead. The next day, the state medical examiner's office completed an autopsy to ensure there had been no foul play.

There are, I think, positive and negative reactions to most things in life, and a lot of the reactions are choice. I am choosing to let the experience of Pete's death inspire me not only to be a better person but also to really live my life. We both spent so much time working that we missed out on a lot of time doing the things we wanted to do, pursuing our passions, and enjoying friends and family.

Two weeks after Pete's death, I handed the condominium over to the bank and moved to Florida, intending to start living the good life, or at least to eventually start living. Over time, I learned to be happy working one fun job (bartending) and spending the rest of my time playing volleyball, swimming in the pool or ocean, and just having fun. I became a SCUBA diving instructor and started doing my favorite hobby for a living. Then, I began to travel and learn things firsthand. With the encouragement of a girlfriend and my new philosophy on life, I went to college and became a teacher. College was something I had never thought I would or could do—neither had my teachers. However, teaching is definitely something I was meant to do. If not for those life-altering events, I would not have pursued that field or career.

This holistic transformation has allowed me the means, the time, and the motivation to see and do everything I want to do in all aspects of my life. It has brought me a balanced life—one that has the true success I had always strived for, including great relationships, a lifelong desire to learn, and an ability to explore and see the world. I am going to keep Pete's spirit alive by keeping my own spirit alive. Because my transformation began with Pete, I will always take some part of him along with me, wherever I may roam.

# QANTAS: AIRPLANES & AIRPORTS

There I sat, stuck in a small airplane seat, on the way to Singapore. I say stuck because there was absolutely no place to go and nothing to do physically. Even the smallest movement was difficult because, as luck would have it—thanks to Murphy's Law—I was trapped next to someone who really should have paid for two seats.

I have always thought that they should have little Stairmasters instead of seats on any flight that lasts more than twenty minutes. I bet it would cure jetlag. All the passengers could arrive at their destinations *pumped up* and ready to go as opposed to feeling like slugs. My alternative plan would be to replace all of the seats with beds. The planes could probably still accommodate just as many people if they set it up like sleeper cars on a tightly packed train. Perhaps they could fit even more if they designed them like the coffin-sized capsule beds popular in the Japanese airports and surrounding hotels. Everyone would arrive at his or her destination well rested. With this type of innovative design, however, there would definitely be an increase in the membership of the mile-high-club.

I was flying Qantas Airlines. I had chosen Qantas because it was said to be the only major airline that had never had a plane crash. I hold this impression by the thinnest of threads since my information is based solely on what the character Raymond Babbitt said in the movie *Rain Man*. Raymond was an autistic man played by Dustin Hoffman. Hoffman did such fine acting that it was easy to believe that he was really autistic and that the statistics he spouted about planes were real.

Like most people, I do not want to crash, but believe it or not, that is not what bothers me when I fly. It is the sheer boredom and discomfort. I feel like I am being punished when I am forced to sit in a restrictive chair and tolerate the people all around me. On either side of me, I am engaged in a fight to see who gets to put his or her arm on the armrest. Why would the airlines force a person to share a single armrest with a perfect stranger? Is this supposed to bring two people closer together? Has anyone ever really found his or her match on a plane? In all of my travels, I have never once sat next to a person I would want to share an armrest with—let alone a kiss.

I have learned through trial and error that if I am fortunate enough to win the armrest battle, I can never leave my seat. I will not go to the bathroom, and I will not reach up to turn on the light. Sometimes I don't even want to leave my seat after the flight is over because I am so happy with my victory. After all, it may be a long time before I am victorious again!

Besides the armrest issue, the space between rows is so very small. Airline etiquette demands that you position your legs so that they do not press against the seat in front of you. For some people, the logistics of this require that they turn sideways. There is, however, no room for that maneuver because there is another person to either the left or the right—or both.

I fervently pray that the person in front of me forgets to recline his chair. If I am blessed with his forgetfulness, I actually have a modicum of space. With that very little bit of room, I can keep my knee out in front of me instead of tucked into my chest, and I can actually use my tray table. If the person in front of me chooses to recline, however, I spend the remainder of the flight with his head in my lap as if I were his dentist. The only difference is, instead of his teeth, I often end up unwillingly examining his head for dandruff or lice, sometimes both.

Out of desperation, I no longer identify with the person behind me, so I put my seat back. The person behind me does the same until a domino effect develops; all of the passengers look like they're doing the wave. In the end, each passenger's head is practically lying on the lap of the person behind him. Just as I finally convince myself that I am comfortable, the lights go on, I hear a *ding*, and I am instructed to place my seat in the full and upright position. It makes me want to scream.

Fortunately, I sometimes have a short flight. If it is less than two hours, I am fine. Anything more than that and I have learned the hard way that I need to be fully entertained. I carry more things with me than a mom traveling with three kids all under the age of ten. I bring books, video games, crossword puzzles, sometimes crayons, and on rare occasions a GI Joe. I just cannot sit still. I am an adult-sized version of a little kid on a long road trip. Are we there yet?

As I have aged, I have found that I do not mind road trips as much as I used to when I was younger. This may be because I have developed a tried-and-true coping mechanism. When I am driving for too many hours, I get bored—much to my passengers' dismay. To alleviate the pent-up hyperactivity that inevitably accompanies the boredom, I turn the wheel over to my traveling companion and run alongside the vehicle for a mile or two. After that, I'm good for another couple of hours inside the car.

While this method is great for long car trips, it obviously does not work with any sort of air travel. I have developed another technique for long plane rides. Whenever I fly, I try to be the last one to board. I spend as much time as possible walking through the airport, enjoying the freedom to do as I please. I stretch my arms and legs and savor being totally alone in my personal space. When I get tired of walking, I sit down on an airport chair and recklessly plop my arms over both armrests. I store up these memories so that I can get lost in them once I am trapped on the plane.

The plane ride is the worst part of my travel experience, but airports, in and of themselves, rank right up there as a close second. The hours spent in airports are such a waste of time. It kind of reminds me of the hospital where I once worked. At any given moment, there is the simultaneous arrival of some people and the departure of others. Regardless of the circumstance, a lot of people are crying.

When I think back, it is easy to recall the longest time I spent in an airport. I was traveling through the South Pacific, and as is my custom, I arrived at the terminal in Fiji with plenty of time to spare before my departure. At the time, I did not realize just how early I was—even for me. I was looking for Vera, a woman I had met upon my arrival. She was the airport's version of a concierge. I wanted to thank her for all the suggestions she had given me when I arrived and for hooking me up with such an excellent getaway. It was exactly what I had visualized when I thought about a perfect island vacation. I found Vera in her tiny office on the second floor of the airport. At that point, she was very happy to see me and blissfully unaware that her job description would extend to entertaining a client until his plane took off—a day and a half later!

I was aware when I left for Fiji that there was a coup going on and that it was ill-advised for travelers to go there. I felt relatively unaffected by the news because I think the popular media in the United States tends to generalize to the point of error, blow things out of proportion, or present things out of context. I also knew that I would be staying on some islands off the mainland, where, I believed, the people remained sheltered and free from most political problems. Regardless, I did not cancel my plans because, well, I'd never been to Fiji, and I'd heard that the diving was spectacular. Just to ease the minds of my family and friends who knew that Fiji was my first stop, I told them that I was skipping that part of my trip and going directly to New Zealand.

What I did not count on was that not many other people would ignore the advisories as I did. Apparently, 80 percent of the travelers did cancel their vacations, and no planes were flying in to Fiji. That meant that, until they could get some bodies to fill a plane, none would be flying out.

For the next thirty hours, Vera did her best to try to amuse my hyper little self. First, she gave me the definition of what a coup was. I really should have looked it up before I went there. Then, she shared with me what this coup meant to her and her family. She also explained how the coup affected the reputation of her country.

I learned a lot of other personal things about Vera and her family. The conversations were very interesting, but as that first evening arrived, I got the sense that she would have liked to go home to them. I released her from her babysitting duties in exchange for the rights to the big chair in her office. Unlike the airports in the United States and Europe, this airport had no air conditioning. I was uncomfortably hot the entire time. As comfortable as Vera's chair was, I could not sleep. I was miserable.

The next morning, Vera entered her office with the same bright, enthusiastic smile she had when I first met her. How did she do it? The thought of reluctantly entertaining someone with my attention span would have definitely bought me an extra hour or so in bed.

Vera and I had another day together in which I immersed myself in the details of her Fijian life. We talked of family, traditions, and holidays. She shared with me the pros and cons of tourism and dealing with tourists. This made me think about how I thought about and treated the locals in the places I had traveled. Her words helped me understand how some residents do not like tourists and why. I try to keep this in mind when I travel—it helps remind me to tread lightly and respectfully.

Learning about other people and their cultures was one of the reasons I was traveling, so I guess the time spent without a bed and some air conditioning in this little airport in Nadi, Fiji was not totally wasted. However, I cannot truthfully say the same thing about the thirty-four hours I once spent in Heathrow Airport in London waiting for a friend to arrive.

I had been backpacking around Scotland, Northern Ireland, and Ireland, and I had then taken the ferry from Wales back to England. When I reached the airport, it was late, so I decided to save a few bucks and just sleep in the terminal. It was worth it because I would have no worries about being there to meet my friend, Cindy, when she arrived at eight the next morning. Cindy and I were taking a bus to England's coast and then picking up a cruise ship to go through Scandinavia and on to Russia.

Before I arrived at the airport, I thought that a sleepover in the terminal would not be that bad. I imagined the light from the Burger King sign casting an almost cozy fireside glow over several benches along the wall. At that hour, I thought I would have my pick of any seat in the house. I was pretty sure that there would be other well-lit restaurants where I could relax, get a drink and a snack, and read in unhurried pleasure. At the minimum, I figured I could read until I passed out on an airport bench. Well, I was wrong. There were no benches, at least not that I could find. There were, however, seats. At first, it appeared as if every nook and cranny was filled with people of all shapes and sizes. If a person did not occupy a seat, then it was filled with the bottles, bags, and boxes of the person one spot down. I had never expected that so many others would have the same idea about saving some money by forgoing a night in a hotel.

After some searching, I discovered that the airport did actually have benches, but they were divided every twenty or so inches by armrests, making it impossible for anything larger than a house cat to lie down. I had no choice but to sit straight up in a hard fiberglass seat. After all my struggles on the plane to carve even an inch of space on my armrest, there I was with vacant armrests as far as the eye could see! Unfortunately, I was exhausted and unable to appreciate the irony. As I surveyed the area, I desperately wanted to rip out the armrests so I could lie down and sleep.

With the passing of each miserable hour, my desire to be horizontal increased. I lost count of the number of deafening overhead announcements heralding the arrival and departure of flights about which I cared not. The only thing worse than my seat or those announcements was the continuous litany of garbled, incomprehensible security reminders.

Ordinarily, I prefer colder temperatures to hot. I rarely get cold, but while I was at Heathrow I was shivering. The nighttime temperature in the terminal had to be just above freezing; although the iced tea I was nursing to try to keep me awake did not become frozen solid, the ice cubes never melted. I think keeping the heat down was a ploy to keep people awake. Over the course of a few hours, I emptied my pack and put on whatever clothes I had in there. After donning my entire wardrobe, I was still chilled.

When I could not sit or slouch a second longer, I lay down on the floor in front of my seat. Almost immediately it seemed, just as my body was melting into the hard surface, I was scolded by a security guard and told I was not allowed to lie down. At least that's what I assumed he said. I never could understand proper English, at least not when someone from "the motherland" speaks it.

I have to admit that I felt like a bum trying to catch some *z*'s in a local park. The night dragged on, and I periodically walked around trying to warm up and wake up. I must have looked as bad as I felt, based on the glances I got from the other zombies who were sharing my nightmare.

The endless night finally gave way to morning, and the time came for me to make my way to the arrival gate. As the arrival time drew near, I was elated to discover that Cindy's plane was not delayed. A delay would have surely sent me off the deep end. I anxiously watched as folks walked through the gate; some passengers were greeted by friends and family, others appeared relieved to be home, and still others just looked happy to be in London. I watched each person get off that plane, but none of them was Cindy.

I stood there, pathetically alone, for a good long time. I was totally deflated. I could not believe my bad luck. What next? Should I jump off the London Bridge? A bit extreme, but I was at my wits' end. After a few deep and shaky breaths, I picked my lip off the same floor I was not allowed to sleep on and headed for the appropriate airline desk. I mustered up as much patience as I could and checked to see if my friend had been on the flight. For security reasons, the airline staff would not give me the information, and that was about it for my patience. Frustration and discomfort mixed, and I started causing a ruckus. I am never intentionally rude to people, but I was on empty and did not know what else to do. My voice grew louder with each word as I explained my situation to a nice but uncaring woman at the counter. As I showed her the confirmation papers with both Cindy's and my names, she glanced at our itinerary, smirked, and pointed to a date at the top of the paperwork. As my eyes followed her finger to Cindy's departure date from Georgia to London via New York, I realized my error. Cindy was indeed scheduled to arrive at Heathrow at 8:00 a.m.—but not until the following day! When it finally clicked that I was a day early, there was nothing left for me to do but apologize for my rudeness, gently tuck my tail between my legs, and shuffle away from the counter. When I looked at my watch and saw it was already 10:00 a.m., I realized that I only had twenty-two and a half hours to go!

With the daunting prospect of such an interminable wait stretching out before me, I needed to stretch out and get some restorative sleep. I paid a ridiculous amount of money to store my luggage for twenty-four hours and then walked outside the terminal doors. I sat down on a green bench to thaw out. I breathed in the exhaled cigarette fumes from the smokers around me and opened up my magazine. When the person next to me inhaled as much nicotine as she needed to last through her upcoming flight, she left. I quickly lay down in the fetal position, put the magazine over my face like a happy bum, and drifted off to sleep. Ahhhh, no armrests!

Most of the time, it is safe to say that I am not a people watcher. I don't usually give a hoot what anyone else is doing. However, while killing time in an airport, "people watching" does seem to be an excellent way to pass the time. I was in a small, hot airport in Honduras once with my dive club, "Scuba Toons." Our flight to Roatan, one of the Honduras Bay Islands, had been delayed. We set our luggage on the floor and lay on top, waiting, in a boredom-induced comatose state.

With little else to occupy my time, I started looking around the room. Although most of the other travelers looked gloomy and uncomfortable, one person in particular looked worse than the rest. I watched as a drug-sniffing dog daintily tinkled on his luggage. The man stood by without saying a word. He remained silent not because he didn't like his luggage and not because he had drugs sealed in a waterproof baggie inside his suitcase. He remained silent because the soldiers who owned the dog were carrying assault rifles. I am sure that this was a bad airport experience for this man, but for me it was just a rather funny little diversion. It offered a little entertainment to relieve me during my miserable delay. In the not-too-distant future, the tables would turn, and I would find myself serving as the entertainment for a long line of passengers looking for a diversion.

My worst airport experience was at Tel Aviv, in Israel. I had been traveling for my summer vacation, and from the time I boarded a minivan in Egypt to travel to Israel, things had gone poorly. The seven-passenger van was already packed with ten people. Nobody seemed to mind when we pulled off and picked up more stragglers on the side of the road. I did not know who these people were, but I remember thinking that they had to be friends of the driver. In reality, I think the only criterion for pick-up was that they smoke; every single one of them smoked. This was what I got for traveling on a shoestring.

Once I arrived in Israel, I walked across the border, paid somebody with a uniform some money, and waited for another bus to take me to some staging area where I waited for yet another bus. The third bus would get me to Jerusalem, and it was a lot nicer than any of the others. We were even able to stop at the Dead Sea for about fifteen minutes. I took advantage of this time and went for a swim. I wanted to see if I really could float effortlessly because of the high salinity. I could.

Swimming (or floating) in the Dead Sea seemed like a good idea at the time, but I spent the rest of the day with diaper rash. From the time I got off the bus in the Holy Land, and with every step I took thereafter, the dried salt rubbed away layer after layer of my skin like vicious sandpaper. My thighs chafed, and I was cranky. Neither played a role in the way I was treated there, but it may have played a role in how I reacted.

From the time I got off that bus until the time I got off the one that took me to the airport, everyone with whom I came in contact was rude to me. People were literally bumping into me on the sidewalk as they passed by me. When I concluded that it was no coincidence (after the fifth or sixth overt shove), I started bumping back and swearing at the aggressors. They all just gave me the same hostile look. In addition to the sidewalk gauntlet, I consistently got the wrong information, even from the professionals. For example, I asked the lady at the ticket counter if I needed to change money for the bus to the airport and was promptly told that the driver would accept my US dollars. When I handed the bus driver my money, however, he abruptly said that he did not take American money. When I explained that the lady at the ticket counter told me he would, the driver yelled at me and said, "This is not f***ing America!"

The chafing, the bumping, and the rudeness all contributed to my arrival at the airport four hours before my flight. My early arrival might also have been because I had visited ten countries in sixty-seven days, and I was eager to be done with this trip so that I could process all my recent experiences. Maybe I was also anxious to get on a flight that would land me back on familiar ground in New York. Mostly, I think it was because I had had a pretty poor experience in Israel and just wanted to get the heck out of there.

Not long after my arrival at the airport, the security-conscious Israelis became suspicious of me for some reason. Maybe it was because I showed up at the airport and checked in so early. Maybe it was because I had so many other travel vouchers attached to my ticket. I am not sure what criteria they went by, but it was immediately clear that I had become a person of interest.

First, a nice lady in uniform approached me and said, "Sir, please step out of the line and follow me." Still within earshot of the other passengers, she asked, "What is the purpose of your travel?" I calmly responded, "Pleasure; this is my vacation."

She smiled innocently enough, but the questions began to seem more like an interrogation. "What places have you been visiting?" she inquired.

Initially, the interrogation posed no problem because I was very early for my flight and had the time to answer her questions. I even thought it was kind of cool. The other passengers in line instantly regarded me as suspect. I could almost hear them saying to one another, "I thought that man looked strange." "There was just something about him," another would claim.

As I was listing off my previous destinations, other security personnel joined her, and the drilling went on and on. I was still all right with the security questions, even when they became more personal. I believe some of the additional officers were there simply for hands-on training. At one point, when there were six people around me, the original officer asked if I had proof of my activities over the last two months. I started to become a little annoyed, and the smile began to disappear from my face. She asked if I had been keeping a journal, and when I responded yes, she asked if she could read it. I handed her the book without thinking, and as she began to flip through and read random pages, I realized that earlier in the day I had stopped at a coffee shop in town, and I had written down what a rotten time I was having. I had recorded in excruciating detail how poorly the local people had treated me, and I remembered expressing displeasure with my experience in Israel.

I wanted my journal back before she got to that part, but I did not dare to ask for it. I was afraid that asking for it back would create some additional suspicion of guilt and escalate her interrogation. I knew that if she took exception to anything I had written about her country, she had the power to keep me from my flight and make my visit even more uncomfortable—and longer. From that moment forward, I resolved to withhold writing any negative opinions in my journal, at least until after I had left the particular unpleasant country.

I sweated as the other security officers asked additional questions. Many of the questions were repeats, and I was getting angry. They told me to calm down and moved me to a hallway behind a locked door. I wanted to take the focus off the journal that the first officer was still reading, so I began to ask questions. I had become very defensive and asked if they believed I was a terrorist carrying a bomb. I opened my small carry-on backpack and emptied it onto the floor. As the agents went through every nook and cranny of my belongings, the officer reading the journal decided to join them. Maybe my stuff looked interesting—or at least more interesting than my memoirs. Regardless of why she stopped reading, I was relieved. I wished I had done this earlier and saved myself the frustration and stress.

My ordeal lasted for over an hour, and when they were finished with me, I went outside to sit on a bench and calm down. I still had about forty-five minutes until it was time to board my flight. I took out my journal and wrote about the incident and the miserable people who had given me my worst airport experience ever. In retrospect, I had not quite learned my lesson, but I figured there was little chance that they would ask to read it again!

As I soared over the Pacific reflecting on those past air travel tribulations, I realized that there were worse things than being crammed on this long flight to Singapore. No matter what, at least I had the assurance of Qantas's top-notch safety record to relieve my fears of crashing. Besides, I needed to think about more important things than past flights—like strategies for the unavoidable battle over the armrest.

# RECRUIT: MOVE OUT, NOT UP

At eighteen years old, I took my first flight ever. Yes, this was my introduction to travel. I left a cold Connecticut winter for the windy and much colder climate of Great Lakes, Illinois. It was December 22nd, three days before Christmas. I was not going on vacation; at that time I still had not been on a vacation. Nor was I flying home for winter break after my first semester at college like many of my peers. Finishing 149th in a high school class of 153 had not exactly put me on the academic path.

No, this plane was taking me to boot camp! In pure desperation for something to do after high school, I joined the US Navy. I was lured in by the commercials that showed Navy Seals jumping out of helicopters into the ocean. They said I would see the world—but before I could do any of these fun things, I had to make it through two months of boot camp as a recruit.

**Recruit:** (n) a scared, confused youth sporting two millimeters of hair who is yelled at continuously as he is made to do physical and menial things (things that his mom never made him do) until he either becomes a man or cries, quits, and returns home to Mom, where he will never again do either a push-up or such tasks as making a bed with hospital corners, ironing, and folding clothes to produce clean, crisp creases, and scrubbing the floor until it's as clean as the kitchen table.

This definition also applies to women; however in the entire time I was in boot camp, I never saw one. I don't know if seeing women during that time would have made things easier or harder for me.

The navy changed the name of boot camp to basic training, because, I guess, someone thought that the term boot camp had a negative connotation, and the navy would not stand for that. The first eight weeks of boot camp, a term I intentionally use for its negative connotation, were a sort of trial period. Not that it was the kind of trial period that gave any of us recruits a choice. It was not as if we could have said, "No, I don't like this military thing. I think I'll go home." The only choice we had was how much effort we put in and how much of the rigorous training we were willing to endure. The fundamental goal of basic training was to try to stop me from being a punk. Oh yeah, and to divest me of any pride I had ever had. This objective was not mine at all; it was, however, the main focus of the drill instructors.

I did not take the SATs in high school. I honestly did not know what it was or why I would volunteer to take a test that was not required (not that a required one would have had much of a chance of getting done either). I did, however, have to take one standardized examination to get into the navy, the ASVAB test. I took it simply because my recruiter told me I had to. As one can guess, my scores placed me somewhere between a high school dropout and an orangutan. Therefore, my choices in the navy were limited. For me, it was ordnance or a naval janitor. No offense intended, but I did not go through boot camp and get a short haircut to become a janitor. I could have easily become a civilian janitor and worn a uniform that was much more attractive than the one the US Navy designated for its crew.

My main drill instructor, also known as our company commander, fit every stereotype of how drill instructors are portrayed in the movies. He behaved exactly as, and even looked a little like, Gunny Sergeant Hartman from the movie *Full Metal Jacket.* He screamed non-stop for no apparent reason, and he swore like … well, like a sailor. He talked a lot about sex with inanimate objects and called us all types of names. He kept us *scared straight* for sixty-something days.

"Don't believe a f***ing word your f***ing recruiter said." Those were the very first words I heard from my drill instructor after we piled out of the government bus that had picked us up at Chicago's O'Hare Airport. It was the first couple minutes of basic training, and we were already being yelled at. I did not know what we could have possibly done wrong, but I knew I only had seven weeks, six days, twenty-three hours, and fifty-eight minutes left. The freezing winter rain that poured down on us was demoralizing, but it did not seem to affect this mean son-of-a-sea-corker as he made us line up outside and then yelled these encouraging words and a few others. He made it clear that our recruiters had misled us, but he made it even clearer that we could not do or say another word about it.

**Recruiter:** (n) sniffling, slimy, lying rat who convinces young adults that they can have whatever they want in the service—knowing full well that when the recruit gets out in four years he, the rat, will be hiding in a hole someplace else, safe from retribution.

We got up at the crack of dawn each morning to the sound of the drill instructor literally beating the metal garbage cans with a nightstick and spewing forth a litany of profanity. Everything was always a huge rush. We dressed in seconds and then had to *double time* to breakfast, although we were not allowed to call it breakfast; we referred to all meals as chow. For most of the meals, we devoured our food as we walked through the serving line. Whatever we had not consumed by the end of the chow line, we threw in the trash barrels, and *double timed* our way back outside. Somehow, no matter how much we rushed, we were always late for something. This was not good for my digestion, but it could have been worse. We took our rifles to chow, and one unfortunately appointed recruit had to stand guard over all of our weapons—he did not eat at all!

We learned how to march, dress, and clean. We learned how to do everything with rifles except fire them. Looking back, I understand why we were not allowed to shoot our guns. I believe there were more than a few young men in my group who would have buckled under the physical and emotional strain. It did not take a great deal of imagination to picture one of those men going postal on the drill instructor, like Private Pyle did in *Full Metal Jacket.* I suspect that none of the other recruits would have been too heartbroken if that had happened, but we were glad that the live ammunition was out of our reach for fear that the stressed man would miss and clip a few of us recruits as well.

We got a lot of physical exercise in boot camp. If we got in trouble for anything at all, we would do additional "training" at night after the other recruits were done for the day. I had what was described as a bit of an authority problem, so I ended up going two or three times for that additional training. I can still smell the odor of the huge gymnasium as ten or so other free-spirited recruits and I did crunches, push-ups, and flutter kicks until our stomachs cramped and our arms felt like spaghetti. The yelps of pain did not encourage the drill instructors to stop the punishment. They yelled, called us names, and really got irate when someone would slow down, collapse, or break down. It was made clear to us that if we did any of those things too early in the punishment, we would be required to come back the next night.

When the drill instructor felt that he had abused us enough, he would escort the stiff victims back to their individual barracks. More than the smell of the gymnasium, I remember the feeling of sliding directly into bed with a sweat drenched T-shirt and underwear. This was the most disgusting, uncomfortable feeling, but after what I had just been through, I would melt into my bunk and fall fast asleep. I am proud to say that I never had to go back the next night. I never stopped exercising, and I definitely never broke down. I am honest enough to admit, however, that I could not move the next day. Even now, I cannot imagine going back twenty-four hours later and doing it all over again.

Although I do not remember all the things I got in trouble for, I do remember one rather vividly. My drill instructor had an assistant, the *ass. drill*, I guess one could call him—I know I did. The ass. drill's physical appearance was so goofy that it was hard to take him seriously. He had huge Dumbo ears and a long saggy mouth. When he barked out orders, his ears and lips would wiggle for some moments after he stopped yelling. As difficult as we had it and as scared as we were, I could always find amusement by looking at the ass. drill's face. It was a bit of relief in an otherwise stressful environment. One time, my amusement was too much to contain, and I laughed not only out loud but also, unfortunately for me, directly into his floppy face. Needless to say, I went to bed very sweaty and sore that night.

I vaguely remember several men from our company who had to serve time in that gymnasium, and I recall very well the five that did not complete basic training. Two teenagers from the Bronx, whose urine tests came back positive for cocaine, were ejected. I guessed they regretted listening to their intelligent friends who probably assured them that the drugs would be out of their system by the time they got to boot camp. I am not sure what is worse—that they did cocaine just before starting boot camp, or that the navy waited until these recruits were two weeks from completing boot camp before giving them the boot!

There was an older man, almost thirty, who was actually kicked out of our company because he was deemed mentally unstable. I cannot really disagree with the decision. I remember talking to this guy and thinking he was a nut-job. He appeared to be untrainable. No matter how the instructors tried, they could not teach him to fold his clothes correctly. All the recruits thought he was pretending to be an idiot just to get a section eight (now called a 5-13) discharge out of the navy. I know the company commanders thought so too because every time he screwed something up they would yell, "You've got to be f***ing bullshitting me!" I thought the poor guy was just misunderstood until one day on a smoke-and-Coke break I saw him eat his own cigarette butts. He was one of the reasons we were all really glad we did not get to shoot the rifles.

About halfway into our training, two guys just could not hack the abuse anymore and decided to go AWOL (absent without leave). Apparently, they climbed over the barbed wire fence that surrounded the training facility and followed the railroad tracks all the way to Chicago. Those left behind are never told the fate (or success) of the ones who go AWOL. It was probably bad for morale, but we were all pulling for them. In the end, I made it through basic training and graduated with the rest of the young men in Company 378.

Upon completion of boot camp, I was no longer a young punk kid. I emerged from basic training a disciplined eighteen-year-old man. I could vote and drink before I went into the service—the clichéd way of determining when someone is an adult in the United States—but after basic training, I could fight for my country. Ironically, I did not want to fight. Unfortunately, per the agreement that the sniffling, slimy …

oh, you have the definition—recruiter persuaded me to sign, the navy owned my every thought, feeling, and action for the next four years. Therefore, regardless of whether I wanted to fight or not, that is what I had to do, or at least learn to do.

Boot camp had, in fact, removed the punk from me, and replaced it with a whole new attitude. Sadly, they also removed any pride I had as well. What happened to the few, the proud, the … oh, that's the marines. Bat-shit, I joined the wrong branch! No fear though, the navy would soon replace the pride they had stripped from me with "military pride." To accomplish this task, we needed an enemy.

Orders to the Naval Aviation Weapons Training Facility in Millington, Tennessee, would place me in the perfect place to develop the skills to fight. It was here that I would be allowed to play with bombs, missiles, and, finally, guns. Actually, I learned to build and load bombs, complete general maintenance, and make repairs on the armament systems of F-18 jets. I learned all about bombs, from practice bombs with smoker fuses to armed ones weighing five hundred pounds. The AIM-9 missile was a favorite of many of my classmates with its heat-seeking capabilities, but I favored working with the M61A1 gun. The weapon was situated just in front of the pilot in the nose of the plane. The gun was huge and so were the 20 mm rounds that came out of it.

At first, the field of aviation ordnance may not seem like the preferred choice for a peaceful person like me. However, at the time, I was more hyper than peaceful, and I was just looking for something exciting to do. As it turned out, I did not really qualify for much else. The only A my high school report card ever saw was in physical education. If I were graded for every gym class I attended in a single day, I would have been valedictorian. Unfortunately, high school required all kinds of other subjects that really did not interest me at the time like math, English, science, and social studies.

It turned out that the weapons school was more of an education than I thought it would be. As I took classes, studied, and passed exams, I not only learned how to build bombs and load missiles, I also learned how to construct academic self-esteem and discipline. In high school, I routinely skipped class and went to gym. If I skipped class in the navy, I'd be going to physical training rather than physical education. I had had enough of that in boot camp, and that was one education I did not care to repeat.

With my weapons schooling successfully behind me, I could begin the wonderful life of traveling around the world with the US Navy, just as my recruiter promised. Off I went to my first assignment, the naval air station in Lemoore, California. California is a great state with plenty to do for anyone, but Lemoore was not exactly booming with beaches, palm trees, or Sunkist. In fact, aside from the cotton industry, there seemed to be nothing there.

My major gripe with the armed forces, though, was the promise of travel. In the four and a half years I served, I almost never left the United States. Every couple of months, we would take a military flight to Fallon, Nevada, or Yuma, Arizona, to drop a bunch of bombs. On one of those deployments in Arizona, we crossed over the Mexican border into Boy's Town. I am not sure if this was the actual name of the town or if it was nicknamed this because of all the prostitutes hanging around. I was just happy to go someplace where I had never been. However, because we were in the military, we just went to the nearest bar, got drunk, and tried to avoid getting into a fight with the locals. The only thing I remember about my first trip to Mexico is that my friend threw up under the table, and the ordnance sergeant dipped his tortilla chip in it and ate it. How's that for some great role models?

My next duty station was Jacksonville, Florida. Florida, too, is a great state with plenty to do—just not near the base. I was assigned there before the football stadium was built. This area of Florida is where I learned the term "damn Yankee." I actually did know the term, but I had never been called one before. I was not aware that anyone had been called one since the Civil War.

By the time I had moved to the base in Florida, I had four months of training in ordnance and two years in a training squadron. I was now an expert on the navy's newest jet, the F-18. I was moving up the ranks, and I had become a petty officer. I had a crew of my own to teach and lead. I loved the hard work. I loved coming in from the flight line after a long, hot day of humping bombs, troubleshooting problems, and performing scheduled maintenance. It was something to be proud of, and I started to really feel good about the possibility of a naval career. I remember even buying a Navy bumper sticker for my truck that read, MOVE UP, NOT OUT.

The United States was not in the midst of any major conflict at the time, so things got stale on the bases. However, military pride still had to prevail, so we found other enemies. The enemy, pathetically enough, became other branches of the service. Because I was based in a marine training squadron, the conflict that was concocted for us was the navy vs. the marines. In slang terms, it was squids vs. jarheads, respectively. The word *squid* came from the relaxed way a sailor marched and the word *jarhead* came from the shape of a marine's head because of his funny haircut. The conflict was obviously nothing at all like the middle school playground tussles that periodically erupted when two kids would call each other names. Oh no, this name-calling battle was very grown-up stuff.

The problem with an army that has no enemy is that there is no place to release the pent-up, testosterone-laden desire for conflict. When I was stationed in California within a marine squadron, the conflict was obvious and easy to delineate: navy vs. marines. In this new squadron that consisted of only sailors, it was harder to find ways to compare personal "mast" size. With little else to discriminate against, the battle lines were drawn based upon one's rate (job title). It went against human nature. In most instances when people meet, they search for common ground: age, occupation, or interests. In the armed forces, instead of being united by similar age, choice of military branch, and years served, simply choosing a different job within that same branch almost guaranteed we would be at arms with each other. I never understood it, and more importantly, I never bought into it.

Rank was an even greater point of conflict than rate. To begin with, rank is always posted on the uniform and is extremely important to all parties. The rank emblem defines the rules of engagement when two or more parties interact. It seemed to be the single deciding factor in any type of communication. An officer would instantly exert power and authority over enlisted personnel. Among the enlisted, the number of stripes specified the pay grade, and the individual with the most, flourished. An E-5 (enlisted grade 5), dominated an E-4; an E-3 trumped an E-2; and even an E-2 looked down on an E-1.

In all fairness, the disrespect I had for several of my superiors was not unwarranted. I had no problem with the officers under whom I worked. They were educated, motivated leaders and I respected them. However, many of the enlisted personnel that ran some of the individual shops or departments were miserable losers who seemed to do nothing but try to make life for those under them as crappy as their own. I had no respect for these enlisted personnel because they were terrible leaders who spawned poor future leaders. They did not have to learn or qualify to be leaders. Those with longer service seemed to feel that it was not only accepted but also expected to disrespect those who had less time. I do not handle unnecessary, blatant disrespect very well (never have and never will), and do not believe anyone should. I do understand the pecking order and its importance in the military; taking orders without question has its place as it can and does save lives. However, the constant authoritative posturing that goes on is, in my experience, unnecessary and only serves to undermine the cohesiveness within each unit by ensuring a constant, unnecessary battle.

As one of the petty officers in my shop, I had a great rapport with the people who worked under me. Our collegial relationship was never a problem. My crew respected me on the job and understood exactly what I expected of them. They knew that if the vans were loaded, we would be working our rear ends off all day. When we came back to the shop at the end of the shift with everything complete, it was a good day. They also knew that they would be disciplined if they got out of line. It was simple and as stress-free as possible with a minimum amount of authoritative crap. Instead of being lauded as successful, efficient, and respectful, the appropriate camaraderie I had with my crew only served to antagonize the staff above me. They were hated because they believed that being jerks was the only way to engender respect. This was their brilliant philosophy, and they wanted me to pursue it too. It really angered them when I chose not to act like they did, so my immediate superiors started busting my posterior.

I learned that, in the military, when someone of higher rank or service wants to get you, they are going to. They got me. My chief ordered me to perform an unsafe act concerning the arming of a five-hundred-pound bomb. When I blatantly refused, despite his repeated and increasingly louder "request," he wrote me up for disobeying a direct order. It was more dramatic than that, but those are the basic facts. I was sentenced to Captain's Mast, a proceeding similar to appearing in court before a judge. I stood there before the squadron's commanding officer, listened to the charge brought against me and to the punishment issued. Although I had Navy safety manuals that showed that the act my chief ordered me to do was unsafe and against Navy regulations, I was not able to present the facts, nor was I able to speak at all.

I was fined and knocked down a pay grade. Because of my disciplinary record, which included a few fights at my previous duty station (jarhead verses squid conflicts), I was also informed that if I got written up once more before my tour of duty was over, I would be dishonorably discharged. Now, I did not like the military and wanted to get out. In fact, I had even gone so far as to rearrange my Navy bumper sticker to read MOVE OUT, NOT UP, but I did not want to go out on a dishonorable discharge—and certainly not with only six months to go! That is exactly what I told my executive officer (second in command) when he asked me two weeks later if I was trying to get myself kicked out of the military.

I was in the executive officer's quarters because I had gotten written up again. The second write-up did not surprise me because I had seen it coming. Shortly after I left Captain's Mast, my chief had told me that he was going to get me, and it was only a matter of time. He said that I had made him look bad in front of his superiors. I imagine that it was because I had the safety manual ready to prove he was incompetent. I told the executive officer about the chief's threat, but he could not do anything about it because I had questioned authority, and in the military, authority is not questioned.

Sometime between the Captain's Mast and the second write-up, the executive officer must have read the section in the manual about the proper and improper way to arm that specific bomb, based on the configuration of the aircraft and in relation to the other weapons it was carrying. He knew that I was correct; even more important—he knew that my chief was wrong, possibly dead wrong.

The executive officer went to bat for me, and I was grateful. If this man had not put himself on the line for me, I think I would have been even more embittered about the military—if that was possible. He took me out of the ordnance shop because he suspected that I would not stand a chance. He sent me out to sea, where he was convinced I could not get into any trouble.

I spent the last few months of my enlistment on an aircraft carrier called the *CV-43 USS Coral Sea*. It was a very impressive ship. I have seen this vessel in at least two movies. The way it stored and stacked jets and helicopters was amazing. It was like a busy parking lot in New York City, but most of the time, the flight deck ran as smoothly as a well-choreographed dance with the men from each shop wearing different-colored shirts to identify their roles; I wore red for ordnance!

A flight deck is also a dangerous place. We were told that at least one man per cruise loses his life. Sometimes, the unfortunate person was dismembered by the mighty catapults that shoot the planes off the ship. Other times, an inattentive victim got blown overboard by the mighty afterburners of the jets. Most unfortunate, I believe, were the low-ranking individuals who were sent at night to empty the trash overboard—don't get me started on that environmental issue. If one of those poor souls popped up from the water after his three-story plunge, he would only be able to watch in disbelief as his safe haven steamed away into the dark, the loud ship's engines drowning out his desperate screams. A man overboard would be difficult enough to recover during daylight hours since it takes thirty minutes just to turn a carrier around. The chances at night are so near impossible that I do not think an attempt is even considered.

I loved being on the ocean, and I spent as much time on deck as I could. I loved simply looking out at the endless ocean and dreaming. This occupied only a small percentage of my time; mostly I had to be on hyper-alert when I was on deck. I was bored in the shop and did not like the conditions on the ship. The work was hard, but for me, the time off from work was harder. We would work twelve hours on, twelve hours off. There was absolutely nothing to do when we did not have to be in the shop or on deck. During flight operations, we could not really hang out on the flight deck because it was already crowded enough with just the one crew. We could not hang in the shop because it was very small and again, the entire other shift would be there. The quarters were cramped and hot. We all slept in bunk beds that were not only stacked too close together, but too close to the steel ceiling, which was just below the steel flight deck. The air throughout smelled like jet fuel, and the drinks on board (referred to as bug juice) tasted like jet fuel. Although I was on the ocean and traveling, I was not happy.

The one-month "work-ups," as they were known, were merely training for six-month deployments. The work-ups had the advantage of being shorter, but there were no stops in foreign ports. We would train for a month and then return to our base. During my second tour of work-ups, my discharge day arrived. I was lifted off the carrier by a cargo helicopter, along with some supplies and a few other personnel that were leaving the ship for one reason or another. As we lifted off and made a hard bank, I watched the huge, battleship-grey carrier grow smaller and smaller. This was it for me. I did what I needed to do to fulfill the biggest obligation I would ever commit to. I did not like it, but I had done it—honorably.

I had just turned twenty-three when the navy released its grip on me and I was honorably discharged. It took two full years to finally feel free and out from under the military's giant thumb. The sense of elation totally overwhelmed me, and I felt like I owned and controlled my thoughts and emotions again, or at least was allowed to have them. This was an amazing feeling that I swore I would never give up again. My visions of traveling the world would have to wait a while longer. The military was just not for me in any sense. I am grateful for what I got out of it, but it took many things from me, too. I needed the discipline, but I needed my pride as well. I was thankful for the structure, but not at the expense of my spirit. I was glad I moved out—and not up.

# ST. MARTIN: HOLLAND & HONEYMOON

I had experienced some rough seas during the night, and, with the arrival of morning, I was feeling terrible. I remember taking two Dramamine tablets to reduce my uncharacteristic nausea. Even now, I am not clear on why I also chose to drink champagne. I do know, however, that I had more champagne than Dramamine. In hindsight, mixing the two seemed kind of counterintuitive, but at the time it seemed reasonable. Needless to say, I will never try this mixture again, now that I can personally verify that the outcome is so much worse than either a hangover or motion sickness—even combined!

I was traveling around the Caribbean on a cargo boat when we docked at a port in St. Martin. I thought it would be a great way to see a good part of the Caribbean. Shortly after we'd docked, a sailboat pulled up alongside and tied off to us. We laid planks down in between the two vessels so that we could more readily transport goods from our boat to theirs. Even in port, the water remained rough and an eye (a metal ring through which the mooring rope is passed) had already been ripped off the bow of the smaller boat.

Most of the time, we transported our goods directly to an island. In some cases, especially with the small islands, we were not able to dock in port because the water was too shallow or the docks were too small to accommodate our cargo boat. On rare occasions, as with this particular case, we supplied sailboats that did not really have a home per se. While the people on the islands ordered all their basic necessities and anything else they could not get, make, or grow on the island, the people on the sailboats mostly received just food, toilet paper, and a disproportionate amount of alcohol.

The bad weather made the ocean so rough that the dive shop that was located right off the pier had cancelled the day's SCUBA diving trips. With SCUBA temporarily out of the question, I needed to find something else to do so I would not go crazy sitting on a docked boat. With limited options, I decided to walk around Phillipsville. I had heard that they had excellent shopping. I would certainly never consider myself to be even an occasional shopper. Besides, I really could not purchase anything since I did not have room for even a sugar cube in my sea bag. I did not know how long I'd be on this Caribbean adventure, but I did know it would be long enough to preclude collecting gizmos and trinkets.

I had met a young couple from Texas on the ship, and the wife told me that they were also going shopping. It was not much of a coincidence, considering the limited bad weather options. They asked if I wanted to accompany them, partially, I'm sure, because I was traveling alone. Poor me, huh? I agreed to join them because I loved to listen to their Texas drawl—mostly hers. I am from the Northeast, Connecticut specifically, where I have been told we talk fast. I guess it must be true because, normally, I get kind of impatient listening to anybody south of say … Pennsylvania. Now, as I stared at this lady's light, freckled face, I never wanted those vowels to taper off, so of course I agreed to accompany them.

The three of us cruised up and down the entire strip of Front Street and Back Street. The melodic quality of the woman's voice soothed my spirit for only so long before I became restless. I do not like shopping to begin with, but going with other people and looking at what they are interested in, well, let's just say I could have used an additional dose of Ritalin.

We were making our way back to the docks when it occurred to me that we had seen an unusual number of people with orange hair. When I saw a young man with orange clogs, I sensed that something was amiss. Within a few minutes, I noticed more and more orange everywhere. It wasn't until we reached the pier that I realized what was happening: World Cup soccer—and Holland was playing. The game was being televised in a little bar on the pier, and the Dutch Navy was in port. I should have realized what was going on sooner, since I had had a relationship with a girl from Holland, and I had experienced firsthand that nation's obsession with soccer—and the color orange.

When we arrived at the docks, the scene was chaotic. The bar was rocking, the area in front of it was a maze of orange, and the navy guys were periodically throwing each other off the pier and into the Caribbean. After a day of shopping, I needed to let loose. With my decision made, I told the nice couple it had been a pleasure shopping with them, and, as quickly as possible, I walked them safely to the boat.

I returned to the docks with excited anticipation and boldly dodged the orange throng on the pier—only to pass the threshold of the bar and enter a sea of orange that made the outside crowd seem like a small church gathering. The bar was a small, drab wooden tiki-style hut that had no business being at the edge of a main strip or at the entrance to a pier. If I did not know better, which I didn't (and still don't), I would claim it was erected just for this particular soccer match celebration.

As I entered the bar, some drunken, orange-haired fellow handed me four ten-ounce Heinekens. Before I said a thing, he took one of the beers back, poured it on my head, and smashed the bottle on the floor. Was this the Caribbean way of recycling? I did not have time to react before several other orange guys were patting me on the back like I was a long-lost friend. I realized that everyone was ordering four of these little beers at a time, and, judging by the actions of my fellow patrons, the sacrifice of one beer per round was not considered alcohol abuse.

The pub's employees seemed to frown on this little bit of amusement, but I guess the money being thrown around reduced their displeasure and made it all worthwhile. After all, if the Dutch were smashing a quarter of what they were purchasing, beer sales would be flying. Good thing I had my shopping sneakers on instead of my usual summer flip-flops.

I loved these Dutchmen because their excitement was both contagious and welcoming. Within a couple of minutes, I was almost as fired up as they were. It was hard not to be. I was throwing down Heinekens like they were free. Oh, yeah, they were! I could not keep up. Everyone was buying such a massive quantity of beer, and it seemed as if there were always at least eight beers in front of me at any given time. No one ever said, "Is this one mine?" We just drank. Wanting to fit in with the crowd, I downed each beer in just one chug. This was unusual for me because I am a self-described lightweight. The little bottles held two ounces less than an average beer—and we were drinking them as if they were shots. I have never drunk like that before; nor have I since. This was foreign peer pressure, and it was much worse than the domestic variety.

No sooner did the Heineken from my first beer bath stop dripping into my eyes than a second was poured over my head. This second bottle, however, was from no stranger. It was not even from a Dutch dude. This shower came from Julio, our ship's first mate. It opened a floodgate, and with it came three more beers for me to down—as if I needed them.

Julio joined my orange friends and me as we celebrated the victory of Holland. I cannot remember what team they played that day. I had beer in my eyes, and my orange wig, gladly donated by some other enthusiast, was pulled too far down over my face to watch the small television. Besides, my eyes kept scanning the floor because I had to keep checking it for broken glass. I do know that, since that day in June, when it comes to *futbol*, I always cheer for orange—as long as the United States isn't playing, of course.

My second visit to St. Martin was for my honeymoon. Well, it was not exactly my honeymoon. In fact, I have never even been married. It was a friend's honeymoon, and I had a great time! I had spent a month in the Caribbean on a cargo boat, followed by a week or so traveling on mail boats. I was not quite finished with my vacation, and I still had a couple of weeks before I had to go back to work. A female teacher friend of mine had been secretly married to a Cape Coral, Florida police officer. Apparently, her parents did not approve of him because he was a cop—or maybe it was because he was short, I cannot remember which it really was.

Regardless of the reason, my friends had been living secretly sinless for over a year as husband and wife. I guess this was long enough so that when they did get publicly married, they planned a honeymoon that was less romantic than the average horn-dog's. In fact, when she told her friends about the trip to St. Martin, she extended an invitation to anyone who wanted to tag along. I did not know if she was just being nice or if we were really supposed to take her seriously. Since I was in the neighborhood (the Caribbean), I thought, why not take them up on it? Needless to say, I was the only one who showed!

When I arrived, the happy couple had already been there for three days and had yet to leave their room—but not for the reason you'd think. Unfortunately, after their arrival they'd heard that St. Martin was a dangerous place; therefore, they did not want to venture far from the safety of their room. I have discovered that as soon as one bad thing happens somewhere, that is all anyone hears about for the next decade or two, no matter how many good things occur. I tried to get them to buy into this philosophy, but they would not budge past the threshold of their honeymoon suite.

I finally convinced them to at least go to a few of the time-share seminars that were prevalent in the area. We endured forty-five minutes of painful sales pitches, during which we pretended we were interested in buying a condominium. In return, we received valuable rewards for our time. When my teacher friend claimed that she did not have that much trouble faking it, I let her statement go without comment, simply because they were on their honeymoon.

For the next week, we alternated between sitting through the seminars and cashing in on our rewards. Our payoffs consisted of a snorkeling trip to the beautiful island of Anguilla on a luxurious sailboat, a dive trip to the little island of Saba, and plenty of coupons for food and poker chips at the casino down the street.

After this exciting week of adventures, my friends loosened up a bit and even planned to spend their final full day shopping along the "scary" streets of St. Martin. I agreed to go along, simply because they had agreed to do all the fun things I wanted to do. After browsing aimlessly through what seemed like every shop on the strip, the day was done, and I needed a drink.

When we got back to the hotel, we made our way down to the pool bar. The new missus headed back to the room before she even had her first drink. I am not sure why she left; fortunately for us, it was before the bartender announced the start of a Miss Tan Contest.

As luck would have it, the new hubby and I were asked to be judges for this auspicious event. At first we refused, as any respectable man would, but when the bartender offered to buy us each a drink for this unrewarding service, we quickly agreed. I was a little nervous at first, not having judged a contest of this nature previously—or since. *What questions would I ask? How would I determine what attributes were important?* We quickly learned that the winner was simply the woman who showed the most tan—or was it the one who wore the least clothing?

After the contest was over, the winner came over and gave me a big kiss on the cheek. My friend had to refuse his because he was petrified that he'd get caught. After all, he was on his honeymoon. As promised, we received our payment of free drinks from the slimy-looking bartender. While we reminisced and giggled like two schoolboys, we heard the bartender announce, "It is now time for the Mister Tan Contest!" Our giggles turned into nervous laughs and our chests deflated. I sank so low onto my underwater barstool that I was ready to take out the straw from my tropical drink and use it as a snorkel.

"I really do not want to do this," I said to the bartender as he attempted to bribe us with more free drinks if we entered this contest. My friend agreed that he was not going to become eye candy, even if it did mean free booze. A group of ladies, including the winner of the previous contest, came over to us, pulled our heads above the surface of the pool, and pleaded for us to enter.

They did not necessarily want us in the contest because we were good-looking "Mr. Tan" type material or anything. It was just that everyone wanted a contest, and there were not too many guys around to enter. On the other hand, the wayward hubby had been on the water for two full days developing his tan, and mine had been in the making for almost two months—we definitely qualified!

We ultimately caved in, and, after slamming our free drinks in advance, we proceeded to subject ourselves to the gawking of rambunctious, rowdy women. Apparently, the same contest rules used for women applied to the men. I was falling "behind" in points to some beach "bum" next to me, "butt" I "clenched" the title when I smiled and mooned the judges, exposing the tattoo of Bugs Bunny SCUBA diving on my big white cheeks!

I probably would not have been able to do any of this if it were my actual honeymoon. My cop friend got in trouble from his wife just for being there. I think she cut him off for the rest of the year when she discovered that he had participated in the contest. Not surprisingly, these friends stopped calling me right after this little escapade. I guess they thought I might have been bad for the relationship. I never returned to St. Martin, and I have not been invited to another honeymoon since.

# THAILAND: MONKEYS & MALE HOOKERS

I opened my eyes, and I saw millions of monkeys. I knew I was dreaming, and I could not wake up—not that I wanted to because it was such a cool dream. I love monkeys, probably more than the average person does. However, I do not want them to take over as they did in the movie *Planet of the Apes*—but that is exactly what they have done in the small town of Lop Buri in Thailand.

I was taking a train from Bangkok to northern Thailand for a three-day hiking trip. I had just awakened and was casually looking around the train car. Nobody appeared to be paying any attention to the chaos outside the window, which made it all the more likely that I was dreaming. Except that I was not dreaming. There were, in fact, monkeys running on the grass, sitting on all the structures, and hanging from all of the trees. I do not recall if I saw even a single person outside of the train, but if I did, the people would have been outnumbered a thousand to one by the monkeys.

I had arrived in Bangkok about five days earlier. I took *tuk tuk* rides to temples and other attractions around the city and then went diving with Larry's Dive Shop. I ended up diving in Pattaya because there was a big storm in Phuket, where I had intended to go. Phuket was a better diving location, but it was also prone to more violent weather. In fact, this area was hit by the huge tsunami in December 2004.

At night, I watched Thai boxing matches at one of the many outdoor bars in downtown Bangkok. The diminutive Thai men were amazing. They would get the spectators fired up with their skill, while the even smaller Thai ladies got the spectators liquored up. The fighters were quick and nimble, but they never delivered any damaging blows, making the fights look more like exhibition matches.

At some point during the evening, coincidentally when the crowd was at its wildest and the booze was flowing fastest, a little Thai guy would challenge someone from the bar to take him on in a boxing match. As one can imagine, the room was flowing with testosterone. The combination of sweat, beer, blood, and sexy women was enough to get any man off his barstool to rise to the challenge of a duel.

I am totally into doing new things and have given myself permission to *go for it* on many occasions, especially when traveling, because I believe I have a different kind of mindset. I am convinced that mistakes are meant to be made on vacations. I can do dumb things, and nobody I see on a regular basis ever knows about it. I can try new things without being permanently judged, and nobody around has any expectations of me.

"If only I were eighteen again." This is the statement I used the first time I visited that Bangkok bar to try to convince myself not to get up and go a few rounds with someone half my weight. "Too old," is what I said to the waitress (not that she understood what I was saying anyway) when she tried to convince me, and half the other men in the joint, to jump into the ring to fight.

For some reason, I just was not feeling the whole "get in the ring" thing. Maybe it was because I was not seeing anyone else do it. I was alone and had no peer pressure—except for the waitress, who was not someone I was out to impress. Besides, there were several groups of guys around me who were definitely drinking more than I was. With all that alcohol, they should have been egging one another on, but they were not.

The search for an opponent continued for about ten minutes, but all attempts to get someone brave enough (or foolish enough) to enter the ring failed. There was booing from the local patrons, clucking like a chicken from the waitress, and whining from both the challenger and the ring announcer. There were even a couple of bribes of a free T-shirt and money offered. The more bribes they offered, the less it seemed like a good idea. *Why are they so desperate to get someone in there*, I wondered.

Unsuccessful in securing any challengers from the floor, the Thai boxers continued to move about impressively and strike with unimpressive punches and kicks. I could not help thinking that, if an innocent foreigner were in the ring, the boxer would change both his tempo and strategy. Before I returned for a second night of this entertainment, I realized that I was correct.

It was, of course, all a scam, as I learned later from the people at the dive shop. After getting some unsuspecting tourist into the ring, the local Thai patrons placed their bets, and the battle would begin. The bets were not on who won or lost—everyone knew that the visiting team did not stand a chance. Bets were placed instead on how many seconds it would take for the Thai boxer to knock out his opponent. The dive shop crew emphasized their warning about the scam by telling me about a jarhead—sorry, a Marine—who had gotten into the ring and who was killed by a blow to the throat. I am not sure if it is true, but, like most stories, there probably is some grain of truth in it. I guess that the rest of the guys in the bar that night must have heard the same story, because no one was ready to jump up and volunteer.

When the little Thai men had finished with their boxing exhibition, I returned to my hotel, sat at the pool, and observed the travelers returning after a long night out. Some simply stumbled to their rooms, others were accompanied by a beautiful young woman—or two. There was a guard shack at the entrance to the hotel that monitored who entered the grounds. When the "women of the night" walked in, the guard would take their identification, and he'd give it back when they left later in the evening. I assumed that this was to protect the hotel guests.

The next morning, I was sitting on the outside patio, eating breakfast, when a young guy who appeared to be about twenty-five years old sat down at the table next to me. When our eyes met, we gave each other the macho head nod that guys tend to do. This brief, nonverbal acknowledgement meant, *Hi. Good morning. How are you? How was your night?* and several other greetings, all rolled up in one efficient motion.

With all that information conveyed, there is usually no need to disrupt the peaceful silence. In this instance, however, we did start talking because I had recognized him from the previous night. He was one of the lucky men who had returned to the hotel with a lady friend.

Even though I had already asked him how his night was with the head nod, I decided to ask again to get some specifics.

It turned out that his name was Johnny, and he claimed to be a salesman from Seattle. I got the impression, however, that he was an up-and-coming politician from somewhere in the New England area. I assumed this because he did not have an accent—which is to say his accent was the same as mine. Only a politician (or a politician's son) trying to be extra-careful to protect his reputation would need to fly all the way to Thailand to get some extra nooky.

Johnny started telling me about his experiences from the previous evening. I will leave out the salacious details of what he told me because this book is not X-rated, but it turns out that, while he was exploring the woman he was with, he found that she had a few extra parts he had not expected to find. It was at this point that I realized that my assumption about the identification procedure at the guard gate had been wrong. This security measure was to protect the prostitute in case the franks and beans made their way out of the skirt and the "john" went postal!

Johnny was in one of those uncomfortable situations where anything he did after that would be deemed wrong. Did he kick his butt, kick her out, castrate him, pay her, or not pay him? I asked him what action he took, but I was not really listening to the response because I knew it would be a lie. He probably did what any drunk twenty-five year-old man loose in Thailand would do: he finished!

After finishing his story, there was really nothing much left for either of us to say. The once-enthusiastic conversation had nowhere to go from there, so Johnny went about his business. I forced down the rest of my morning meal—except for the sausage. Like the Thai boxing challenge, I was glad I had decided not to take part in this type of thrill.

Later that morning, I took a train up to Chang Mai, where I would spend the next three days hiking in the jungles close to the Burmese border. Once I arrived in Chang Mai, I walked through the streets and down a small alley to arrive at the agency that had arranged my trek. I met my guide, who introduced himself as Jackie Chan. We loaded our gear, climbed into a beat-up truck, and drove to the end of civilization. Just shy of an hour later, we crawled out of the truck and began our walk into the lush forest.

When we arrived at the start of the trail, there stood another local man to help guide us on our trek. It was a great hike that brought us along paths that were sometimes so overgrown that they had to be cleared by the trail guides' machetes. We stumbled upon waterfalls, and cooled our over-heated bodies in the cascading water. Each evening, we ended our hike at a local village and stayed the night in a thatched hut.

On the first night, the women and children of the village greeted us with crafts that they had made. We were escorted to the hut that our group would share. Once all of our gear was stowed securely away, we all took a quick tour around the grounds. Our guide, Jackie Chan, pointed out the hut that was used specifically for having sex—strictly for the purpose of making babies, of course.

Later, we went inside the big main hut and ate dinner with the men of the village. I never thought I would eat squirrel, especially after watching a member of the village carry it in from the woods on a stick. It was pasty and a bit gamier than I preferred, but it was the only protein offered, so I ate my share. During the meal, the chief told us stories of his people, and Jackie Chan translated. They were stories of the tough times his people had experienced, but it was not until the following day that I would truly feel for these people, at least the women.

Moments after leaving the village the next morning, we passed the fields belonging to our host tribe. I noticed a small hut along the edge of one of the fields and casually asked if the workers used it so they could periodically have respite from the sun. Jackie Chan smiled and explained to us that when a village woman was pregnant she still had to work the fields. If the lady went into labor, she would go into this hut to have her baby. He added that the woman was then expected to go back to work in the fields. He concluded his information session by letting us know that, in this area of Thailand, when a mother had twins, the acting midwife would kill one of the babies because they still believed that one twin was possessed. I did not have the stomach to ask how they determined which one to kill.

After a second day of trekking, we reached another village. Of all the indigenous villages I have visited throughout the world, this one stands out from the rest. It was located deep in the heart of the jungle, and its occupants seemed ambivalent about our arrival. The women and children carried on with their chores of cleaning and tending to the animals. A few of the elder ladies appeared to be working on a blanket. I thought it was strange that I did not observe any men in the area.

Upon arrival, Jackie Chan spoke to a village woman, and she pointed to the main hut. Jackie Chan immediately went inside, and when came back out, he told us that he had spoken to the chief and that we would be welcomed for the night. I could not imagine there being another village for many miles, and I remember wondering what would happen if a village chief were not so gracious.

As we hung around the village, our guide showed us what responsibilities each woman or child had. He talked about the vegetables these people grew and the way they retrieved water. I watched a young boy, about five years old, sift through berries and chase away a pet pig. Everyone, it seemed, was expected to work.

As the sun started setting, the men began to appear around the camp. I presumed that they'd been out hunting and gathering food. Jackie Chan asked us to sit around a huge fire pit. The men of the village spaced themselves in between us. After two men started a fire in the pit, the women began to cook and organize the night's meal. It was interesting how the children gradually disappeared as the adult men appeared.

The fire was roaring. We tried to make conversation with the natives sitting closest to us, but it was mostly gestures relating to clothing or jewelry worn by either party. As dinner was just about to be served, the chief made his appearance and sat between the two giant logs we all shared. Jackie Chan again translated as the chief said a few welcoming words to us. When the chief's last words had been spoken, the children of the village finally reappeared, and what a grand entrance it was. Each child, in order of height, slithered past the guests, giving special recognition to their leader. Every child in that village was dressed in vibrant colors and decorated thoroughly with trinkets made by village members. It was stunning. My eyes began to mist when they all started singing and performing their traditional dance.

The firelight enhanced the ambiance of this event. It was truly a *National Geographic* moment. I was experiencing firsthand things I had only seen on adventure television. I was living it! I wanted to take pictures. I really wished I had a video camera. Mostly, I just sat, enthralled and engulfed by those magical moments. I did not want to miss a second of it. I regret that I have not one photo of this experience, except the ones burned into my memory.

The next morning, I was surprised, to say the least, when I stepped outside my hut and saw elephants standing there. I love elephants and had recently even ridden an African elephant at a zoo. The ride lasted only five minutes. Although it was great to be in such close contact with the elephant, the time was too short and the price was too high for both the noble beast and me. The noise, lines, and the elephant's general environment detracted from the quality of the experience for both of us. Now, I was about to ride on an Asian elephant all the way to the next village where we would be staying.

I am not sure how the elephants were brought to the village, but frankly, I didn't care. I would be riding those magnificent wild beings through their natural habitat, the jungle, all day long. My ride would be considerably longer than a five-minute zoo ride, and maybe, just maybe, I would finally get my fill.

I was the first of our group to climb onto a rickety wooden scaffold and mount my beast. It seemed so high up and although I should have been a bit nervous for the first few minutes, I was way too excited to feel anything but joy. I could not wipe the "perma-smile" from my face. The young Thai boy sitting on the head of the elephant did not share my enthusiasm. I did not want to spend the next several hours atop my elephant staring at the back of this sullen young man. A few short minutes after takeoff, I asked him if he would please switch places with me. I am sure my words did nothing to enhance the communication. It was the clever international hand gestures that came to the rescue and got my point across. Now I had several reasons why I, rather than the sixty-eight pound kid, should sit up front on the elephant. Up front, I could be the one orchestrating our progress through the jungle. Without the kid in the way, my view of the jungle would be unobstructed except by the occasional flick of the elephant's ears.

The young boy reluctantly traded places with me. I do not think that he necessarily wanted to sit on the elephant's head; I think he was just too lazy to move to the back. Maybe he was overworked, who knows? I guess he would have had to get up pretty early in the morning to have these elephants at this village by first light, but because I never found out where they came from, I didn't know either way. Anyway, the boy stood on the elephant's neck, stepped over me, and tried to give me the stick he used to handle the pachyderm. I refused the weapon. I would never whip my favorite animal for two reasons: I would not want to inflict any pain on him, and I would not want him to get testy and inflict pain on me!

My new seat was awesome. I spent the rest of the journey stroking my elephant's coarse, wiry hair. I stroked him from his head to the soft skin at the top of his ears. I was supposed to steer him by digging my foot into the lower part of whichever ear was facing the direction I wanted to turn, but my elephant needed no such direction—he knew the way.

We rode all day and arrived at the next village just a little earlier than I had expected. I hesitantly dismounted my animal and petted him until the very last minute, when the elephants were led away. I stood and watched until the very last elephant's tail disappeared into the jungle's thick vegetation. As I turned back toward the village, I realized that I still did not know their origin.

As I rejoined my group, we were greeted by some of the younger tribesmen. They said a few brief words to Jackie Chan, and he respectfully waited as some adults made their way over to us from their huts. This village seemed similar to the first one we had visited—until after dinner that is.

Dinner went off in the same manner I had experienced from the first village; we sat around the main hut, and the men ate while the women served. However, after dinner, while the chief was telling stories, his wife walked behind me and began to massage my shoulders. Now, the chief's wife was a big woman with puffy, unkempt hair and a dress that pretty much looked like a circus tent. I guess her looks should have been irrelevant because, well, she was the chief's wife!

My heart started hammering in my chest. Each touch made my shoulder and neck muscles contract tighter and tighter. Scared to death, I looked over at the chief. Even though I received the universally understood male head nod from both the chief and Jackie Chan conveying that this situation was all right, it was not all right with me.

I was extremely uncomfortable. There were five other travelers and four or five other natives all looking at me to see what I would do next. I was embarrassed and sweating more than usual, and that was a whole lot, considering that we were sitting around a hot fire in the sweltering jungle in the blistering summer in tropical Asia. Maybe it had to do with the fact that all the men in the village carried spears. Maybe it was because it was the chief's wife. Mostly, I think it was because I was still thinking of Bangkok, and I was not about to give the chief's wife a package check.

The situation got a little easier when a couple of other women had finished rinsing the plates in a bucket of water. They came over to the circle and joined the chief's wife in her massage antics. Three of us were now being massaged, and the pressure was off me. I never did figure out the purpose of this after-dinner treat. Maybe they just ran out of dessert. I am just relieved there was not a "happy ending" requirement.

The next morning, we hiked to a river and caught some bamboo rafts downstream. After another short hike, we were back into civilization. Following a four-hour train ride past the town full of monkeys, I was back in the land of Thai boxers and male hookers. From one jungle to another!

# UNITED KINGDOM:
## BALD FOR BRITAIN

I planned to backpack around the United Kingdom for a couple of weeks simply because it was something that other travelers told me that I just *had* to do. It seemed like a good enough reason at the time. After all, I had very little knowledge of the world around me, and this hike would be one more step in my education. I wanted to learn firsthand about the ways of others. Although I had quite a few vacations under my belt by this time, this backpacking trip would be my first one not dedicated to SCUBA diving.

On this adventure, I was determined to stay above water and finally be exposed to the kind of foreign creatures that talked. I was intent on seeing real history in the guise of old churches, castles, and monuments. In keeping with the antiquity theme, and because I wanted a light load, I was prepared to do the entire trip wearing the same old pair of jeans and a single T-shirt (I would, of course, bring fourteen pairs of underwear and socks).

My plan was to spend two weeks hiking throughout Great Britain, followed by a fourteen-day cruise from England to Russia via Norway, Sweden, Finland, Denmark, and Estonia. My adventure would consist of two very different parts, so I really needed to pack for two trips. I had my beat-up knapsack and matching attire for backpacking and a proper suitcase filled with casual dress clothes for the cruise.

I left from New York's JFK Airport on a late-night flight to arrive in England first thing the next morning. Before getting on the plane, I put all of my clothes into the suitcase and used the knapsack as my carry-on, filling it only with a couple of books, a journal, identification documents, and two weeks of snacks for the backpacking portion of the trip.

Upon my early morning arrival in London, I took a bus to the hotel where I had booked a room for the night between the end of my backpacking tour and the start of my ocean adventure. I expected the hotel personnel to gladly accept my suitcase, wish me a good hike around their country, and look forward to my return in a fortnight. This was not even close to what happened. Despite my best efforts, the protracted discussion with the desk clerk about storing my luggage deteriorated more and more as time went by. Once the clerk's tone became decidedly snippety, I requested a manager. At least I think I did. He may have just come out from the back room when he heard the frustration seeping out of me, mostly via my mouth. The manager spoke the same words as the clerk, but they were devoid of the snotty attitude vibrantly emanating from the clerk.

I once again explained that I really had no other choice but to leave my bag at the hotel for safekeeping. I could not possibly lug my suitcase around for the next couple of weeks. While it was true that I was not sure exactly how much actual walking I would be doing between buses, trains, and ferries, I was certain that even a little walking would be way too much carrying that cumbersome suitcase.

"Sir," the manager said, "regulations prohibit us from storing luggage for people who are not currently guests of the hotel."

"But I am going to be a guest at this hotel in two weeks. I have a confirmation number," I replied as I started rifling through my paperwork again.

The manager held up his hand to halt the rustling of paper. "But you are not staying here now," the manager countered, "So the best I can suggest is that you store your luggage at the airport terminal."

"For the price of storage at the airport, I could hire a sherpa to carry my suitcase and my backpack," I declared.

"Bombs!" the manager exploded. "That is the reason we cannot keep your luggage!"

"Oh, is that all?" I said enthusiastically. Quickly seizing the moment and before either the manager or clerk could object, I unzipped my suitcase and starting laying out all my garments on the hotel lobby floor. I had no shame, but I think the manager and clerk blushed a bit, especially when I got out my Bugs Bunny boxer shorts.

Although he was clearly embarrassed, the manager did take a good look at my belongings. Then he asked me to pack up and to please follow him into the back room. I was hoping he was going to store my gear and not ask me for to a date because of my sexy underwear. Luckily for me, it was the former. I thanked him profusely, threw my luggage in the back room, and headed out the front door to start my journey.

Because of the long bout with the hotel staff, I only had to wait a few minutes before the bus to Salisbury, England arrived. I took this bus to the first stop on my educational vacation—Stonehenge. I was high as a kite, knowing that in less than an hour I would arrive at this famous architectural wonder. I was also elated that I had overcome the luggage problem and had nothing but my small pack to carry around for two whole weeks. I was unencumbered, I was light, and I was free.

I arrived at Stonehenge before noon and spent the greater part of the day enjoying the ambiance created by the large stones and open field. I had read about the origin of this great structure, its possible creators, and its possible purpose. Some believed it was a sort of calendar or astronomical observatory, while others thought it was a site for ceremonies or even a sacred burial ground for high-ranking citizens. I wondered what purposes my imagination would propose after I had trod upon the ancient grounds.

I had seen documentaries depicting Stonehenge's beauty and mystery, but upon first glance, I must say I was unimpressed. The site was much smaller than I had anticipated. I think what disappointed me even more than the size of this wonder was the people who surrounded it. All I had seen from television was an unobstructed view, and that was what I wanted to see in person. That did not seem all that likely to happen, however. I went there on a bus, and so had many others. It seemed that another bus full of visitors showed up every half hour or so. With camera raised, I impatiently waited for the bodies to get out of my frame, but they never did. My arms were tired and my eyes were strained, so I holstered my camera and retreated.

I did not leave Stonehenge; I simply walked through the field to get some distance. I walked until I could not hear the constant hum of annoying chatter from the less-respectful tourists. Not that Stonehenge is such a holy or sacred place that one should not speak while visiting, but unfortunately the drone of voices did take away from my personal experience.

I finally chose a spot where I could hear no human but could still see the great stones that made up this maze. The stones themselves were very impressive, even from a distance. They were grayish white from thousands of years of unprotected exposure to the elements. The green moss that grew on most of the stones was the same shade as the grass that I lay upon. Although many rocks had fallen from their original places, it appeared that nothing had shifted in hundreds of years. Regardless of the dilapidated condition, its fundamental arrangement was still visible.

I finally was able to clearly focus my imagination. After what seemed like an hour of observing Stonehenge from this patch, I moved to another, with a varied view of the bridged boulders. With the sounds of modern humans diminished by distance, I began to see past the other tourists, who previously had littered my view with loud, bothersome, unnatural colors.

After another long period, I moved again, to yet another angle from which I could admire and daydream. After an initial disappointment with my surroundings, I was now absorbing the site for my long-term memory. I was glad I had given myself time to feel it. I had not taken any real pictures—only the ones in my head. Each blink of my eyes was another click of my imaginary camera.

After a while, I reclined in the grass, ate a snack bar (or three), and read from my book. Having so many hours there was a terrific luxury, and I have since incorporated this lesson into my travel philosophy. I am fortunate enough to have long periods of time to travel, and if I go to a place that really moves me, I stay until I get my fill. Conversely, if I find myself in a location that does nothing for me, after ensuring that I have given it a sufficient chance, I simply move on.

As the day began to come to an end and the tourists started to drift away, I moved closer and captured Stonehenge on film. I caught it from all the angles I had studied throughout the course of the day. I did my best to capture it without the hint of human presence. When I look at my pictures in the years to come, I will admire them even more since they represent my time at Stonehenge without the intrusion of modern voices or visions.

I caught the last bus out of Salisbury, this one en route to the Roman Baths located in the town appropriately named Bath. This trip lasted only about thirty minutes. It was an enjoyable ride, but I imagine that, after a dreamy day like the one I had at Stonehenge, any bus trip would have been. I chose not to talk to the few other passengers who appeared to be doing the same thing I was. Talking would only have taken away from the reminiscing my brain was doing. It also would have prevented me from thoroughly enjoying the English countryside I saw outside my window.

The rolling green hills gave way to the town of Bath just around twilight. I exited the bus and quickly found my way to the indoor entrance to the Roman Baths. I wandered around the baths for a couple of hours, and when I went back outdoors, it was well past dark. I had had a long, full day between traveling overnight, the hotel incident, bus rides, long hours at Stonehenge, and examining the Roman Baths. I was rapidly approaching exhaustion, so I began searching for a place to crash for the night. After realizing that the tiny town could only accommodate a small number of visitors and that there had been "no room at the inn," I began to walk toward the outskirts.

The farther I walked away from town, naturally, the less populous things became. My chances of finding a place to rest my weary head and body were becoming slimmer and slimmer with each step. The establishments that housed tourists were becoming fewer and fewer, and the ones I had passed thus far had had no vacancies. I walked about two miles, arriving in what seemed to be a common neighborhood. The houses were few and far between and there were few streetlights. Many houses had their lights off for the night, and I sincerely wished I had begun my search earlier. It was a long, boring walk, and my mind started to wander. I recalled the short nap I had stolen on the grassy fields of Stonehenge earlier in the day. I wondered if this night would find me exposed to the elements in a much less comforting way. At this point, I was so weary that a night under the stars would not have bothered me much.

I continued to walk in kind of a hypnotic trance, grateful for my light pack. I finally found a building displaying a vacancy sign. It was a bed and breakfast that resembled a common residence more than a business catering to the public. At this point though, I cared little about their qualifications or amenities. I was only interested in a bed, and a bed was all they were offering. The little old man who answered the door appeared to be not only annoyed by my presence, but a bit surprised as well. I assumed that because his place was so far out of town, he did not get many visitors, especially this late at night. His comment about only providing a bed, and not breakfast, sent me on a mental argument about changing his sign from reading "B & B" to just *B*. I chose to keep these thoughts in my head though, only because I could not afford to have him give me the boot.

Apparently, he and his wife had stopped serving breakfast because mad cow disease was making its way through the region, and people had become very cautious about consuming anything related to cattle—meat or dairy. We discussed price, and he showed me to my room. I think that their son had just gone off to college or something, and they were renting out his room. I could not have cared less; I did not care about breakfast either, at least not at that moment. I simply brushed my teeth in the common bathroom, stripped down to my underwear, sank into my well-appreciated bed, and fell into a deep sleep.

I was awakened by a knock on my door at what I thought had to be an unreasonably early hour. It felt early because of how worn out I was. It looked early because of the gray clouds and the dreary day that I viewed from the small window. It was, however, not even close to early. It was closing in on 11:00 a.m. I was quite sure that these hosts did not have any other guests waiting for my room, but they chose to wake me nonetheless. The little man tempted me with some bread that his wife had baked, and I am not sure if he felt he had to in order to get me out of his house.

I wearily threw on the clothes I had peeled off a dozen hours prior and headed downstairs, hoping that I could fill my belly before I hit the road. The last thing I had eaten was a few snack bars at Stonehenge. My last "meal" had been on the plane over from New York about thirty hours earlier, if one could even call that a meal. I was, at the least, looking forward to a nice, hot cup of coffee.

I stumbled down the stairs and was escorted to the living area by a little old lady who, I assumed, was the co-owner of the bed and breakfast. She sat me down on the couch, told me to help myself, and scurried off into the kitchen. I dug into the bread and loaded it with as much butter and jam as I could, trying to replenish my American body with as many calories as it was used to. I reached over to a contraption that I assumed held my morning java. I later learned that it was called a French press. I still think it was a bit past ironic that I was using a French press while in England. In retrospect, I cannot say I was using it. I was fondling it, twisting it, eventually banging it, but I was not using it for anything else other than to make noise, and within a few frustrating moments, to make a mess.

My little hostess appeared from the kitchen, probably drawn from the racket I was making. She noticed me fumbling, and on closer inspection saw my mess. In her proper English words and dignified English accent, she politely inquired, "Is there something I can assist you with?" The American English translation of her query was, "What on earth are you doing, you idiot?"

I allowed her to press my drink for me. If I had only known the name of the contraption, I think I probably could have figured out how to use it. I wondered if it was really worth all the effort. I just wanted to pour the coffee into a cup and drink it. *Maybe it is really good, strong coffee,* I thought. I hoped it would be worth the struggle and embarrassment. When my cup was full, I scooped a spoonful (or four) of sugar into it. I remembered that I would not be offered any cream or milk because of the angry cow thing, so I gave it a stir and took a nice big sip.

It was tea! I hate tea. I despise tea. I have tried to like tea, or at a minimum tolerate it, but I cannot. Tea tastes disgusting to me. I do not even like the smell of it. *How did I not smell this tea as it was being made?* I asked myself. Maybe I was not awake yet. I wanted to throw up after I drank that big gulp of tea, but this nice woman who had just pressed my tea with her poor little weak, brittle-boned arms, was watching for my reaction. Looking into her sweet old eyes, wishing I had sweetened my drink by four more scoops of sugar, I swallowed with a hidden cringe. I looked back at her, smiled, and said it was delicious. I added that it was the best tea I had ever had—and I did not feel as though it was a lie. It very well could have been the best tea ever pressed, but I hated it!

After my bread breakfast, I went upstairs to shower and eat some snack bars. Fresh out of the shower, I reached into my backpack to get clean socks and underwear. As I rooted around in the main section of my pack, I realized that it was totally empty. I kept searching as if there could be an area I overlooked, but there was not. My mind started getting fuzzy; it was trying to comprehend what this meant. Then, it hit me like a ton of bricks: I had put my clothes for both portions of the trip into that one big suitcase and in all the excitement back at the hotel forgot to properly redistribute them. My entire wardrobe now sat snugly in the hotel storeroom. My money, books, passport, and journal were tucked safely in the smaller front pocket of my backpack, so I was not in serious trouble. This did mean, however, that I would not only be sporting the same jeans and T-shirt the entire trip, but also the same pair of underwear and socks.

Under these circumstances, I was thankful that I had decided to shave my head before I left the States for my walkabout. I was pleased with this decision, as I would have also left behind my shampoo. Greasy hair is a sure sign of a dirty traveler—not that the smell I was sure to acquire over the next fourteen days would leave anyone doubtful that I was traveling a bit too light.

Already dressed, I grabbed my hollow knapsack, slid downstairs, and thanked the little English couple for their hospitality. I stepped into the damp early afternoon and was immediately stimulated by the rain dripping on my hairless noggin. Despite the fact that I had a long, wet walk in front of me, I was smiling like I had just consummated a relationship.

I walked the couple miles into town and caught a bus northeast to Leeds. Then, I caught a train to Scotland, followed by another bus that took me to a ferry on its way to Northern Ireland. I spent a week in Ireland tracking down my roots and admiring the green, expansive countryside. I traveled to Wales to see some more castles just in case I had not seen enough in Ireland and Scotland. More trains, buses, and another ferry landed me back in England.

When I got off my last bus and arrived back at the hotel that held my clean clothes hostage, I threw away the disgusting, dirty ones that had served as my uniform for the past two weeks. Backpacking had been a bit stressful because I had to be mindful of bus and train schedules, and I never knew where I would sleep from one night to the next. Once the cruise began, I would have plenty of time to relax, reflect, and process what I had learned.

After a three-hour shower and a restful night's sleep, I showered some more in an attempt to catch up on those I had missed. Initially, I had shaved my off my hair to make things more manageable for the backpacking. On the cruise, there would be more than enough time and opportunity to shower and shampoo, but I found myself shaving the stubbly sprouts of hair on my head again, simply because I liked the feel of it. With this style choice, no one would know for sure if I needed a comb-over or was hip like Vin Diesel.

I had often wondered what it would feel like to have my head shaved completely bald. Surely it was different from the crew cut I had gotten as I prepared to enter the navy. I remembered rubbing my head after that first cut and feeling a neat prickly sensation, as if a shoeshine brush had replaced my scalp. I was still curious about what it would feel like if my head was covered with only skin. Since none of my friends would let me rub their shaved heads, I had no choice but to shave my own if I wanted to find out.

Of course, I had no idea what my head looked like without the usual adornment of a full head of curly brown hair. It was possible that my head would resemble those of several people I had seen who, based on the shape of their bald heads, really should have done anything (including wearing a toupee) before choosing to sport their naked dome. Well, after shaving off all my hair, I was pleased to see that my head was proportional and devoid of any major dents, points, or scars. As far as the cool, unusual feel of it, I spent the first three days of the trip just stroking it! In hindsight, this may explain why no one wanted to sit next to me on the bus.

I was so proud of my bright, shiny head, that while I was in Ireland, on the grounds of the Blarney Castle, I stuck my round, naked head into a plant whose leaves were the size of my body. I was so pleased with the effect that I had another tourist take a picture of me. At first, I thought I looked like a child in a school play getting stuck with the role of a strawberry, but when I had the photograph developed I must say I was a spitting image of a photograph by Anne Geddes—chubby cheeks and all!

# VOLCANOES:
## THE LIMB-SAVING PEE

I have come to realize that having a purpose when I travel really does give me motivation and direction. Initially, my traveling was inspired by plain old boredom. I simply wanted to be somewhere else and hoped that an alternate location would provide something interesting to see or do. For a while, SCUBA diving and exploring the wonders of the aquatic world were the sole reasons for my travels.

Before long, I started looking for additional things to do on land during a trip. I guess my travel theme evolved into searching for natural wonders or unique animals above and below the surface of the water. My basic method of travel design was to choose a country from a map and do a little research to discover its main claim to fame.

In some of these places, the main attraction was a volcano. I was drawn to these areas because they were always good places to hike, they usually provided excellent views, and, sometimes, when they were active volcanoes, they provided energy and animation that equaled the parts of my nature that often ran amok when I was younger.

Each volcano provided a unique experience not only because of its geography but also because of the special hazards exclusive to each site. For example, while hiking Longanot Mountain, a dormant volcano in Africa, we needed protection from wild animals and poachers, and our guide, Peter Gun, offered us this protection.

Peter was the English name he assumed so that travelers like us could focus on other things besides trying to pronounce his Swahili name. Unfortunately, our driver, pretty much the only other human with whom we had contact, had also taken the name Peter. To distinguish between the two, we nicknamed our protector "Peter the AR-15 assault rifle carrying guy." For obvious reasons, we eventually shortened his nickname to Peter Gun.

Several countries have volcanoes as their main attraction. Some countries, such as Costa Rica, have more than one volcano. When I visited this beautiful Central American country, I was actually able to go volcano hopping. Volcano hopping is similar to a phenomenon called bar hopping, where people move from establishment to establishment, on foot, enjoying the different atmospheres and libations—until the bar hopping becomes more of a pub crawl. The main difference I have discovered between bar hopping and volcano hopping is that the fall is a lot farther when you lose your balance doing the latter!

When I was visiting a dormant volcano, I would drive up as far as the road would take me and then hike around the rim. While volcano hopping in Costa Rica, I realized that, on a clear day, if the volcano was active, I could see smoke pouring out from the top of the cone. At night, from the right spot, I could actually see the fiery lava spurting out.

The United States has its own share of volcanoes. Probably none are more famous than those associated with the ring of fire that formed the Hawaiian Islands. Early one morning while I was living in Maui, four fellow teachers and I headed to the top of Haleakala, Hawaii's "House of the Sun." It took us nearly two hours to drive to the crest of the volcano. We arrived just before dawn and were greeted by temperatures cold enough to seep through our blankets. Since two of our group members, Ryan and Gina, were dating at the time, it was very romantic for them. Safe to say, however, the romance was lost on Randy from Rochester, Josh my roommate, and me.

As the sun slowly rose, we were able to make out the unique, craggy outline of the volcanic rocks. Soon after, we were able to see the clouds that filled the crater. It was breathtaking to be above the clouds. When the sun finally rose above the horizon, it cast its beams of light upon the rim, illuminating the rich and vibrant reddish colors of the sandy pathway that had been hidden in the predawn hours.

We did not, however, plan to hike around the rim. We had loaded our bicycles in the back of Josh's truck with the intent of pedaling all the way down to sea level. Of course there really was no reason to pedal; all we needed was brakes—and helmets!

Gina had volunteered to drive Josh's truck down and wait for us at the bottom. Before we left the crest, we all agreed that it was not a race. We would simply take our time riding down to sea level. I think someone even mentioned stopping to take pictures. Not too long after we left the top, though, our casual joyride was splashed with some testosterone and became a race.

It started gradually; one minute someone noticed a cow grazing in a field, and someone else mentioned the picturesque view of the pineapple patches below. Soon, each of us was using less and less brake. We felt the wind buffeting us as we gathered speed. Lance Armstrong would have been proud as we starting crouching on our little bike seats to reduce drag. I would have shaved my legs if I had had a razor with me. In the tradition of all races, none of us wanted to be last.

Before long, we were gaining on Josh's truck with Gina at the wheel. She waved to us in a confused and worried manner as we sped past. We passed several cars, but no cars ever passed us. We were going faster than they possibly could because the road was just one tight switchback after another. We stopped only once—when Randy wiped out.

It was more of a slide than a wipeout, but on tar and on the edge of a mountain, it could have resulted in worse injuries than a scraped knee and bruised pride. It was especially humiliating for Randy to have taken a spill because he was the member of the group who had chosen to give the rest of us advice before we started our descent. "Keep your pedals in the horizontal position while coasting around the turns. If they're in the vertical position, the inside pedal could catch on the road as you lean into the tight turns," he lectured. As we peeled Randy off the guardrail and retrieved his bicycle—which had decided that it wanted to keep going a bit longer after its driver had been ejected—he admitted that he had gotten caught up in the moment and had forgotten to follow his own advice.

Even with the crash, we arrived at sea level in a quarter of the time that it had taken us to get up to the top of that 10,023-foot volcano. After our exhilarating race, we sat on the beach in Paia and watched the surfers hang ten. It was another twenty minutes before we saw Gina—our ride home—finally make it to the bottom. As I sat on the beach and relived the ride down, I realized how lucky we were to be able to coast all that distance with gravity as our only source of power. Next time, I thought, I will take my time.

Of all my volcano explorations, my wildest experience was a few months later, when the same group of us visited the "big island" of Hawaii. It is called the big island because, yes you guessed it, it is the largest island in the chain. Hawaii is the home of Kilauea, a volcano that erupted in 1983 and has been going strong ever since. Even if it were to stop flowing today, it already holds the record as the longest continuously flowing volcano.

When a friend and I had visited this island ten months earlier, we had tried to see the famous flowing lava. Neither of us could afford to take a helicopter ride over the cone to watch the lava flow, so we decided to try our luck and conduct our own search on land. We went to a car rental agency and chose to rent a jeep because of the off-roading we assumed we needed to do.

We drove along dirt roads, trying to find a spot near some exposed lava. It turned out to be a stupid waste of time. Every time we stopped to ask someone for information or directions, he or she mentioned the helicopter option, was unaware of the location of exposed lava, or was generally uninterested in our search. At the time, the lava had been flowing for more than seventeen years, so I guess the novelty of it had worn off for locals. On that attempt, we never saw anything even close to molten, flowing rock.

I had learned from my mistakes, so, before the group of us went looking for lava, we did some research. We talked to people ahead of time who had been there and done that. This time, the five of us rented a nice, comfy full-size car and drove on the smooth pavement to where the road ends.

At the time of the last eruption, and throughout the years since then, lava had poured out of the cone, causing a flow that destroyed everything in its path, including houses, trees, and roads. It was impossible to clear the hard lava, so alternate roads were constructed, and the old roads, with their hardened lava barricades, simply lay dormant, leading to nowhere. We were on such a road and drove until it abruptly ended. I got out of the car, more than anxious to see what lay ahead. I impatiently searched for a way to get up close and personal with the flowing lava. Unfortunately, the lava was no longer flowing directly from the cone and had not been for years. It was difficult, or from my first experience, impossible, to find a burning red river of lava. We learned that our best chance was to watch for steam forming as the lava hit the ocean. This appealed to me because I love water and I wanted to see the violent change as hot lava was cooled in the relatively cold ocean.

We grabbed our gear and walked past the multitude of signs warning of danger and possible death. Living in the United States, I am oblivious to danger signs since they are plastered on even the most innocuous items. Not a day goes by when I am not bombarded by warning signs about the perils of a wet floor in every bathroom, sharp objects, and possibility of ice on bridges—even in the summer, when the temperature exceeds eighty degrees.

Our original plan was to arrive at the end of the road around dusk and hike down to the spot where the lava flowed into the ocean by nightfall. The glow of the molten lava, we reasoned, would surely be that much brighter and easier to spot at night. As it turned out, we could have started our journey a couple of hours earlier and still not reached our goal until after dark. It was a long, slow walk on that surface of hard, irregular lava with only headlamps and the slight light of the moon to guide us. We learned to take several seconds for each step in order to find solid footing. We were sure that someone would twist an ankle before the excursion through this lava field was over.

After almost two hours of walking, we finally began to see smoke rising in the distance. About thirty feet from the cliff edge, we noticed red lava flowing above us. It was amazing, and as gravity would have it, the lava was heading for lower ground. It was more oozing than flowing, so we figured we had plenty of time to see what we had come for before there was any need for alarm.

We smelled the sulfur as it shot out of steam vents all around us. The heat was bad enough, but it was the burning sulfur that completely overcame us. It was so harsh that we had our shirts off and tied around our mouths and noses—except for Gina, who used a bandana instead. The clothing made the air less acrid and objectionable to our lungs, but it did nothing for our burning, watering eyes.

As we neared the edge, we all became more cautious. The hardened lava became even more brittle, and we were not sure of its stability. At this point, the thought of the overhang crumbling away under our feet became our worst fear. If it gave way, we would plummet fifty feet down to the shark-filled waters—with no way out, unless we could make it all the way to the south side of the island. And that, of course, assumed that we did not land on rocks or get shredded by the part of the volcanic cliff that fell with us.

As we got within about five feet of the edge, we saw the steady stream of smoke billowing up from the adjacent cliff. It was not until the breeze blew and the smoke cleared that we were able to watch in utter amazement as the red, molten lava poured into the sea.

Our cameras clicked and a video camera captured our *oohs* and *aahs*. We all stood in awe, gazing at this amazing site—but not for long. One by one, we stepped away from the dangerous edge. I was the last to go because I was so entranced by the scene before me. I watched as, like cherry cough syrup, the lava waterfall flowed. I was mesmerized, just as I had been countless times over the past year by the beautiful blue Hawaiian waterfalls.

Before too long, there was talk of leaving. "We've seen it, taken photos and recorded it, lived to tell about it, now let's not push it," said one group member. I certainly was not ready to leave. I had not had my fill of this amazing phenomenon. It was Josh, however, who prevented us from having to leave prematurely. He spotted a five-foot mound of crumbled lava that had bunched up and collected on the edge, just before dropping into the ocean. We all carefully climbed onto this volcanic perch and celebrated our safe haven. It offered an even better view than the unstable edge.

We continued to watch as the glowing lava poured into the ocean. It seemed to have a life of its own, and when the heat of the liquid lava met the cool fluidity of the ocean water, smoke would instantly form and swirl around the union point. As the smoke rose above the surface, the wind blew it away, once again presenting us with an exceptional view.

Suddenly, the sounds coming from Randy, who was a few feet ahead of us, changed tone from awe to a warning. "Hey guys, look at this, my urine is steaming!" We had been watching the slow-moving lava gradually wind its way in our direction. We had noticed that the massive flow had splintered into two smaller molten rivers that ran on either side of us. Little by little, the lava was slowly closing off our exit, but we thought we had plenty of time before the route would become impassible.

When it finally registered with us what Randy's words signified, we looked at the ground. We saw the lava running not only on either side of us, but also directly underneath us in the spaces between the already cooled, solid lava. We immediately got up and started to make our way in the direction from which we had come. I carefully tiptoed across the unpredictable volcanic ground like I was walking on glass, or more appropriately, hot coals. Aptly enough, curses spewed out of our mouths as we made our way past the danger zone.

About fifteen minutes into our stressful exodus, we stopped and sat down for a rest. We needed to allow our heart rates to slow and let Randy finally finish emptying his bladder. We talked about how stupid our inattention was and how painful it would have been to singe a foot in the lava. I imagined setting one foot after the other into the burning liquid, and then running on my stumps as they became progressively smaller with each step.

It really had been a close call. The lava had managed to singe the bottoms of my boots. I still have the hiking boots I used that day. Their partially burnt soles serve as a reminder of some of the stupid things I have done just to get a thrill. They are a direct reminder of what it would be like to be "two feet" shorter!

# WALL OF CHINA: GESTURES & GASTRONOMY

Many times, I travel somewhere with an agenda already bursting at the seams and chock-full of natural wonders I plan to see and physical challenges I plan to undertake. I will, for example, plan to hike a volcano, take a dip in natural hot springs, and follow that up with more hiking and perhaps a camel ride. Of course, I always plan my activities in an efficient geographical order. Occasionally, however, I travel to a place to simply enjoy one activity or attraction. Such was the case when I took my first trip to China. I traveled specifically to walk the Great Wall, and that was all I did.

I arrived in China with the fairly unusual luxury of being focused on one single goal. On this particular trip, I was using an around-the-world ticket, so my itinerary was flexible. I had taken advantage of this flexibility by staying longer than I had originally planned at a couple of my previous destinations, having discovered more things to see and do than I initially had thought existed at these locales. In the end, though, I found myself coming up short on time. I had to be back in the United States for the start of the school year—my students would have noticed the lack of a teacher at the front of the classroom. To fit the remainder of my planned destinations within my time frame, I had to make some adjustments, and I decided that China was the perfect place to do that.

As is usually the case, I had done my homework. I watched travel videos and thumbed through a Lonely Planet book before my trip to discover what there was to see and do in this hugely populated country. I dutifully selected a number of activities and sites to check out besides a visit to the Great Wall. While the activities I had selected were more appealing than other options I saw or read about, none of them sparked an eager anticipation in my heart. My time crunch made it easy to cut out all the filler activities I had listed. They may have been interesting, but none of them was essential. There was just one thing I could not live without—walking on the renowned wall.

When I arrived at the airport in Beijing, I immediately realized that I was in the most foreign place I had ever been. Unlike Honduras and Fiji, two of the more unfamiliar and exotic places I had just visited, the atmosphere in China made me feel very different and alone. To begin with, everything and everybody was very cold and militant in appearance and nature. There were no smiles or greetings from anyone.

I navigated through customs by following the passenger in front of me, and when I was spit out at the other end, I was instantly lost.

I did not know what to do. Nothing was written in English. For the first time in my travels, I could not find the help I needed. It sounds stupid, and I know I should not have expected it, but I could not find anyone who spoke even a single word of English. To compound this situation, I had not learned how to say anything in Chinese, partly because I would only be in China for a short time and partly because the language is one of the most difficult to study.

With sheer persistence and random luck, I did eventually find what seemed to be a taxi. While I tried my best to convey the Great Wall in a series of gestures, the man in the taxi just stared impassively at me. Clearly, the driver and I would have never won a game of charades. At this early stage in my traveling experience, I retained some mistaken ideas about communication with people from countries other than my own. Not knowing what else to do, I simply yelled, "The Great Wall!" to the driver, as if a louder volume would transcend the language barrier between us.

No sooner had I completed my request, and I was on my way—somewhere. I was not sure where, but the driver seemed to have a clear goal in mind. He seemed nice enough. I am still not sure what that phrase means, but I hear it a lot. Nice enough for what? All I can say is that the driver seemed more laid-back than the rest of the folks I had dealt with in the airport. While I appreciated the taxi driver's disposition, I did worry that if he were too laid-back, I might arrive at the Berlin Wall.

To my relief, after about a forty-minute ride (if I recall correctly), I was deposited at the famous Great of Wall of China. Regrettably, the communication between the taxi driver and me had not improved on the trip from the airport. He got overtly frustrated at my inability to comprehend his pantomime. I finally figured out that he wanted me to just jump into a metal bubble suspended from a cable. It would carry me up to destinations unknown. I was a bit surprised that I had to take something similar to a gondola to the top of the mountain upon which this section of the wall was built. With no one else around, I had no idea what was supposed to happen when I made it to the top. With the driver's increasingly insistent gestures, I reluctantly hopped in, figuring that I might as well stop worrying and enjoy the ride up to the top. Within a few minutes, I was on the summit, and my question of what to do next was quickly answered: pay!

There was a Chinese man waiting for me at the top, and before the bubble carrying me even came to a halt, he was demanding money. In no way did he resemble my mental image. Granted, much of this mental image was formed from movies and gross generalizations, but I could tell that this guy was not a peaceful Asian man, quietly sitting around, waiting to share his wisdom with some Westerner. As a matter of fact, he was not peaceful, wise, or quiet. In truth, his cup did runneth over as the words spilled out of his mouth. His repetition and insistence that I pay immediately made me think he must have expected me to have my money in hand, ready for him to take it. It almost seemed that he would not let me out of the bubble until I gave up the money.

Well, I had no idea what to expect and did not know how much I needed to pay for either the ride or the admission fee. What if I thought the fee was too much? Would they have let me ride the gondola back down or would I have to walk? It all boiled down to whether I was willing to hike down, get a cab back to the airport, and fly out because of being overcharged by a few bucks. I could not imagine spending the rest of my life explaining to people that I "almost" walked the Great Wall of China. Yes, I got all the way there, but I was not willing to spend the money for admission.

I never did find out how much it should have been to enter. I, of course, had not exchanged any money into local currency, so I just kept handing the man US dollars until he was satisfied. It is possible that he just kept motioning for me to give him more and more bills until his guilt (or profit) was so strong that he smiled to indicate I had given him enough. From my nearly empty pockets, I suspect that I probably paid for the next several local families to enter that day. No problem, I thought. It was, after all, part of the traveling experience.

Once I was atop the wall, I saw mostly local people throughout the day. I saw a few Westerners, but we were clearly outnumbered. I am always smiling at people and believe myself to be very approachable. Anywhere I go, I talk to locals, practice their language, and learn something about them. I often say hello to other travelers just to see where they are from and maybe exchange some travel advice. People seem to always want to talk to me. Some wish to practice their English, some just want to welcome a foreigner, other travelers want to ask me where I am from, and still others want to get travel advice about the area from me.

This place was different. This country was different. This day at the Great Wall was different. I spoke with no one and nobody spoke to me. Perhaps it was because, for the first time, I had not taken the time to learn anything about this country. Maybe my ignorance led to this seclusion. Lesson learned. I decided, for that one day, that I would accept the isolation and take advantage of being placed in yet another type of bubble. For the entire day, I remained silent, like one of the old, wise Chinese characters I had seen in movies.

I spent the day silently walking on the wall and trying to imagine the significance of it. I thought about the purpose of its design and the manpower it must have taken to build such a huge structure. I tried to envision all of the people affected by this wall. I daydreamed about those xenophobic centuries during which the Chinese worried about not only physical attack by invaders but also the less violent influence of outside cultures.

As I strolled along observing people, I got the sense that maybe things had not really changed that much over the centuries. Perhaps this wall, long retired from its job as a physical protector, still symbolized an active isolationist worldview. Even with the global economy and communications revolution, this place did not seem to have absorbed very much from the world beyond. The absence of any perceptible recognition of the world beyond its borders could have been the reason China was more foreign to me than any place else I had visited.

Although I spent most of the day on the wall, in all actuality, I probably only walked a couple miles of it. I started at a high point in the wall and walked up and down many stairs. The view was somewhat diminished by a slightly overcast sky. Nonetheless, I stopped often to look out, ponder, and rest. I would have liked to walk farther on the wall. In fact, before I realized that there were stairs, I had thought of taking a bicycle and covering at least ten to fifteen of the more than fifteen hundred miles that the wall stretches. However, treading up and down all those steps prevented me from exploring even five miles, and all that walking on the hard rock structure did a number on my back. Additionally, if I planned on getting a ride back toward the airport, I though I had better return to the section where I had started.

In hindsight, I realize that I should have researched several entrance and exit points along the wall so that I could have entered in one location, walked all day, and exited with confidence at another point. Even now, I am not sure that it is possible to do that. Since I have never attempted to look it up, I guess I am still not that interested in once again exploring China or the Great Wall.

After I felt that I had absorbed enough of the great structure, I caught a ride in a vehicle similar to the one that had brought me there several hours earlier. Getting a ride was not a big deal after all. There were a couple of these cars in the dirt lot, and their drivers appeared to be just waiting for someone like me. I half-heartedly hoped that the gentleman who had driven me to the wall would be waiting, although I am not sure if he actually agreed to be—based on my poor miming skills.

In any event, he was not there. I accepted a ride from the first driver who approached me and somehow conveyed to him that I needed to find a cheap hotel. I give myself no credit for the success of this communication. As a taxi driver, he would have learned the words for airport and hotel in multiple languages. He probably also memorized the words "Great Wall" in these languages. All I could think was, *where were you this morning?*

We fought through traffic that consisted of an interesting mix of cars, bicycles, motorcycles, and rickshaws. In just this relatively short period of time on the streets around Beijing, I witnessed an accident. I guess this was not too incredible, based on the mixture of vehicles and the lack of any regard to lights or signs. Accidents must surely be pretty regular occurrences. It was a small accident: a man on a bicycle misjudged the space he had and cut between two cars. He knocked himself off his bike and almost knocked himself out when he collided with the side mirrors of the smaller vehicle.

The cab driver brought me to a place that I would later learn was only about five miles from the airport. It had been impossible to gauge how far we had traveled from the wall because of the hustle, bustle, and heart-stopping traffic. Somehow, the long taxi ride cost significantly fewer dollars than my gondola ride.

The hotel was nice and the rates were translated into US dollars for the slackers like me who had not bothered to exchange money or even learn the exchange rate. I gave the nice lady at the desk just enough money for one night. I simulated shoveling food into my mouth, and she smiled. She kindly pointed to the restaurant that was semi-attached to the hotel.

The restaurant staff, unfortunately for me, was neither bi-lingual nor well versed in charades. I tried desperately to explain that I could not eat anything with onions. I repeatedly pointed at the word "onion" on the menu, shook my head back and forth, wiggled my finger, and gave what I believed was the international sign for no. With my severe onion allergy, it was more than just a preference issue. The waiter nodded as if he understood me but without much conviction. When he brought my food, the first thing I saw was a huge mound of onions staring right at me! I pointed at the offensive pile and said, "No, No, No!" I asked for another person to speak to. The more emphatically I tried to indicate that I could not have onions, the more emphatically each water boy, waiter, busboy, and manager communicated that they understood my request. Once again, as the food arrived, I saw the exact same pile of onions on the plate, now moved to the other side and with a piece of lettuce thrown over it as a disguise. The owner had come out to see what the fuss was all about, and I tried one last time to explain myself. I got out of my chair and pointed at the onions, shook my finger, wagged my head from side to side, and waved my arms to make baseball's "you're out" signal. The crowd watched my behavior in rapt attention as the owner assured me that he understood my seemingly simple request. At this point, I even thought I saw Mao Zedong giving me the okay sign through the serving window.

Within a few moments, out came my plate—and there they were in all their glory, mocking me. I had worked up an even greater appetite during my dinner theater performance, but I was now more exhausted than ever. After this third and final vain attempt at getting any food that did not contain onions, I paid for a meal consisting of two Cokes and several slices of bread, and I headed for my room.

I took a long, hot shower and brushed my teeth with the little Chinese toothbrush and the tiny tube of Chinese toothpaste they had left for me in my room. Feeling a bit cleaner and a lot lighter in spirit, I looked around my room and was happy to see a telephone on a small table by the bed. Before I crashed for the night, I called the airline to change my flight dates. Several months earlier, when I had booked my entire around-the-world ticket, I had allotted myself four days in China to experience the Great Wall. I had done it in one, so I made arrangements to fly out early the next day. It was a piece of cake because the United Airlines representative spoke excellent English!

# XCARET: RUINS & CENOTES

I arrived at Xcaret prepared to map out all the ruins of Mexico. On this trip, I had planned to see as many of the ancient ruins as possible. Xcaret and its sister park, Xel-ha, are eco-geological parks located south of Cancun, Mexico. I was especially interested in seeing their huge models replicating all of the major ruins in Mexico and Central America. It was a great starting place for our seven days of exploring. With all the choices so clearly laid out before me, I immediately gravitated toward Tikal, the biggest ruin by far of all those represented.

I smelled a major road trip on the horizon, but my travel *amigo*, Tony, quickly vetoed me. He is the type of guy who will usually go anywhere at any time without any questions, but he quickly pointed out that Tikal was in Guatemala, and we were currently in Mexico. If we made that trip, we would spend the whole time driving and probably never even get to see the ruins. Reluctantly, I agreed that perhaps Tikal was not the destination for this particular travel adventure.

Using the numerous models as inspiration, we used a page from my journal to draw a crude map of the ruins that we planned on visiting. The finished product was somewhere between a third grader's treasure map and a cartographer's first draft. In all honesty, our drawing was closer to the former than the latter, but it served our purposes nicely.

I had arranged this retreat at the spur of the moment. I had just returned home from a summer vacation filled with exciting travels—but I had spent the whole time without once setting foot in the water. That was definitely a first for me and not a good one. Therefore, my initial reason for this trip was to get wet! I wanted to dive as much as possible to get my water fix. My secondary purpose was to play Indiana Jones and explore the ruins of an ancient world.

With our map drawn and our plan complete, we spent the remainder of our day in Xcaret making the most of what the ecological park had to offer. First thing the next morning, we rented a Jeep, loaded it up with junk food from the petrol station, and began our journey south. I took the wheel and my navigator, Tony, held our map with pride … and with more than a little confusion.

After visiting a couple of the smaller archeological sites, the Mexican sun was really getting to us. It was about ninety degrees, and the sun was relentless in both its light and intense heat. The ground was parched, having long since given up on any attempt to retain what little water it had, and now the heat not only hit our heads on the way down but also scorched our feet as it ricocheted upward from the baked clay soil. We were more than ready for submersion into some refreshing water.

As we drove along, we saw billboard-sized signs that had pictures of what looked to be clear, cool water. These watering holes, better known as *cenotes* in Mexico, were not of interest to us at the start of our day. In fact, looking at a *cenote* seemed like a waste of our time. After four hours of baking, however, it seemed like our primary mission. I am fairly certain that the pictures of water did not improve artistically with each sign that we passed, but to us they became more and more tempting until they resembled a mirage. Only a fool would ignore a mirage, and, after a very brief discussion, we agreed that we needed to visit one.

We made a U-turn and backtracked until we got to the last *cenote* sign we had seen. We turned off the main road and onto a narrow, unpaved one that led into a little dirt parking area. For approximately thirty feet, we followed a small footpath that was being strangled with plant life. Then, like a scene out of some old movie, we arrived at a small clearing. The mirage was real!

It turns out that *cenote* is the word for deep, water-filled sinkholes formed by water seeping through the porous soil above. The Mayans considered these sacred holes a gift from the gods. This one was located in a place where no one would ever expect to see it. Most of the water was hidden deep beneath the surface in a labyrinth of tunnels and caverns. We barely got into the refreshing pool before we got out and went back to the jeep to grab our masks and snorkels. It was too tempting to pass up, and we began our exploration of what lay beneath.

I have to say that snorkeling in these *cenotes* was enjoyable. It was amazing to see the maze of tunnels and small caves, but as fun as it was, it was also a bit annoying. Each time I began to really feel a thrill from my intense examination of the surroundings, my little voyage would be abruptly halted by my mammalian desire for air. I really could have used a dive tank, but I immediately stopped that train of thought because I had promised myself that I would never do any cave diving.

By the time we finished our semi-frustrating exploration, we were more than adequately cooled off and ready for the next leg of our journey. As we walked back to the Jeep, I turned back to look at the clear, blue *cenote*. It seemed to be calling out to me, tempting me to stay and explore more deeply. I hesitated only for a moment before I continued up the little dirt path. We set off down the road to continue following our homemade map of the ruins.

We had only driven a few miles when we saw yet another *cenote* sign. It was a big, colorful sign with a painting of a jaguar on it. Regardless of the fact that we had only been driving for a couple of minutes, I was already hot again. Plus, I really wanted to stop and check this one out. The cool thing about traveling with less than a full-blown plan is the flexibility to just do what I feel like at any time. We figured that the ruins could wait because we needed to go *cenote* hopping!

My co-pilot was always game for anything, so he happily agreed to put the map down for awhile—I don't know if he really understood it anyway. We backtracked a bit and drove down another dirt road to find the *Chac Mool* (jaguar) *Cenote*. We immediately saw a small group of people, who were clearly not locals, sitting at a table. We stopped ostensibly to get directions, but we were also curious about the gathering.

It turned out that these people, who seemed to be a bit nervous, were being briefed on the safety measures needed while SCUBA diving in the local caves. The instructor was an older Mexican man of about sixty years. He spoke pretty good English, and his audience seemed to respect his expertise. As one of the divers was giving us directions to the *cenote*, the guide chimed in, "*Amigos*, why swim when you can dive? Would you like to come join our group?"

My brain said "No," but my lips were much quicker. "Yes, that would be fun," I blurted out. Tony did a double-take, and his eyes nearly bulged of his head.

As I have already mentioned, Tony was game for almost anything. For all the stupid suggestions I have made on our trips, his response has always been, "Uhh, okay." Cave diving, however, was different. Both Tony and I lived in Florida, a state known for a robust dive community and a lot of cave diving. From our experience, it seemed as if most SCUBA-related deaths had something to do with caves. Reading such stories in both the local newspapers and dive books always freaked us out. We could not imagine the panic and terror of being trapped in a small space, unable to find the exit.

The outcome is straight out of a horror movie. Many divers panic uncontrollably until they drown; some, with acceptance and resignation, watch their pressure gauge as the air runs out. A few veteran divers have had the wits to actually carve final farewell messages into the cave walls. Later, sometimes much later, when the limp diver is pulled from the den, the rescuers read those last words for the victim's spouse or family.

None of these scenarios appealed to us. Several years earlier, Tony and I had been diving in caverns located in central Florida. As we swam deeper into a sinkhole and farther and farther away from the natural sunlight, we reached an area that transitioned from cavern to cave. Beyond this point, we would no longer benefit from the security of the light from above or the direct access to the surface. A sign had been posted as the walls of the cavern narrowed to form the entrance to the connecting cave. It was adorned with a frightening image of the Grim Reaper. What was completely horrifying was the tally beneath the image indicating the number of divers who had died while exploring the darkness of that cave.

We both mentioned that being trapped in a cave was not the way we wanted to exit the earthly stage of our existence. It was on that day, ten years earlier, that we had agreed to never penetrate a cave underwater. And it was on this hot August day that we were about to do just that!

Although we had brought some of our own dive gear with us on this trip, I did not feel like spending the time to drive the forty miles back to our hotel to get it. Besides, we had to rent tanks, weights, and wet suits anyway because they were too bulky and heavy to pack. While we did not need a wetsuit for the warm ocean, we would in the much colder water of the underground caves. We decided that it would probably be easier and cheaper to just get the complete package deal. The instructor sent us to the dive shop and gave us a time to be back to do a later dive.

We completed a streamlined version of the orientation to Mexican cave diving and were about to take the chance that we had promised each other we would never take. The confident words from our guide offered only a small measure of comfort. At the time, I was severely claustrophobic and had not yet developed any coping mechanisms for panic. I was about to be trapped in a cave underwater for forty-five minutes. To say the least, I was nervous.

My nervousness dissipated, however, when we climbed into what looked like a clear puddle. As I walked out toward the center of the puddle, I had to pull myself under a huge boulder and between a couple other smaller rocks. It was a total GI Joe moment—better than anything I had imagined as a kid! I saw the bright, water-filled caverns below me, and I submerged. Our decent from the surface was at a fairly sharp angle compared with traditional diving and continued for about sixty feet. The light slowly dimmed and then abruptly disappeared as the water and air above our heads was replaced by water and rock. In that one clear, precise moment, I recognized that we were in a cave filled with water. There was no direct access to the surface and that life-giving air.

I kept waiting to get nervous again. I had thought that I would be thinking of my inability to surface if I panicked or my regulator malfunctioned. Luckily, the nervousness, when it came, was completely overshadowed by excitement. It turns out that my love of excitement and adventure in this case far surpassed my preconceived notions and fears.

In that moment, I was Jacques Cousteau. I was a wet Indiana Jones. I was deep in the caves and deep in my own little movie. I imagined all sorts of scenarios including accidentally discovering this cave and exploring it for the very first time. I turned off my dive light, if only for a few seconds at a time, and enjoyed the dark unknown. I was alive. This was real. I thrive on the feeling I get when I am afraid to do something but do it anyway. Experiencing the unknown is what does it for me. Maybe I did it to prove to myself that I could conquer anything. Maybe it was simply so I would not live in fear or feel weak every time the subject of cave diving was discussed.

Focusing on a task helps prevent me from panicking when I am in an otherwise stressful situation. On this dive, we were told to watch for a halocline, the area where salt and fresh water collide. In this cave, the salty ocean water was covered by a layer of fresh water originating from the springs above us. The fresh and saltwater layers did not mix but rather persisted as two distinct zones because the water was so still. When I came upon this phenomenon, I actually positioned myself so that the interface between the layers was even with the middle of my mask. I had clear visibility on the top half of my mask and blurry on the bottom. Then I tilted my head vertically and saw blurry with my right eye and clear with my left. This activity kept me busy and my mind occupied for quite some time.

Eventually, we moved on and followed one cave into an area that allowed us to surface. We found ourselves in a small underground bubble with a circumference no more than twenty feet around and height that did not extend beyond a couple of feet. This small room, delineated by rock and water, echoed with silence until we started making childish *ooh* sounds; then the moment was gone. The ceiling above us was made of hard but porous limestone. Roots from the plants above had actually bored holes through the rock in search of water. It was an eerie sight that resembled a scene from a Steven Spielberg film.

We stayed in this underground grotto for about five minutes. During the first few minutes, I shared my comments and listened to my fellow divers' reactions. Then, I drifted away to savor my own thoughts and reflections. I remember thinking how exhilarating it was to experience this amazing place. If I had not been willing to take a dare and move out of my comfort zone, I would have missed one of life's rare treasures.

We swam away from that peaceful place, and when we surfaced a second time, the dive was over. It was time to extract myself from the water and move back onto dry land. We had survived. It was a good day. I had won and, more importantly, my anxieties were lost in that perilous underwater cave. I cannot live my life without trying to conquer my fears. Now that I have triumphed over these fears with this activity, I can safely say that I will never do it again … probably.

# YASAWA ISLANDS: CANNIBALISTIC CATERPILLARS

I was looking for a place where people just wanted to peacefully enjoy their simple island life. I thought perhaps I could find a place where folks still did things the old-fashioned way—although in Fiji I had to be careful, as they were the last people to end the practice of cannibalism.

The first person I met in Nadi was a big brown man with a huge afro. He welcomed me to his beautiful country, and I tried not to notice that he was wearing a flowered skirt, the traditional dress of Fijian men. I told him that all I wanted to do was SCUBA dive. He smiled and in the deepest, yet most gentle voice, he said he would introduce me to Vera.

Vera was a petite, exotic woman sporting long, straight, black hair with just enough gray to give her a little character. She periodically displayed a shy smile that widened exponentially at the mention of her family. She was soft-spoken but very knowledgeable and professional. She arranged for me to stay in a little bungalow located on a small island off the mainland. She even drove me to the docks where I picked up the transport boat to take me to my destination, the Yasawa Islands.

Yasawa is a group of about twenty volcanic islands that form an archipelago in Western Fiji. This was also a spot where I expected to enjoy getting a taste of the simple, relaxed, old-fashioned life … so long as I was not on the menu.

I took a small boat carrying fruits, vegetables, and some other necessities to a few of the islands in the archipelago that were inhabited. I do not think it was that long of a distance, but it took about two hours to get to the tiny island where I would be staying. It seemed a lot farther because of the uncomfortable boat ride, the result of both the rough seas and the small, junky, diesel-smoke-filled vessel whose motor had all the power of a wind-up toy.

I did not mind the wavy, bumpy ride because it was a small price to pay for a chance to meet the awesome people with whom I would share this island. There were five others traveling to the same destination. Ester and Felix, a sweet couple from Switzerland, were the oldest of the group. Neil and his friend Eric were bartenders from Idaho who became the group's suppliers of Kava, an herbal drink noted for its calming effects. Amy was from Belgium and totally into photography. They all had entertaining stories of past destinations. I just listened and learned. As they shared their tales, my "must see" list grew considerably.

These five travelers were all looking for a place to just relax and get away. Most of them had had to wait several days in Nadi because this transport boat was the only way to get to these smaller islands, and it made a run only twice a week. I really lucked out because I had no previous knowledge of this small paradise, and yet I was on my way there just hours after my arrival in Fiji.

From the moment I stepped off the boat, I knew this was a place where I could live. It was simple. An inviting white sand beach led to plush green trees and grass all around me. At the edge of the beach, I saw palm trees interspersed among four quaint little bungalows. A native of the island greeted us and led us to the bungalows that my companions would occupy for the next few days, and I would enjoy for the next week.

Part of me felt spoiled for having asked for a private hut. After watching Amy disappear into the trees on her way to another set of bungalows on the other side of the island, I saw four fellow travelers cram into a bungalow the same size as my own. Then, they began the process of deciding who would sleep on the beds and who would sleep in the hammocks. After watching their negotiations continue for things as important as personal space, I was pleased I had paid to have a place all to myself.

The cost of a bungalow was very low, and I could not, and still cannot, understand why one would choose to save a few bucks by bunking with three others. It was more perplexing when I saw these same people spend at least the cost of a bungalow on a couple of beers later that same evening. I was glad that, in the course of my limited travels, I had already learned the benefits of getting a private room when I stayed in hostels.

Now do not get me wrong, it is not that I do not like rooming with others. Well, actually, yes it is. I started traveling later in life when my lifestyle and personality were already pretty well developed. Plus, I do not really have the lifestyle of many hostel-goers. The plain truth is that I just do not feel like I fit in with that general crowd. They are interesting and fun to travel with, but at the end of the day I feel like an old Resident Assistant in a college dorm. I like to get up at first light, go all day, and then retire early—while those around me seem to be just gearing up.

When I had stayed in crowded hostels in the past, it always seemed as if there was some unspoken contest that had three distinct competitive categories. The first was who could get home the latest, the second was who could come back the drunkest, and the third category was who could make the most noise while trying to find his or her own bunk. I have never chosen to participate, but it has been my personal observation that each of the three categories draws a large number of willing contestants.

I have chosen, however, to stay in hostels because I like the cost, camaraderie, and learning opportunities that they afford. I enjoy listening to the experiences of fellow travelers, but I just do not want to hear slurred stories at 3:00 a.m., especially when the dialogue is interrupted every five minutes or so for the storyteller to vomit on my backpack.

It should be no surprise, then, that as I watched the four fellow travelers fight for territory in that tiny hut, I was glad to be alone in my own bungalow. That feeling of quiet, self-satisfied pleasure would change, however, on the very first night.

The first order of the day was not to unpack but to begin my island adventure. I threw down my gear, and I started to explore the small island. I climbed on the rocks at the water's edge, hiked up the small mountain, walked along the beach looking for cool stuff, and visited the little SCUBA shack to make arrangements for the first available dive.

At dusk, I made my way back to the little bungalow compound. The man who oversaw the bungalows had prepared a dinner of rice and vegetables for our small group. I gladly joined the others. The vegetables were, as always, mixed with onions, so I loaded up entirely on white rice. My allergy to onions quite possibly would have required a trip to the hospital, which could have short-circuited my entire vacation. I had no medical coverage as the school year had ended, and I would not be returning to my job. Looking back, I guess you could say I was unemployed but enjoying a round-the-world vacation. Cool.

During our meal, I listened to tales from the wanderlust years of Ester and Felix. I watched their aged faces light up as they relived those golden memories. I learned about the mishaps of Neil the bartender, whose main goal appeared to be getting plastered in every country before going back to his local bar to share his experiences. Most of all, I listened attentively to Amy.

Amy had been traveling for five months. I liked her stories not necessarily for what she said but for how she said it. Her soft, charismatic voice flowed as if every word and event was poetically called upon at just the right moment. I watched her soft lips and slightly crooked mouth spill out each word as if it were special. She had a natural face that probably never saw makeup and certainly was not the less for it. Her hair was dark blonde and uncontrolled except for the blue bandana that tried unsuccessfully to tame it. Her clothes were baggy, and I could not tell the definition of her body. Maybe in this particular case, I did not care. She was talking, my ears were glued to her every word, and my eyes fluttered back and forth between her sweet mouth and her soft eyes.

Time passed quickly, and before I knew it, the caretaker announced that the generator would, as always, be shut off at 10:00 p.m. He suggested that we should all be settled in or at least keep flashlights available if we needed or wanted to get around at night. I, of course, did not have a flashlight. I was a tenderfoot traveler and not yet savvy enough to foresee the need for one. Besides, I planned on being in bed well before lights-out to ensure that I was up for my morning dive.

I said good night to the group and then specifically to Amy, who had joined us for dinner. I hoped that she would ask about sharing my private bungalow before the trip was over, but for now, I would follow the dirt path alone to my humble little abode.

Upon entering, I glanced around at the simple surroundings. Then, I grabbed my Wayne Dyer book and sat down on the sandy floor of my bungalow and read. I needed to sit directly under the window to take advantage of the last hour of the outside lights. For me, a flashlight and alarm clock are still optional when I travel. A book, however, is mandatory.

In the final minutes of light, before the generator was due to be turned off, I made one last trip down another dirt path to the bathroom. I brushed my teeth in the little sink outside the outhouse, and, at the last possible moment, I used the toilet. I desperately hoped that this draining would carry me through until daylight. With no flashlight, I would never find my way to the bathroom in the middle of the night.

I finished going and jumped up and down many times so as not to leave even a single drop in my bladder. I am glad none of the other guests stumbled in to use the bathroom at that point. They might have thought I was doing something I shouldn't have been. I did not want to take a chance of stimulating my bladder so I didn't even wash my hands—not that there was any soap available.

For that week, with careful planning, I ended up making it almost every night without requiring an additional trip to the bathroom. The only night I could not hold it until morning, I simply aimed out the window, which was merely a cut-out in the thatched wall of the hut, and relieved myself. I did not go out the door because I could not find the wooden door latch in the dark. Those were the good old days. At this point in my life, if I needed a flashlight to make a trip to the bathroom each time I awoke with a full bladder, I would go through a set of batteries every night. Now when I am traveling, I am sure to keep an empty water bottle by my bedside. My refill of the day may taste a bit bitter, but it's cheaper than all those batteries.

I made it back to my place and prepared for my first night in this little tranquil paradise. I crawled into the twin-size bed and pulled the mosquito net, which hung from the ceiling, securely around me. With the sound of the waves crashing against the gentle sloping beach, I exhaled slowly and anticipated a long, dark, quiet sleep.

It hit me like a bullet and woke me with a violent start sometime in the middle of the night. I cannot describe the instantaneous adrenalin rush and horror that washed over me when I was awakened by the sensation of something gnawing on my penis! "What the f***!" I yelled as I reached down into my Bugs Bunny boxers and felt this fuzzy thing. I pulled it off, squashed it, and threw it across the small room, all in one spastic motion. I jumped to my feet and tried to leap out of the bed, but all I managed to do was nearly hang myself in the mosquito net. "Son of a …"

I finally managed to disentangle myself from the netting and crawl toward the opening. To avoid another up-close encounter with the marauder, I leaped as far as I could from the bed to the floor. In my agitation, I misjudged the distance and sailed too far across the room. I hit the nightstand—the only other piece of furniture in this eight-by-eight-foot room—with my thigh. "Damn it!" I yelled. *That's definitely going to leave a mark,* I thought.

I limped toward the window, hoping for a little light from the moon. Bang! Ouch! Crap! I stubbed my big toe on the foot of the bed. Another mark, and I had not even found my attacker yet. This was becoming a comedy act. I sure was glad I had gotten my own bungalow. I was even more pleased that Amy had not come to my room. Anyone watching me would have been laughing his or her butt off. Nobody could see this, though, because there was no moon, there was no light, and I surely was not laughing.

In fact, by this point in the saga, I was really freaking out. My battle wounds were mounting, and I couldn't see a darn thing. My mind was in hyperactive overdrive. *What was this creepy thing, and where was it hiding?* Suddenly, I realized that when I tossed the critter across the room, it probably never even cleared the closed mosquito net. The bug had to still be in my bed! That meant that the villain and I would be all alone in this tiny room until sunrise.

What was I to do? I could not stand up all night like a sentry in the middle of the room. I could not passively wait for the light of day. I had no idea what time it was; I would not have been able to see my watch even if I had one. For all I knew, it was shortly after ten and I had only been asleep a few minutes.

I finally mustered up the courage to climb back into bed. I felt around in the blanket and netting, but could not find the intruder. I crawled into bed and tried to relax, but I could not. I needed to know what had bitten me and if it was poisonous. There was nothing I could do to take my mind off those questions; I just lay there wondering if I would wake up dead. With the profound lack of light, I could not even read to take my mind off my worries.

Everyone else in the compound was sleeping—not that they would have been any help. The caretaker did not sleep on the grounds; he was, no doubt, off in his own bungalow with his family. In the pitch dark, I could not get to anyone even if I wanted to. I would not be able to find out how much trouble I was in until morning, and, worse, I could not see if that disgusting creature was still alive and in bed with me. My midnight mantra became a series of increasingly more vehement repetitions of "Oh crap, oh crap, oh crap."

My imagination got the best of me. I started picturing myself lying in bed experiencing agonizing pain, paralyzed, and unable to speak from the venom in this tropical weenie-biter. In the morning, the locals at the dive shop would have just thought that I had slept in or decided not to dive. The others at the compound would have assumed

I was diving all day. Come nighttime, they might even have thought that I skipped dinner in fear of encountering some onions. Maybe no one would find me until the second or third day, when someone might become curious enough to check on me.

After many long hours reviewing that scenario, I finally began to see the soft light of daybreak. I realized that I was in a sort of trance. I hoped it was from the lack of sleep and exhaustion from being in a state of nervousness for so long, rather than an effect of the critter's poisonous attack. At least I was not dead, I reasoned.

I got up, put some shorts on, and began to look for the thing that had molested me so many hours earlier. At first, my eyes fell on something by the end of the bed, but it turned out to be part of my foot—a piece of my toenail that I had left behind in my earlier collision. After searching the rest of the floor, which only took a few seconds, I hesitantly glanced back onto my bed. Then I spotted it, right at the bottom edge of the bed. I suspected that it had not gone far. Apparently, it only bounced off the inside of the mosquito net. I then realized I had been sleeping with it all night!

The little creep was a caterpillar—a squashed, dead, caterpillar. I was once told that if a snake ever bit me, I should try to capture it and bring it to the hospital so they would know which anti-venom to give me. Based on that advice, I scooped the insect up onto my book, and headed off in the direction of the picnic table where we had eaten the previous night.

I waited there impatiently until the caretaker showed himself from the edge of the trees. I approached him like a kid running to his mom to show her a bug he had just found. He quickly advised me that this caterpillar was not poisonous and that I would not die. I felt the stress just pour out of my body. I could finally rest. As relief flowed through me, worry was replaced by an energy that was all positive. I was alive, rejuvenated, and had some diving to do.

I left the caterpillar's remains with the bemused caretaker, and ran to the bungalow to grab my SCUBA gear. I cut through the woods to another beach, and walked along the quarter mile stretch of sand to where the Zodiak awaited my arrival.

I made this stroll to the dive boat each morning and afternoon for my entire week in Yasawa. Sometimes, I went again at dusk to make a night dive. Each time I walked this beach, I was sure to be greeted by the few Fijian families that lived on the banks just above the sand. "*Bule*," they would smile and call as I walked by. "*Bule*," I would say back with an excited smile, knowing that, as I shared in this untroubled lifestyle, nobody had it better than I did.

Regardless of the language barrier, the smiles we exchanged said it all. I think that a sincere smile is all that is ever needed, no matter what country I am traveling in. These particular people, regardless of the size of their family, were very happy to be living where they were, in their little bungalows approximately the same size as the one I was temporarily residing in.

Life was good on this island in the Yasawa chain. With its sparkling ocean, beautiful beaches, good fishing, and even better diving, one might even say it was paradise. It would be relatively easy to settle down there. I could live in a bungalow, get married, and raise some kids. *Hmmmm*, I thought. *Maybe I could see what Amy is doing for the next forty or fifty years.*

# ZIP LINES:
## WAY TO TRAVEL

Standing on a platform seven hundred and fifty feet above sea level at the edge of a mountain, I was strapped into a harness and hanging onto a little bar. The bar was attached to a cable that spanned a valley and connected the mountains on each side. I was about to run off of this platform and experience, for the first time, the wonderful world of zip lines!

I was part of a small group that consisted of a friend of mine from Florida, a married couple from California, and me. When the guide asked who would be first to try the line, the married couple quickly claimed to have kids that should not be left orphaned if the suspension cable broke. Thus, they suggested that either my buddy or I go first to test it out.

I had just learned how really expendable my life was in their eyes. I cannot say that it surprised me though. Being single had somehow made me expendable in the eyes of every parent or spouse that I had come across in my travels. Even some of my closest friends had forced me to be the guinea pig while trying new endeavors. It was always the same comment, "Larry, you go first." And their rationale was always the same: "I have kids," "I have a wife," "I have a husband." Even my single friends had reasons at the ready: "My dog needs me." "Who will feed the goldfish?" "What will become of my ficus?"

At least these people had a reason why they did not want to go first, legitimate or not. My so-called friend, on the other hand, just flat-out refused. It was not even up for discussion or debate. He pointed to the tram from which we had just emerged and said, "I will turn this tram right around and go straight back the way we came before I go first." Thus, by process of elimination, I was nominated to go first for this experience. Of course, this suited me just fine. Just like a little kid, I have no patience to wait. Therefore I really do not mind going first. In fact, in most cases, I prefer it!

Zip lines are the best way to see the canopies of the great rainforests. I had wanted to ride one ever since I saw Sean Connery glide through a South American rainforest in the movie *Medicine Man*. When I heard this adventure was available in Costa Rica, I booked a flight. Then I figured that, if I was going to visit Costa Rica, I might as well first stop off in Panama to visit the famous canal and possibly see a three-toed sloth. Seeing unusual animals is a good excuse to travel. I hoped that this country would allow me to observe the slowest animal on earth in its natural environment.

Unfortunately, I did not get a chance to see a wild sloth in Panama. I did not even get the opportunity to see one in captivity. Therefore, on my long tram ride up the mountain that morning, I silently peered off into the dense rainforest that lay below me and looked intently for the three-toed sloth in Costa Rica. I searched in vain for the entire hour. I usually try my best to be in the moment and live in the present. I should have been thinking about zipping down the mountain I was climbing, but instead I was hunting for something I would not see and reliving my time in Panama.

I had spent my first day in Panama at the locks of the canal. I educated myself about its construction in the three-story museum and learned about the fee that each vessel was charged to pass through. I spent a good deal of time taking pictures and watching the many boats, including a cruise ship, make their way past the locks and through the canal.

The next day, I was at Panama's Summit Botanical Gardens and Zoo located in the Soberania National Park section of the Gamboa Rainforest. It is a fairly small zoo, only six hundred and twenty acres, but it is home to over fifteen thousand species of plants and animals. Unfortunately, I did not have the time to go hiking in the rain forest to find a wild sloth. I had hoped that this zoo would allow me to at least see one even if it was in a captive environment.

I was so disappointed when I learned that the establishment had no live sloths. In fact, I felt truly ripped off because sloths were native to the area. With all the animals and plants to see, I found myself drawn to a stuffed, two-and-a-half-foot-tall, three-toed sloth. This creature must have weighed close to sixty pounds when it was alive, but it was not alive. As I was staring at the exhibit, all I felt was disappointment.

I had come all this way to see a living sloth before the taxidermist got to it.

I was imagining this animal in a living state, probably moving only fractionally faster than in its stuffed state, when I was distracted by a documentary that illuminated a screen the size of the entire front wall. At least the video offered a less stiff version of the critter. I had come all the way to Central America to see a sloth, and I decided that watching a video and sitting next to a stuffed one would have to do.

I watched as my furry friend sluggishly climbed a gigantic tree. I began to remember why I first became infatuated with this goofy looking animal. At this point, I was mesmerized by the video, absorbed in admiring the grace of this unusual creature, and wishing I could pet one, when … swoop! An eagle twice the size of the sloth ripped it out of the tree and carried it away just as a smaller eagle might do with an undersized fish.

I was dumbfounded. I was amazed at the size of the bird, but I was also sad because I love sloths. My mouth hung open as the lady running the projector laughed at my reaction. After the film, she motioned for me to follow her outside. I was hoping we were going to see the eagle and the sloth, both smiling, arm in arm, sitting in a couple of actor's chairs, awaiting praise for their performance.

Well, I did not see that, but what I did see was a real live harpy eagle. It had the face of an owl with a big, black, pointy, sharp beak. Panama's national bird was, for lack of a better word, *gigantic*. It was over three feet tall, and its wings extended to almost seven feet across. Its talons amazed me—they were the same size as a grizzly bear's claws. I learned that it is known as one of the world's most powerful eagles. It is capable of flying up to fifty miles per hour over short bursts and nests a hundred to two hundred feet above ground in the treetop canopy.

Everything I learned made me think that the harpy eagle was an extremely impressive creature, and up to that point, I had been unaware that it even existed. When I did see it, I was blown away by its stature.

In fact, initially I suspected it was just another stuffed specimen. After a few minutes of admiration, I drew out my camera and took a couple dozen photos. With the photographs, I would be able to prove to myself and others that this bird did, in fact, exist. Once I was satisfied, I put my camera down and simply stared, captivated by this bird.

There comes a point in each of my trips when I can feel that if the trip ended at that moment it would be all right. Usually, the feeling comes just after I have gotten my fill of a certain location, or fauna, or flora. In this case, that feeling came after my time with the harpy eagle. Nonetheless, I toured the remainder of the zoo until it was about closing time. I made my way past the monkeys, jaguars, and pumas. Everywhere I walked, I crossed paths with leaf-cutter ants. I followed their paths that led from an unfortunate plant to their burrows. The little buggers looked like they took a knife and carved out pieces of the leaf many times greater than their own body size. They then carried the huge chunks over their heads, and marched in formation to their home. It got me thinking about the next leg of my journey.

The next day, I took the one-hour flight to Costa Rica. I rented a jeep to travel along the coast to do some diving. Along the way, I stopped and hiked along the various volcanoes and visited the hot springs. I enjoyed the scenery and the feel of the wheel beneath my hands, but all the while I was focused on the main reason I came to Costa Rica: to ride the zip lines through the rain forests.

Now here I was, about to slide down the first of a series of cables and land on a platform somewhere on the other side of the valley. The cables were positioned back and forth on either side of the mountain, each end attached to a tree at a lower elevation. I was told that, in order to slow down just before landing on a tree platform, I should twist my body to either side, simply causing more friction on the cable. I was also advised to keep my feet up in a fetal position if I wanted to get more speed. I asked myself if more speed was really what I wanted or needed as I flew from one mountain to another.

I really was not afraid to get this ride started, but I had been wondering how I would figure out when it was time to slow down for a platform approach. Because of the elevation, thick clouds surrounded us. I was wondering what would prevent me from being stopped, abruptly, by a tree trunk. I imagined splattering spread-eagled into a tree and slowly sliding down to the ground *George of the Jungle*-style. Before I could ask the tree guide about stopping techniques, he gave me a shove, and I stepped off into thin air. At the time, I did not know what *vamanos* or *andele* meant. In fact, I did not even catch on when, just before he pushed me off, he yelled, "*Uno, dos, tres*!"

I disappeared into the clouds and immediately my thoughts disappeared too. I lost all sense of where I was and what I was doing. Because of the clouds that engulfed me, I saw only white. It was like being in a dream. Add to that the fact that we were so high up, and I might even consider this experience heavenly.

Because of the slack in the cable, there was a precipitous initial drop. Once my stomach caught up with me, it was not scary anymore. It was just thrilling. At that point, a two-foot long strap attached to a two-inch thick cable supported my weight. My face was wet from the moisture in the clouds. I smiled as I licked the condensation from my moustache. The notion of gradually becoming wet without rain or shower water falling on me was incredible—mysteriously incredible.

The distance from one platform to another was anywhere from thirteen hundred feet to twenty-two hundred feet. I am not exactly sure how long the first leg was. When I finally emerged from the clouds after a long, silent, pleasantly lonely glide, a tree guide was already waiting for me. A guide standing on the platform motioned for me to slow down. He had a rope attached to the cable that would prevent me from kissing the tree.

The lady in the group went next. She must have lost a bet with her husband. She probably didn't even try to gamble with my friend, as he was likely tied off to the tram until the very last minute. Even though she was instructed not to use the brakes on this first stretch because the cable was not very taut, she apparently decided to put the brakes on the entire way. To make a long story short, she had to be rescued and hauled to the side where I was standing by both of the guides. Apparently, pushing or pulling a person up a cable is a tiring task. Neither gentleman was very *feliz* when they finally made it to the platform.

The ironic part was that her fear caused her to be in a much more frightening situation than she would have been. If she zipped right along, she would have been to the other side in about a minute. Instead, she dangled seven hundred and fifty feet above ground, alone, in a haze of clouds for about five minutes, and then spent another fifteen minutes dangling as she was being ignominiously towed.

I do not recall which run I thought was more exciting. Perhaps it was the first couple of cables, as they were definitely the highest distance over the valley floor. On the other hand, the next couple of cables provided me with a breathtaking view. I was below the cloud cover and could see how high I really was. The dew from my trip through the clouds had long since dried upon my face as I cycled between screams of excitement on the faster, steeper runs, and utter silence on the slower, seemingly endless ones. I desperately attempted to capture each moment with all of my senses and store them away to remember and savor. These were the highest zip lines in Costa Rica, and I stayed "high" the rest of the day and into the night from that experience.

Before leaving the country a few days later, I would also conquer the longest zip lines that Costa Rica had to offer. The longest zip lines system consists of sixteen different lines and platforms and covers over four miles. This venture, although not as adventurous as the previous, was still a lot of fun. In this case, a tram was not necessary; I merely climbed the initial tree, clipped my harness to the zip line, and jumped. The lines led me through many areas and heights around the cliffs and mountains. The last few platforms gradually led back to ground level. I saw all the same lush green forests and had a chance to take video and even some photos while soaring through the air.

All told, my means of travel to date include automobiles and airboats, bikes, bush planes and buses, camels, cruise ships and cargo ships, dogsleds and donkeys, elephants, ferries and fishing boats, gondolas, helicopters and hitchhiking, icebreakers, jet skis, kayaks, locomotives, mail boats and motorcycles, Naval aircraft carrier, an outrigger canoe, pontoons and planes, quarter horses, rickshaws and bamboo rafts, subways, sailboats and snowshoes, trams, *tuk tuks* and tractor trailer trucks, U-hauls (too many times), vans, whitewater rafts and wave runners, an *xebec*, yachts and yaks. I always knew that zip lines could be used as a *reason* to travel, but I had never thought of them as a *means* of travel—until now. With this last realization, zip lines completed my round of travel adventures from A to Z.

# Afterword

Looking back, I realize that I began my life with a strong desire to be free—mostly from being poor. I gave up my personal freedom in the US Navy, trying to get farther from material poverty. Through education and travel combined, I have found the true, life-sustaining freedom that my spirit not only craves but also finds necessary to both survive and thrive. It is a freedom of spirit, unfettered by convention or the need to make more money.

I know that my travels have brought me to places in my mind and heart that no one, even I, thought existed. My experiences have taught me the value of discipline, balance, perspective, patience, knowledge, humor, and beauty. I can discriminate between being risky and understanding calculated risks as well as acting foolishly versus living courageously. I now understand why it is necessary to invite new things into my life and not push so hard against the flow. Through these lessons, I have found more success than I ever dreamed possible.

My life has expanded exponentially. It began filled with limitations and as a series of wasted opportunities and misdirection, culminating in the cataclysmic events that nearly killed me. I have had the good fortune to have a rebirth that has led to a life worth living. My path was different from what I expected, but each experience along the way either reinforced my choices or spurred me on toward personal growth and learning.

As a teacher, learner, and curious human being, I have consciously chosen to continue to learn about the world around me through firsthand experience—and what an amazing experience it has been so far. Along the way, I have seen that there is more to the earth than the human mind could have imagined, and I have found what truly makes me happy.

# About the Author

Larry Shortell was born in central Connecticut in 1964 and graduated from Rocky Hill High School in 1982. His world travel and documentation of natural wonders began with a tour of duty in the US Navy. After his honorable discharge, he moved to Florida to pursue his career as a SCUBA dive master and EMT. He ultimately became a dive instructor, and his travels led him to more exotic places.

Successful completion of a BA in special education from the University of South Florida and an MS in education from Cambridge College in Massachusetts opened a door to another type of travel. Larry's position as a special education teacher in Florida, Alaska, and Hawaii provided him with an opportunity for intense study and photographic documentation of the natural world.

Larry has also lived in Tennessee, California, the Galapagos Islands, and Argentina, and currently resides with Lisa, his "girlfriend-plus," and teaches in Connecticut, where he weaves the images and stories of different cultures and places into his classroom. Since the start of his traveling, Larry has completed two around-the-world trips, explored more than eighty countries, set foot on all seven continents, and visited each of the fifty states in the United States.

To contact the author, e-mail junglelarrystravels@yahoo.com

To view the author's travel photographs, please go to
http://my.att.net/p/PWP-larryshortell